BIOGRAPHY

Fiction, Fact and Form

Ira Bruce Nadel

MACMILLAN
PRESS

First edition 1984
Reprinted 1985, 1986

Published by
THE MACMILLAN PRESS LTD
London and Basingstoke
Companies and representatives
throughout the world

Typeset by Wessex Typesetters Ltd
Frome, Somerset

Printed in Hong Kong

ISBN 0–333–33426–4 (hardcover)
ISBN 0–333–42644–4 (paperback)

BIOGRAPHY
Fiction, Fact and Form

Steve [signature]

Wellcome Unit for the
History of Medicine.

Manchester University
July 1990.

By the same author

VICTORIAN ARTISTS AND THE CITY *(co-editor)*

JEWISH WRITERS OF NORTH AMERICA

VICTORIAN NOVELISTS BEFORE 1885; VICTORIAN NOVELISTS AFTER 1885 *(co-editor)*

To my parents
and
Josephine

Contents

Preface

My involvement with biography began when I sought to test the principle that biographies had an existence as independent literary texts free from their anomalous treatment by literary history as documentary works judged for their accuracy and not art. However, criticism provided little elaboration of this view and almost no commentary on the style, structure or language of biography. Indeed, most studies of biography contained only descriptions of the research problems or discoveries of the biographer – or, if the work possessed a critical impulse, concentrated on the historical rather than aesthetic development of the genre. Yet, I believed that biographies required a critical reading as works of imagination and language if they were to be accepted and understood as works of literature. In an effort to amplify this dimension of biography, I framed a series of questions and explorations of which this book is the result.

In part the problem for me was how could one attribute value to biography if the traditional moral defence of the genre, expressed by Dr Johnson when he told Boswell that 'I esteem biography as giving us what comes near to ourselves, what we can turn to use', was found unsuitable. What formal or theoretical properties could define the literary nature of the genre? I have tried to identify them by examining language, structure and theme in biography, in addition to such historical changes as the institutionalization of biography in the nineteenth century and the appearance of the professional biographer. Of particular concern has been the presentation of fact. Conscious of the discrepancies between fact and its representation, I have analysed tropological patterns and narrative techniques in biography in order to understand the transformation of fact into what I call 'authorized fictions'. Paul de Man's remark that 'metaphors are much more tenacious than facts' plus the work of Hayden White coincided with my efforts to analyse the aesthetics of biography and I have found the work of both critics stimulating. And although I draw on biographies from various periods, I concentrate on those written from 1850 to the present and limit my reading to literary biography alone.

Many have listened, encouraged, questioned and contributed to my ideas and to them I wish to offer my thanks. In particular, George Simson, editor of *biography*, has been a steadfast critic always ready to challenge and probe. Leon Edel, through his writing and teaching, furthered my interest in the subject. His arguments for the centrality and art of biography have been important guides for this study. Michael Holroyd was generous in sharing with me his concerns about biography, the result of his extended experience. James Olney remains an inspiring critic of life-writing who showed me how language and autobiography interact; he also manages that rare feat of continuing our dialogue on biography and autobiography in spite of great lapses of time and distances of space. W. E. Fredeman has been a colleague who has both directed and illuminated certain paths of scholarship for me and is a continual example of the intellectual rigour found in nineteenth-century studies today. Arthur Mizener, Daniel R. Schwarz and M. H. Abrams were all important influences on my earliest conceptions of biography, criticism and literary history. S. K. Heninger, Jr listened to many of these ideas in their initial stage and always posed lucid questions that challenged my assumptions, while N. John Hall responded to what must have been prolonged monologues with good humour and grace. My wife Josephine continues to give me a better understanding of life and literature. Doreen Todhunter is, as always, typist extraordinaire.

I am also grateful to the Social Sciences and Humanities Research Council of Canada and the University of British Columbia Humanities and Social Sciences Grants Committee for support. An earlier version of Chapter 3 appeared in *George Eliot: A Centenary Tribute*, ed. Gordon S. Haight and Rosemary T. VanArsdel (London: Macmillan, 1982) and a portion of Chapter 5 dealing with Lytton Strachey was published in *Prose Studies*, vol. 4, no. 2 (September 1981). I wish to thank the editors for permission to use this material. I should also like to acknowledge the British Library for permission to use material from the Macmillan Archives, the Bodleian Library, Oxford, the Victoria and Albert Museum for material in the collection of John Forster and the Huntington Library for letters from their Forster and Carlyle collections.

Vancouver   I. B. N.

Facts relating to the past, when they are collected without art, are compilations; and compilations no doubt may be useful; but they are no more History than butter, eggs, salt and herbs are an omlette.

Lytton Strachey, 'Gibbon'

Nothing happens while you live. The scenery changes, people come in and go out, that's all. There are no beginnings . . . But everything changes when you tell about life; it's a change no one notices: the proof is that people talk about true stories. As if there could possibly be true stories; things happen one way and we tell about them in the opposite sense.

Jean-Paul Sartre, *Nausea*

The biographer, after all, is as much of a storyteller as the novelist or historian.

Leon Edel, 'The Figure Under the Carpet'

*Tension between factual life &
sympathetic representation — surely a false
dichotomy.*

Introduction

How biographies are written and what form they have assumed in
the last century and a half are the general subjects of this book,
which developed out of my concern over the lack of critical
discussion of biography among readers at the same time as the
importance and publication of biography has dramatically
increased. The need to understand the literary techniques and
strategies of biography parallels its emergence today as perhaps
the most popular, widely-read body of non-fiction writing. But for
too long criticism has centred on the content rather than the form
of biographical writing, undermining its literary properties. This
study attempts to redress that emphasis by focusing on a series of
compositional problems and their solutions in the writing of
biography. It concentrates on such topics as biographical portraiture, experimentation and poetics. The goal is to show that
biography is a complex narrative as well as a record of an
individual's life, a literary process as well as a historical product.

An episode from *The Life of Charlotte Brontë* by Elizabeth Gaskell
illustrates the complexity and need for an analytic reading of
biography. Recounting a visit to Haworth, the Brontë home, in
1853, Gaskell narrates an unusual incident. To display the talents
of her dead brother, Branwell, Charlotte brings out, one evening,
his life-size portrait of the three sisters. Gaskell comments

> not much better than sign-painting, as to manipulation: but the
> likenesses were, I should think, admirable. I could only judge of
> the fidelity with which the two other were depicted, from the
> striking resemblance with Charlotte, upholding the great frame
> of the canvas, and consequently standing right behind it, bore
> to her own representation, though it must have been ten years
> and more since the portraits were taken.[1]

Here, the biographer is in an unique situation: she is able to
compare a portrait of her subject with her subject, incorporating
the entire scene into her text, creating yet another witness to the

1

event, the reader. Gaskell is observing while she is observed; Charlotte Brontë, meanwhile, is both a presence and an image. Symbolically, one may choose to see Charlotte as the figurative supporter of the entire family, as indeed she was, being the best-known and longest-living member of the group. Upholding the group portrait emblematically demonstrates Charlotte's role as survivor in a family that suffered the deaths of two sisters and a brother. But the scene possesses another meaning.

In the effort of comparing the real and the represented, Gaskell enacts the process of biography, which is the visual, mental and verbal comparison of what we read with what we think we know of the subject. The scene, in its active effort of comparing and creating (the narrator simultaneously recreates it while participating in it), represents the act of biography. Gaskell's reaction in matching the real Charlotte with the represented – there is a 'striking resemblance' proving the fidelity, she notes – is actually what occurs in biography. Fact and image attempt to unite, although content and structure often threaten the union. The reaction of the reader, based on literary and historical understanding, validates or rejects the work; in this case, Gaskell confirms the likeness which her complete analysis in the paragraph elaborates.

Most importantly, the scene illustrates what we seek in biography, the knowledge that the resemblance between the subject in the biography is equivalent to his empirical existence. But the complexity of the scene increases with the presence of the biographer, who is both an interpreter and an object of interpretation. As narrator and author, Gaskell adds two more roles to that of a character. And standing before the author, the real Charlotte, representing an historical self, holds up her timeless self-portrait, detached and silent behind it, but inviting comparison and comment. Self-consciously, Gaskell and the reader gaze at the objects, the painting and the person. As witnesses, we become aware of multiple perspectives in much the same way that we sense the complexity of vision in Velázquez's 'Las Meninas'. In that painting of the Infanta Margarita, the position of the painter, the reflected image of King Philip iv and his wife Mariana, and the unidentified courtier silhouetted against the rear stairway, plus the outward stares of various figures, challenge the viewer. So, too, is Elizabeth Gaskell challenged by Charlotte Brontë in the scene with Branwell's painting. Readers of biography, however, often receive a text too passively; they are unaware of being placed in an interpretative position, although the very nature of biography demands it.

One way biography challenges the reader is through its narrative style. Readers of biography consistently ignore, however, what is written in favour of what is written about, treating the narrative transparently. Such a response values the content more than the form, but realizing that the narrative of a biography frames the subject and affects our vision provides us with a greater awareness of the complexity and richness of biographical form. One must remember that, especially for biography, third-person narrative, on which it relies so heavily, 'best produces the illusion of pure reference'. But, as Frank Kermode reminds us, 'it *is* an illusion, the effect of a rhetorical device'.[2] Biography, because of its concern with actual people in a definable historical period, with identifiable qualities and details, nonetheless sustains an illusion of reality, particularly in its stress on order and completeness. Yet this is one method by which biography manages to resolve its paradox of achieving completeness by selectivity – through narrative strategies which, in turn, alter our relation to fact.

The aim of this study is to make us more aware of what it is we do when we read and, possibly, write biography. In brief, we participate in a life through numerous means which can be literary, psychological or historical. But the moment we begin to read the life of someone, we begin to compare, seeking that enviable position of having our subject stand before us as she tells us her life-story without interference or distortion. The aim of the comparison is to validate the truth of the biography in historical as well as literary terms. What I shall later call the corrective impulse of biography is actually the process of validating biography. Belief in the authority of biography results from continual correction and comparison, through new evidence or interpretation, of the biographer's account with those of others. This, in turn, legitimizes the reader's belief in the authenticity of the life. Elizabeth Gaskell's witnessing the real and imagined Charlotte Brontë parallels the action of the reader of biographies who consciously and unconsciously seeks moments of comparison in the life which, if they are not in the text, he will provide. The biographer satisfies this through his impulse to correct. But the actual presence of the narrator as a character in the biography,

such as Boswell in his *Life of Johnson* or Elizabeth Gaskell in her
Brontë alters the nature of the account, confusing its narrative
structure and response of the reader. Understanding such
changes and analysing such moments of correction, however, are
the tasks of the critic.

The issue is that of resemblance and one response by readers is
closer attention to the presentation of fact. Traditionally, fact has
validated the biographical enterprise for readers while imposing
limitations on writers. The difficulty, however, is that the best
ordered facts cannot substitute for 'our love of sharp incident,
revealing anecdote, suspenseful narrative, even explicit analysis
of motivation if those are given us with insight and with style'.[3]
But in doing so, the biographer reveals something of himself in the
process, employing methods of personal literary expression.
Consequently, the signature of the biographer is as important to
recognize as that of his subject. The former signs himself through
literary means, the latter through the record of his life.

Facts are to biography what character is to the novel – a
fundamental element of composition providing authenticity,
reality and information. As early as 1761 Gibbon noted several
uses for fact in his study of literature: those that prove 'nothing
more than that they are facts'; those that 'may be useful in
drawing a partial conclusion' where one might be able to judge
'the motives of an action, or some peculiar features in a character';
those – the rarest – whose influence prevails throughout an entire
system and are so 'intimately connected as to have given motion
to the springs of action'.[4] But in biography, the role of fact has
received little notice. Nonetheless, Izaak Walton employed fact to
make his *Lives* more credible and dramatic, Boswell defended his
life of Johnson because of his more accurate facts, Carlyle justified
the length of his *Frederick* because of the volume of facts, Strachey
supported his *Eminent Victorians* because of his interpretation of
fact, while Virginia Woolf struggled with her life of Roger Fry
because of the facts.

But facts are not conclusions nor are they meant to be. Often,
they are manipulated, altered or misused to sustain an interpretation or characterization: Walton, for example, omitted the date
of Donne's will in his 1640 life to maintain the impression of
Donne's preparedness for death (the will was actually written
only three months before Donne died in March 1631); Boswell
omitted details on Johnson's youth and early manhood, concen-

trating four-fifths of the biography on his last twenty years; Carlyle begins *Frederick* announcing the abstruseness of fact and the need to interpret it symbolically 'to try for some Historical Conception of this Man and King . . . An Enterprise which turns out to be, the longer one looks at it, the more of a formidable, not to say unmanageable nature!'; Strachey, among his many shifts of fact, places a crucial conversation between Henry Edward Manning and his spiritual guide Miss Bevan, 'in the shrubbery', adding a suggestive detail when no evidence for such a setting exists; similarly, Strachey describes Florence Nightingale's dying in a 'shaded chamber' when, in fact, her room faced south, had no curtains and was open to the fresh air and sunlight. But to sustain the romantic quality of legend, Strachey creates a mysterious room. In *Roger Fry*, Virginia Woolf continually battles with fact, asking 'how can one cut loose from facts, when there they are, contradicting my theories?' Readers of biographies, however, rarely question facts because, as one critic has noticed, 'it is the spirit of the age to believe that any fact, no matter how suspect, is superior to any imaginative exercise, no matter how true.'[5]

Fact in biography, however, introduces critical questions regarding the nature of life-writing and literary form. To what extent is fact necessary in biography? To what degree does it hinder the artistic or literary impulse of the biographer? To what degree does the biographer alter fact to fit his theme or pattern? How does fact gain meaning? In 1834 Carlyle perceived these difficulties when he asked: 'What are your historical Facts; still more your biographical? Wilt thou know a Man, above all a Mankind, by stringing-together beadrolls of what thou namest Facts?' What insights can fact alone tell us about the subject? Nietzsche in 1885–6 believed 'there are no "facts-in-themselves," for a sense must always be projected into them before there can be "facts"', a philosophic concept that casts suspicion on their validity.[6] Certain biographers and readers have long shared this scepticism, but until recently they have been subsumed by the ready acceptance of the illusion of fact and order in biography. However, contemporary theories of fictional form and narrative technique have clarified our awareness of order and belief, presentation and authenticity, in biographical writing. Nonetheless, such an attitude must combat the domination of fact in biographical expression.

The importance of fact in biography corresponds with the

seventeenth-century rise of science, the eighteenth-century emergence of empiricism, the nineteenth-century dominance by history and the modern emphasis on individual experience rather than a collective tradition. More specifically, it is aligned with a shift away from legend, hagiography or panegyric in life-writing to a concern with the record of a person's life as that record becomes more accessible and unavoidable. Facts, evidence, establish the authenticity of a life, as realism – aligned with objectivity – replaces romance. Walton's *Lives*, Fuller's *History of the Worthies of England* and Aubrey's *Brief Lives* indicate the emergence of realistic detail through the use of records, documentation and interviews which contradict an earlier tradition of impression, remembrance or fabrication. Research and investigation soon become the *sine qua non* for eighteenth- and nineteenth-century biography which relied more heavily on fact than on the identification of values between biographer and subject, or the interpretation of character and narrative presentation. The development of institutions such as the Royal Society became 'perhaps rather a mnemonic than a cause . . . for [the] tyranny of Fact' as reality, itself, became anatomized into fact.[7]

As realism grew in the novel, paralleling and often imitating the factual form of biography, the usefulness of biography also became more evident. Fascination with the Plutarchian and then Johnsonian interest in 'domestic privacies' increased the authoritative and instructive nature of biography while adding to its pleasure. Boswell exuberantly demonstrated this in his *Life of Johnson* (1791); David Masson exhaustively illustrated it in his seven-volume life of Milton (1859–94). To provide such intimate detail, letters grew more important for the biographer and he used them more extensively in his accounts. The acceptance of the multi-volume life in the nineteenth century, inflated by lengthy excerpts from letters, reflects the importance of documents to validate a life, a defence as well as a justification of the biographical form. Undigested and often inaccurate, these facts were nonetheless assumed to be appropriate.

Such a concentration of fact-gathering and investigation did not abate in the post-Stracheyan world of biography, despite the influence of psychology on interpreting and selecting rather than reporting and informing. Research has relentlessly continued as libraries and archives swell with records, letters, tapes, photographs, diaries and journals. Contemporary biographers have gleefully used this expansion of facts as justification for new biographies.[8] Biographers, however, are in danger of suffocating from the collected mass of material, becoming lost in minor details, adhering too strictly to chronology and failing to separate what is the important from the trivial. However, since the mid-nineteenth century, there exists a counter-tradition attempting to free the biographer from the compendious life for the shaped, interpretative life where perspective, dimension and a point of view control the material.

Beginning with Lockhart's *Scott* (1837–8), biographers have departed from facts – or at the very least, altered them to exhibit a figure more consistent with their image rather than record of him. This commitment to an organic portrait, originating in sympathy and sustained by the imaginative vision of the biographer, substitutes a Boswellian emphasis on understanding for a Baconian stress on collecting data. Such a biographer goes beyond his material to maintain an intuitive sense of his subject, although this often means the manipulation of data. John Forster exhibits this habit in his life of Dickens, conflating letters and altering texts. Lytton Strachey exploits this practice in his liberal interpretation or, on occasion, refusal to include facts, as in his decision not to incorporate Queen Victoria's late correspondence in his biography because it altered his conception of the mournful Queen presented in the last third of the life. Virginia Woolf, however, implicitly defended such departures from the record when she introduced the phrase 'creative fact'.

Appearing in her essay 'The Art of Biography', partly a defence of *Queen Victoria*, 'creative fact' became a popular watchword. 'Almost any biographer', wrote Woolf, 'if he respects fact, can give us much more than another fact to add to our collection. He can give us the creative fact; the fertile fact; the fact that suggests and engenders.' For Woolf this is the greatest asset of the biographer, making him equal to the novelist in creative power and importance. More recent biographers have expanded this approach. Phyllis Rose in her biography of Woolf, for example, defines a life in a non-factual way: 'A life is as much a work of fiction – of guiding narrative structures – as novels and poems, and that the task of literary biography is to explore this fiction.'[9] This displacement of facts and their inability to explain the configurations of a life highlight an entirely new approach to life-writing where the value of biography derives from the appraisal and presentation, rather than the accumulation and accuracy, of facts.

The importance of 'creative fact', however, skirts the problem of whether those works which exceed factual detail through their allegiance to conception rather than record remain biographies. Two questions emerge: what makes a fact creative? and does this creativity impair the authenticity of biography? Although some readers initially turn to biography as a reference tool or critical handbook seeking personal detail, literary criticism or cultural history, they often discover dramatic conflict, psychological analysis or structural experimentation. Characterization and point of view frequently overtake the mere presentation of material as the biographer recognizes that personality and character often subsume chronology and objectivity. The best biographies re-invent rather than re-construct. Biography is fundamentally a narrative which has as its primary task the enactment of character and place through language – a goal similar to that of fiction.

A biography is a verbal artefact of narrative discourse. Its tool, figurative language, organizes its form. A biographer constitutes the life of his subject through the language he uses to describe it and transforms his chronicle to story through the process of emplotment. This occurs through uniting discrete facts of the life with certain modes of plot structure so that the parts form a new whole identified as 'story'. However, the transformation of events into story takes place, as Hayden White has explained, through 'the suppression or subordination of certain [events] . . . and the highlighting of others, by characterization, motific repetition, variation of tone and point of view, alternative descriptive strategies, and the like . . .' These are all techniques associated with the emplotment of drama or fiction – but also biography. Four basic modes of emplotment suggested by Northrop Frye – Romance, Tragedy, Comedy and Satire – alter biography from a mere record of past events to a meaningful literary form through the use of conventional structures of fiction. As White details, 'by the very constitution of a set of events in such a way as to make a comprehensible story out of them, the historian [and biographer] charges those events with the symbolic significance of a com-prehensible plot-structure.'[10] Biography as a symbolic structure employing formal elements of language, fiction and narration – this summarizes my understanding of the genre.

Directing the choice of emplotment for the biographer, giving meaning to his subject's experiences, is, as White explains, 'the dominant figurative mode of the language he has used to *describe* the elements of his account *prior* to his composition of a narrative' (p. 94). The particular figurative language, controlling metaphor or narrative mode in a biographical text becomes the basis of my later discussion of biographical theory outlined in Chapter 5. At this stage, it is essential to recognize the primary element of language in biography and its role in determining its form; indeed, language and modes of narration, not content, structure a biography. Not facts, but the presentation of those facts establish the value of biographical writing. In the composition of biography, fictive form rather than historical content dominates as the events of a life become the elements of a story. 'We make sense', says White, 'of the real world by imposing on it the formal coherency that we customarily associate with the products of writers of fiction . . .' (p. 99). This fictive power directs the composition and reading of biography, explaining how biography translates fact into literary event and why biography continually interests readers. Emplotment provides fact with fictive meaning while gratifying our desire to resolve our own sense of fragmentation through the unity or story of the lives of others – and implicitly our own. The fictive power of 'story' provides us with a coherent vision of life.

The patterns of modern fiction and contemporary biography have close connections; factual biography depends as heavily on conceptual paradigms and narrative patterns as fiction. But the suggestion that aesthetic coherence is incompatible with the truth of correspondence in biography undermines the literary nature of biography.[11] The most successful biographies employ facts as parts of an aesthetic as well as logical or expository whole. Boswell provides a pattern of interpretation as well as a factually accurate account of Johnson's life. Furthermore, the impulse of biography is often corrective, revising facts and details or replacing legend with fact – which, in turn, relies on literary forms of expression. Biography triumphs over experience by structuring the confusions of daily life into patterns of continuity and progress.

In transforming the unselective moments of a life into a pattern, the biographer establishes both an explanation and a theme for his subject. Fact becomes metonymic, a part relating to another part involving reduction, by virtue of the need to select and interpret. Every biography manifests its inherently literary resources through its style, tone and point of view and seemingly contradicts the nature of its pure historiography. This opposition between the requirement of presenting facts in a literary fashion versus their basically unimaginative character occurs through the process of emplotment. The situation parallels Pirandello's definition of a fact: 'A fact is like a sock which won't stand up when it's empty. In order that it may stand up, one has to put into it the reason and feeling which have caused it to exist.'[12] For a fact to exist in a biography it needs an imaginative as well as referential dimension which the process of writing provides.

Objective biography is logically and artistically impossible. 'Observation is always selective' as Karl Popper reminds us. Every observation, he explains, requires 'a chosen object, a definite task, an interest, a point of view, a problem' otherwise it is valueless. Lytton Strachey recognized this when he urged that biographers adopt a 'subtler strategy' and write with a 'becoming brevity' and 'freedom of spirit'. The modern responsibility of the biographer is 'to lay bare the facts of the case, *as he understands them*'.[13] As Strachey suggests and Popper confirms, totally objective knowledge or reporting does not exist. Popper argues that we do not think inductively, but deductively, beginning with an hypothesis which then shapes our discovery and use of facts. What we know or learn is the result of how we approach what we seek. Emil Ludwig, biographer of Napoleon, Goethe and others, stated the case in 1927 when he said the biographer 'begins with the concept of a character and searches in the archives for what is at bottom the corroboration of an intuition'. James L. Clifford recognized this when he cited Edgar Johnson on the general method of biographers: 'he knew that most biographers, including himself, started with some well-developed idea of what his subject had been like, and inevitably chose his evidence to support this pattern.'[14]

Harold Nicolson predicted the decline of biography as a literary form because of the modern age's absorption with fact. The conflict between a demand for all the facts in opposition to their artificial presentation would split biography and destroy its synthesizing quality.[15] But contemporary biographies have disproven Nicolson's assertion, demonstrating new ways of uniting the drive for creativity with the need for fact. Yet, the role of fact in biography has remained unclear. Essentially, that role is tripartite: to establish information, verisimilitude and truthfulness. The first is the simplest: to convey information and detail; the second is the most evocative and representational, generating a mood or atmosphere; the third is the most difficult and perhaps the greatest test of a biographer: establishing a sense of the character and personality of the subject.

An understanding of biography in these terms necessarily redefines the role of the biographer, transforming him from a journeyman or manufacturer of lives into a creative writer of non-fiction. The historical association of biography with journalists or historians, rather than novelists or dramatists, is both an oversimplification and misunderstanding. In his need to find a structure, point of view, method of characterization and descriptive technique, the biographer is akin more to the creative writer than the historian. This awareness in turn brings tremendous satisfaction to the biographer, as Leon Edel expressed in the introduction to his final volume of *Henry James*: 'I found my personal reward in the imagination of form and structure – after all, the only imagination a biographer can be allowed.'[16]

In a letter to Edmund Gosse in 1893, Robert Louis Stevenson colourfully summarized the challenge, satisfaction and achievement of fact in biography:

> I like biography far better than fiction myself: fiction is too free. In biography you have your little handful of facts, little bits of a puzzle, and you sit and think, and fit 'em together this way and that, and get up and throw 'em down, and say damn, and go out for a walk. And it's really soothing; and when done, gives an idea of finish to the writer that is very peaceful. Of course, it's not really so finished as quite a rotten novel; it always has and always must have the incurable illogicalities of life about it . . . Still, that's where the fun comes in.[17]

Not every biographer experiences the 'fun' Stevenson describes, although they often imitate his physical actions. Nonetheless, the tension between the freedom and imprisonment of facts is the source of the frustration Stevenson narrates. The various methods of solving that dilemma by biographers will be a continuing subject in the pages that follow.

Chapter 1, 'Biography as an Institution', traces the development of lives in a series and the emergence of the biographical portrait in nineteenth- and early twentieth-century biographical writing. The presence of the professional biographer in the nineteenth century is the subject of Chapter 2, with the example of John Forster, the biographer of Dickens, Goldsmith, Landor, Swift and others. Chapter 3 explores the changes that occur when more than one biography of a person's life exists. George Eliot, the subject of over twenty-six biographies, is the example. Biographies written by writers, largely novelists, form the fourth chapter, which focuses on Mrs Gaskell, Trollope, Virginia Woolf and others. 'Biography and Theory' comprises Chapter 5 and explores the use of literary tropes, narrative method and myth in an effort to identify principles of biographical writing. The final chapter outlines departures from traditional biography and new efforts in experimentation from mock biography to group biography. Uniting all is the problem of fact and the nature of its aesthetic as well as structural function in biography.

1 Biography as an Institution

A biography should either be as long as Boswell's or as short as Aubrey's.

Lytton Strachey, 'John Aubrey'

It is appalling how small even the most extensive knowledge boils down when it is pithily used.

George Bernard Shaw to Archibald Henderson

The extremes Lytton Strachey proposes for the length of biography highlight the problem Bernard Shaw expresses which persists throughout the history of the genre: the proper size and scope of life-writing. In the nineteenth century, this issue was especially acute as the Victorian attraction to history, leading to the inclusive life, opposed the plea for an interpretative life indicated by George Eliot in 1852.[1] Initially, the analytic life was a minority voice as large, multi-volume biographies dominated Victorian lives. However, a tradition originating in short Latin lives, renewed by antiquaries of the sixteenth century, popularized by Aubrey's *Brief Lives* in the seventeenth, dignified by Johnson's *Lives of the Poets* in the eighteenth and culminating in works like Strachey's *Portraits in Miniature* in the twentieth reasserted the centrality of the brief life. In the nineteenth century, the form reached its apogee in collective lives, biographies in series and biographical dictionaries. Their extraordinary sales and continued influence is a measure of their importance.

In the nineteenth century, three publications demonstrate the institutionalization of biography in the brief life: Samuel Smiles's *Lives of the Engineers*, John Morley's English Men of Letters Series and Leslie Stephen's *Dictionary of National Biography*. Collectively, they confirm the importance of brief lives extended by such later writers as Edmund Gosse and Lytton Strachey. Critically, these works display the important tradition of short, analytic lives in advance of the modern preference for such biographies, as well as the constant tension in biographical history between the size and

13

value of a biography. The issue is literary and moral since the perception and acceptance of the subject's life is frequently in proportion to the length and detail of the biography. The question for the reader of the brief biography becomes whether or not the shorter life is as accurate and truthful as the longer; or, to reverse the emphasis, can overwhelming detail also provide an overall sense of character and pattern for the life? In short, does thoroughness of detail prevent the imaginative penetration of the life of the subject?

In his biography of John Sterling, Carlyle quotes the following passage written by Sterling from France in 1836:

> I have also lounged a good deal over the *Biographie Universelle* . . . As to the *Biographie Universelle*, you know it better than I. I wish Craik, or some such man, could be employed on an English edition, in which the British lives should be better done.[2]

Some forty-nine years later, Sterling's wish would be met by an English version of the *Biographie*, the *Dictionary of National Biography*. The appearance of the *Dictionary of National Biography* in January 1885 was the culmination of nearly three-quarters of a century of fascination and attraction to brief biographies or biographies in series. And it is this form of biography that became better known and more widely read than any other in the period.

As early as 1827 the need for brief lives evaluating rather than chronicling a subject was recognized. In the 'Preface' to the *Universal Biographical Dictionary* (1800), John Watkins wrote

> Instead of lamenting with the great Lord Bacon that 'the writing of Lives is not more frequent,' we could, perhaps with more propriety, wish that the practice were either limited or better directed . . . Of late years, thanks to the officious zeal of friendship, and the active industry of literary undertakers, biographical memoirs have become as multitudinous, prolix, and veracious as epitaphs in a country churchyard.

Carlyle continued this criticism in his essays on Scott and Boswell, suggesting that authors be paid for *not* writing fulsome lives.[3] A review in 1857 predicted what occurred over the remaining years of the century as biography grew to unmanageable proportions:

As biographies swell almost to bursting with minute details, under the process of accumulation, it is easy to foresee that we shall have to revert again to that abridged style of biography, of which Johnson's 'Lives of the Poets' are models; – a style which gives us conclusions, but spares us the premises; a style in which the biographer's industry appears in the completeness of the character resulting, rather than in a repetition of all the details from which it is drawn. We want to see a portrait, not an inventory of the features possessed by the subject.[4]

This passage is an important summary because it suggests the kind of biographical style that emerged through individual works and collective lives. The turn to 'the completeness of the character', a revision and expansion of the eighteenth-century idea of 'the character' as a prose form rather than the repetition of details, indicates the need for an interpretation not an accounting. The call for a portrait suggests an artistic effort by the biographer instead of an historical recording. What these and other critical passages represent was the need for biography to redefine itself. In an age of expansion, it must look to limitation. Instead of ballooning with details, it must concentrate on meaning; instead of containing undigested material presented as 'facts', it must possess design and awareness of the ambiguity of its information. But where were the Victorians to find a model of such biography? In a word, they located it in Plutarch.

The importance of Plutarch for the development of English biography at large is, of course, a commonplace but his value for nineteenth-century biographers has generally gone unnoticed. Yet, more than any other figure with the possible exception of Boswell (in part because of Croker's 1831 edition of *The Life of Johnson*), Plutarch dominates the composition and style of nineteenth-century biographical writing. What North's 1579 translation of the *Parallel Lives* meant to Shakespeare and his age, and Dryden's 1683 version meant to Boswell and the eighteenth century, the many editions and translations of Plutarch through-out the nineteenth century meant to a generation of Victorian biographers. The emergence of the literary portrait, brief life, biographical dictionary and collected lives in the nineteenth century owe their popularity to the example of Plutarch. His influence directly shaped the nature of biography in a form other than Seutonian fact-gathering in a chronological order that often mushroomed in the Victorian age into a pseudo-scholarly 'life and letters' account. Character not chronology was the appeal of the Plutarchian style as the singular question Plutarch asked – what sort of man was he? – became the focal point for brief biography.

The importance of Plutarch for nineteenth-century biography is most easily recognized by the numerous translations of the *Parallel Lives* in the period. Their appearance throughout the century suggests that nineteenth-century biography virtually began and ended with Plutarch. In 1800 William Mavor, editor of the late eighteenth-century biographical compilation, *The British Nepos*, translated and edited a school edition of Plutarch; in 1892 W. W. Skeat published *Shakespeare's Plutarch*. The intervening years witnessed a plethora of remarkable editions beginning with *The Female Revolutionary Plutarch* (1803, 3 vols) and the companion volume, *Revolutionary Plutarch* (1804, 3 vols), accounts of military and intellectual leaders of the French Revolution. In 1816 Francis Wrangham edited, in six volumes, *The British Plutarch*. By 1834 *The Cambrian Plutarch*, comprising *Memoirs of some of the Most Eminent Welshmen* by John Humpfreys Parry appeared. In 1846 *The Modern British Plutarch* was published, subtitled *Lives of Men Distinguished in the Recent History of Our Country for their Talents, Virtues or Achievements*. Charles Duke Younge's imitative *Parallel Lives of Ancient and Modern Heroes* appeared in 1858 while in 1860 Arthur Hugh Clough's revision of Dryden's translation appeared and remained in print throughout the century. W. C. Taylor revised Wrangham's 1816 version at mid-century.

Literary references to Plutarch begin with Mary Shelley citing the *Parallel Lives* in *Frankenstein* (1818) as one of the master texts for the monster along with *Paradise Lost* and *Werther*. Allusions to Plutarch appear in *Sartor Resartus* (1834) and in *Our Mutual Friend* (1865), where Dickens has Silas Wegg read Plutarch to Boffin who found the *Lives* 'in the sequel extremely entertaining, though he hoped Plutarch might not expect him to believe them all'.[5] Historical references to the *Lives* include Rousseau, who began to read them at six (and supposedly memorized them by eight), and Napoleon, who carefully read Plutarch throughout his career, as did Beethoven. Macaulay's criticism of Plutarch as a historian in 1828 (although he re-read him with pleasure in 1837 while in India) and Edward Fitzgerald's assertion in 1837 that Plutarch unquestionably 'must have been a Gentleman' are further examples of his prominence. J. A. Symonds read only Plutarch

and Fielding during an 1873 trip to Italy and by 1876 read the
Parallel Lives every morning with his daughter after breakfast.[6] At
the end of the century General Gordon recommended Plutarch as
a handbook for his young officers, while George Bernard Shaw
advised his first biographer in 1905 to avoid a 'theatrical
biography' and keep 'to the lines of Boswell's Johnson and
Lockhart's Scott, not to mention Plutarch'. In an 1873 statement,
R. C. Trench summarizes the importance of Plutarch for
nineteenth-century biography: 'Vivid Moral portraiture, this is
what he aimed at, and this is what he achieved. It is not too much
to affirm that his leading purpose in writing those lives was not
historical but ethical.'[7] Expanding an eighteenth-century tradition of anecdotes and tags from Plutarch, the nineteenth century
discovered in his work – the *Moralia* as well as the *Lives* – the
ethical model and moral focus that provided biography with the
integrity that made it as welcomed by readers as it was admired
by writers.

The virtues of Plutarch as a biographer can be summarized as a
concentration on the illuminating incident, the use of the
substantiating quote, the employment of structural *topoi*, an
emphasis on selective description and a concern with evaluation
rather than extended narrative. An emphasis on individual
human qualities rather than the influences on a life further
resulted in the attractiveness of brief and/or collective lives
written anecdotely but with design. In more detail, the elements
that influenced nineteenth-century biographers – always with the
moral reinforcement of exalting virtues and examples buttressed
with precepts – begin with the frequently cited concentration on
personal details. The acceptability of personal anecdote found
confirmation in Johnson who planned, but did not complete, an
edition of the *Parallel Lives* and, of course, Boswell who cited
Plutarch as his authority several times in his *Life of Johnson*. But
the Plutarchian ideal also taught the suppression of uncomfortable or too revealing facts in an effort to maintain nobility of
character.

Another aspect of Plutarchian biography that attracted the
historical interests of the Victorians was its reliance on, and
recognition of, scholarship. This appeal to authority provided
authenticity for the interpretative life which sacrificed detail but
not references. Criticism of the shortcomings of previous scholarship also occurred, as John Forster illustrated in the 'Preface' to

his second edition of *Goldsmith* when he castigated the errors in
Prior's life of Goldsmith. The ethical nature of man, fundamental
to Plutarch's methods, as well as the heroic grandeur of his subject
also strongly interested the Victorians. The opening of Plutarch's
'Alexander' would evoke approval from Victorian biographers
and readers alike:

> For it is not Histories that I am writing, but Lives; and in the
> most illustrious deeds there is not always a manifestation of
> virtue or vice, nay, a slight thing like a phrase or a jest often
> makes a greater revelation of character than battles where
> thousands fall, or the greatest armaments or sieges of cities . . . I
> must be permitted to devote myself rather to the signs of the
> soul in men, and by means of these to portray the life of each,
> leaving to others the description of their great contests.

For many biographers such as Carlyle in his *Life of Sterling* or Mrs
Gaskell in her *Life of Charlotte Brontë*, this emphasis on portraying
the 'signs' of a man's life rather than a description of the facts is an
important manifesto.

Excelling these features of biography for the Victorians,
however, was Plutarch's belief that the primary purpose of
biography was moral – that a life-narrative existed to instruct. His
life of Pericles states the view explicitly:

> Moral good is a practical stimulus; it is no sooner seen, than it
> inspires an impulse to practice, and influences the mind and
> character not by a mere imitation which we look at, but by the
> statement of the fact creates a moral purpose which we form.
>
> And so we have thought fit to spend our time and pains in
> writing of the lives of famous persons.[8]

Nineteenth-century biographers upheld this position as a defence
of, and rationale for, their writing. If a biographer should choose
to reverse this emphasis, as some accused Froude of doing in his
life of Carlyle, a furore would be likely to explode. But nowhere
was the moral purpose of biography made clearer than in the
various collected lives that emerged in the century. In 1859, for
example, Samuel Smiles, a popularizer of lives in a series, wrote

> Biographies of great, but especially good men are . . . most

instructive and useful, as helps, guides, and incentives to others. Some of the best are almost equivalent to Gospels – teaching high living, high thinking, and energetic action for their own and the world's good. British biography is studded over . . . with illustrious examples of the power of self-help, of patient purpose . . .

Anticipating Smiles, Francis Jeffrey in 1835 described biography

as the most instructive and interesting of all writing . . . teaching us . . . great moral lessons, both as to the value of labour and industry, and the necessity of *virtues*, as well as the intellectual endowments, for the attainment of lasting excellence.[9]

The didactic character of biography, restating Goldsmith's view from the 1762 'Preface' to *his* abridgement of Plutarch, remained an important link between Plutarchian and nineteenth-century biography. So, too, did the habit of suppressing uncomfortable or disturbing facts about the subject that would disrupt or alter his integrity. What Plutarch explains in his 'Lucullus', that 'the shortcomings and faults which run through a man's conduct . . . we should regard rather as the defects of goodness than the misdeeds of wickness', became the justification for uncritical lives.[10] This negative dimension of selectivity found support among Victorian eulogistic biographers like Mrs Richard Burton or Mrs Kingsley in their lives of their husbands, or in J. W. Cross's edited and intensely respectful portrait of his wife, George Eliot. But as the century progressed and Plutarch was found to be factually inaccurate while distorting the truth, his influence waned.

Nonetheless, Plutarch's stress on distinguishing traits in collective biographies that grouped lives thematically or topically had a great impact on the composition and form of nineteenth-century biography. The condensed life with a moral purpose, contained within a volume or series of similarly styled lives whose brevity permitted only anecdotal illustrations of personality, resulted in a long and popular set of titles that shaped nineteenth-century life-writing. And linked to the emphasis on the Plutarchian form was the reprinting of a crucial set of collective lives beginning with selections from Aubrey's *Brief Lives* (1813). Thomas Fuller's

Worthies of England (3 vols) appeared in 1840, while J. H. Newman's edition of *Lives of the English Saints* began in 1844. By 1862, and following, *Men of the Time* started, the forerunner of *Who's Who* which continued the popularity of biographical dictionaries originating in the eighteenth century with the awesome but incomplete *Biographia Britannica* which only reached the letter F.

Spin-offs such as G. L. Smyth's *The Worthies of England* (1850), an imitation of Fuller, or the 1872 edition of *Lives of the Saints* edited by S. Baring-Gould and the fuller 1898 edition of Aubrey maintained the fascination with brief lives, sharply drawn with one or two dramatic incidents. Works on genealogy began to become important at this time, notably Debrett's *Peerage* begun in 1803 and Burke's *Peerage* with the first edition appearing in 1841. The formalization of biographical writing in a series occurred in many fields as seen by the *Foreign Office Lists of Diplomats and Consular Year Book* (ca. 1852), *Lives of British Physicians* (1830), *Lives of Eminent Missionaries* (1832–5), *Lives of Eminent Zoologists* (1834), *Lives of the British Admirals* (1833, ff. by Robert Southey), *Biographies of Eminent British Statesmen* (1831–9), *Lives of Indian Officers* (1867) or *Heroes of Industry* (1866). Tradesmen also became popular subjects and titles like *Lives of the Electricians* (1887, 2 vols) or *Lives of Distinguished Shoemakers* (1849) and *Heroes of the Telegraph* (1891) soon appeared in print. One publisher even announced *Wrecked Lives; or, Men Who Have Failed* as a form of negative reinforcement to Victorian success.[11]

Collective biography also became a subject for serious literary figures as well as popular compilers. Hazlitt published *Spirit of the Age: or Contemporary Portraits*, Carlyle, *On Heroes and Hero Worship*, Thackeray, *English Humorists of the 18th Century*, Emerson, *Representative Men*, Arnold, *Essays in Criticism*, and Sir James Stephen, *Essays in Ecclesiastical Biography*. Strictly speaking these are not biographies, if we reserve the term for a complete account of a subject's life, but they are attempts, in the Plutarchian manner, to provide the character of a subject in his time associated with his finest accomplishments. When Carlyle rhetorically asked in *The French Revolution* 'where are the Plutarchs?' the answer was not in the grand histories of noble men but in the numerous collective lives that stressed the highlights of a life, often through anecdote, establishing a strong counter-tradition to the life and letters style.[12]

Plutarch contributed one additional dimension to biographical writing: a self-reflexive awareness of the role of the biographer. At the beginning of his life of Timoleon, he explains that in writing the life of another, he discovers something about himself:

> It was for the sake of others that I first commenced writing biographies; but I find myself proceeding and attaching myself to it for my own; the virtues of these great men service me as a sort of looking-glass, in which I may see how to adjust and adorn my own life.

Attention to understanding the life of the subject became, for Plutarch and his followers, attention to self-discovery. It was not until 1910, however, that Freud, in his biography of Leonardo, restated Plutarch's idea when he suggested that writers often choose their subjects 'for personal reasons of their own emotional life'.[13] In the *Parallel Lives*, the nineteenth century found endurance in suffering, the pursuit of goodness through morality and a recognition of man's temporality. These virtues tended to shape the substance, as Plutarch's technique aided in forming the style, of a series of biographical works that, in turn, prepared biography for the changes initiated at the end of the century by Lytton Strachey and others.

It was Samuel Smiles, physician and railway administrator, journalist and biographer, who perhaps most clearly demonstrated the Plutarchian ideal of didactic and moral biography in the Victorian age. In *Lives of the Engineers* (1861–2), *Industrial Biography* (1863), *Men of Invention and Industry* (1884), and *Life and Labour: or Characteristics of Men of Industry, Culture and Genius* (1887), Smiles upheld the principle that biography instructs through noble example. 'Good rules may do much, but good models far more, for in the latter we have instruction in action – wisdom at work', he wrote in his popular tract and guide to his biographies, *Self Help*.[14] Through his accounts of the public accomplishments of men of engineering and science, Smiles satisfied Victorian England's need for heroes who rose to greatness on the morals of good behaviour. After John Forster, according to one historian of biography, Smiles 'came nearest to being a professional biographer' and his contribution to changing the status if not perception of biography cannot be discounted despite the excessively moral presentation of his subjects.[15]

That Smiles was a popular and influential writer has been made clear by, among others, Asa Briggs in *Victorian People*; that Smiles had an important role in the development of biography has been less noticed. Like Plutarch, Smiles favours collective biography and, at least implicitly, structures his lives in the parallel manner of Plutarch. He also concentrates on the heroic dimension of his subjects, repeatedly showing their ability to triumph against adversity, often achieving prosperity as well as fame. His ability to write clearly, if at times simply, captured the interest of the public; they saw in his *Lives of the Engineers* or *Industrial Biography* proof that self-discipline, persistence, common sense and courage could mean success as much as genius, inspiration and imagination. No biographer was more Victorian in embodying the virtues and values of the age than Smiles. And as a biographer, he spent as much effort on the literary composition of his lives as on their historical accuracy. In matters of tone, point of view and narrative, Smiles is as capable as Trollope, Hardy or, at times, Dickens. For A. O. J. Cockshut to emphasize the inabilities of Smiles as a writer is to negate his role as a biographer whose sense of structure and presentation of subject matter equalled the demands of his time and his wide readership. In his celebration of work and its virtues, Smiles confirmed the Victorian ethos through triumphant examples.

In the concluding paragraph of *Past and Present*, Carlyle predicts the rise of the labourer and the general advancement of man via his activities:

> Ploughers, Spinners, Builders; Prophets, Poets, Kings; Brindleys and Goethes, Odins and Arkwrights; all martyrs, and noble men, and gods are of one grand Host: immeasurable; marching ever forward . . . noble every soldier in it; sacred, and alone noble. Let him who is not of it hide himself; let him tremble for himself.[16]

Nobility is work, defined by the conduct of men in the march of progress. The recorder of this movement is Smiles, who documents its progress in *Lives of the Engineers*. In men like Brindley, who proudly and valiantly pursue their goals of technical advancement and human improvement, Smiles translates Carlyle's prediction of the future into achievement and shows its arrival. Smiles, however, was not the first nineteenth-century writer to provide collective biographies of contemporary successes.

In 1830–1 George Lilie Craik, the Scottish journalist, anonymously published for the Society for the Diffusion of Useful Knowledge, under the direction of Charles Knight, a two-volume work that initiated Victorian biographical studies of self-improvement and success. Entitled *The Pursuit of Knowledge Under Difficulties illustrated by Anecdotes* (note the prominent Plutarchian mode), the book contained biographical sketches in dictionary form of English and foreign scholars, artists, scientists, engineers and inventors who succeeded against great difficulties. This work of inspiration and guidance gradually became a popular success reappearing in 1844. A year later a three-volume edition was published, followed by a two-volume version in 1858, revised and enlarged in a new one-volume version in 1865, finally reprinted in 1881 and 1906. In 1847 a supplement illustrated 'by female examples' appeared. John Sterling's reference to Craik in his 1836 letter to Carlyle indicates something of the general awareness of his work. In his autobiography, Charles Knight quotes a letter by Craik that highlights the impetus for both the *Pursuit of Knowledge* and, by slight extension, the work of Smiles. Discussing tentative titles, Craik writes 'our title must be, not Anecdotes of Self-Taught Genius at all, for that is greatly too limited, but *Anecdotes of the Love of Knowledge*'.[17] Such a distinction is common to all the examples he adds, while the title combines a Plutarchian stress on anecdote with a Victorian emphasis on self-improvement. Henry Brougham, founder of the Society for the Diffusion of Useful Knowledge and the Queen's Attorney General, however, altered the title to *The Pursuit of Knowledge Under Difficulties*.

As a boy, Smiles read Craik's book and even memorized passages. In the 1840s, beginning with his lectures to the young workers of Leeds, Smiles began to consider a work parallel to Craik's focusing not on literary but commercial and common successes illustrated by 'examples of conduct and character'. Demonstrating the value of George Stephenson's great word – 'Perseverance' – Smiles sought to show how success can be 'accomplished by means of individual industry and energy' which we all possess. George Stephenson, railway engineer and inventor, was one of his early examples and Smiles's personal acquaintance plus curiosity and admiration of him led to his research and publication of his *Life of George Stephenson* (1857), perhaps the first Victorian biographical bestseller.[18]

After giving up a career in medicine, Smiles became editor of the *Leeds Times*, and first met Stephenson at the opening of the North Midland Railway in 1840. Within five years Smiles himself began his more than twenty-year involvement with railways, beginning as an Assistant Secretary to the projected Leeds and Thirsk Railway, eventually becoming Secretary of the South Eastern Railway in London. After the death of Stephenson in 1848, James Kitson, Mayor of Leeds and noted manufacturer of locomotives, approached Smiles to write the life. He demurred, although three years later, in London, Smiles approached Robert Stephenson about writing the life of his father. Little enthusiasm for the project, plus Smiles's own sense of not knowing the region where Stephenson lived and worked, halted any further plans. But when his railways job took him to Newcastle in 1854 for several years, Smiles began his detailed research among Stephenson's associates, visiting locales and examining records necessary to write the life.

Smiles completed the biography in the spring of 1857; it appeared in June and reviews were quick to praise the work for its description of a model life: 'We should like to see this biography in the hands of all our young men', declared *Fraser's*. 'One breathes a healthy, bracing atmosphere in reading this book', added the reviewer. The *Westminster Review* echoed this sentiment noting that the biography would be a popular as well as useful book, while the *Quarterly Review* stressed the importance of the subject, grandly announcing that 'there is no science more worthy of study than the science of railway inter-communication'. Only a few writers, however, commented on the art of the biography. *Fraser's* noted that Smiles was 'so anxious to place the character and career of Stephenson justly before his readers, that he quite forgets himself. We do not know how a biographer could do better.' 'Graphic narrative' is the phrase the *Quarterly Review* favoured for the use of anecdote and political narrative of the opposition to the railway. The style was called 'manly' but the general focus was on the subject matter and organization of the work.[19] The overall popularity and importance of the book, read and appreciated by George Eliot among others, register the new value of biographical writing.

First among these values, which Smiles establishes and sustains, is the social and historical context for the life of Stephenson. The biography begins with a portrait of Newcastle and its environment, describing the economic and social need for railways to aid and improve the labouring conditions of the colliers. But Smiles does not limit himself to these descriptions; he conveys equally well the conditions in Caracas, Bogota and the Southeast Asian jungles where Robert Stephenson worked for three years.[20] A link between machinery and improving the conditions for men emerges as a consistent theme in the life which gives Stephenson the role of protector and reformer – as when he invented a safety light for miners. Supplementing the historical and social settings, written in clear but not excessive prose, are numerous anecdotes that vividly illustrate the character of Stephenson. Whether it is his special attachment to his son, involvement with machinery or determination to improve himself (in passing we are told Stephenson often wrote practice sums on the side of coal wagons while guiding their movement), Smiles always provides detail and example.

Added to these visual scenes are dramatic descriptions of danger, challenge or worry that lead most often to success. At these moments Smiles actually reconstructs dialogue and action, breaking down the authority of the omniscient narrator to provide a sense of actuality for the biography. Stephenson's early success in improving the pumps and saving the mine at Killingth (ch. 3), the dangerous experiment with a new safety lamp for the mines (ch. 6), or the account of a visit to Sir Astley Cooper, opponent to the development of the London and Birmingham railway (ch. 8), are all rendered dramatically by the re-creation of actual conversation or re-told in the voices of other dramatic narrators. These and other scenes, such as the famous battle between the 'Rocket', and its locomotive challengers, involve the reader with the drama of Stephenson's life which is also the drama of England's progress as the railways begin to shape the economic and social direction of the country. Implicitly, Stephenson is a modern knight armed with logic, common sense and engineering know-how.

The style of the biography alternates between popular diction and semi-archaic language. The tone is didactic although it does not weaken the book; by contrast, it provides a new level of appreciation by the audience who, when tired by the cliches of transparent words, discovers strength and education through the

powerful moral interpretations Smiles presents. George Eliot's
remark that reading the life out loud to G. H. Lewes 'has been a
real profit and pleasure' suggests the dual appreciation of the
events and their meaning.[21] The clarity of Smiles's language,
especially on technical matters, balances the generalities he relies
on when celebrating the importance of Stephenson's achievements. The style of Stephenson's own writing is generally clear,
terse and vigorous. At its most successful moments, the biography
blends descriptive language with analysis as in the building of the
embankment at the edge of Chat Moss near Manchester to
complete the Liverpool and Manchester Railway. Told by the
workers that he must give up 'the idea of a floating railway, and
either fill the Moss hard from the bottom, or deviate so as to avoid
it altogether', Stephenson never alters his purpose. 'Persevere!' is
his motto. 'You must go on filling in,' he said; 'there is no other
help for it. The stuff emptied in is doing its work out of sight, and if
you will but have patience, it will soon begin to show' (p. 156).
The metaphysical certainty of Stephenson marks his faith in his
work and confirms Smiles's emphatic theme that determination
will succeed.

Even humour has a place in Smiles's account of what eventually succeeds at Chat Moss. The 'copius stream of bog-water'
flowing out from Chat Moss, he explains, resembled in colour
'Barclay's double stout; and when completed, the bank looked
like a long ridge of tightly pressed tobacco-leaf' (p. 156). But
consistently, it is Stephenson's moral conduct that permits him to
tame nature and generate immense benefits for England.

Smiles, however, does not let the contribution of Stephenson or
the context of his success overshadow a sense of the individual
man. Frequent anecdotes in the Plutarchian manner of illuminating character appear throughout the life. We learn of his pleasure
in stimulating his students 'to educate themselves, . . . to acquire
that habit of self-thinking and self-reliance which is the spring of
all true manly actions'. 'In a word', says Smiles, 'he sought to
bring out and invigorate the *character* of his pupils' (p. 163).
Independence and character are stressed, although personal
details of Stephenson's family life and private relations, except
those with his son, are few. But anecdote reveals the man.

There is, finally, a balanced internal unity in this life; as various
experiments advance the state of engineering, so, too, does George
Stephenson's personal stature and fortune grow. And as various

projects come to completion, so too does Stephenson's life (ch. 18). At the end of his life, he has also renewed his love of nature. And as the biography concludes, Smiles transforms his subject into a universal hero: 'Though mainly an engineer, there was no area of speculation that he did not develop large or original veins' (p. 281). But in the tradition of the *Parallel Lives*, the conclusion of the life of Stephenson is actually a comparison, as Plutarch ended each set of his dual biographies with a comparison of his subjects. For Smiles, it is of father and son, a summary of their strengths, with very little on their weaknesses. But the wealth of the son, the first 'engineer millionaire' (p. 287), somewhat distances Smiles from his subject and in this comparison Smiles displays greater sympathy for the father than the son. It is to the father, principally, that Smiles writes his encomiastic concluding paragraph in a tone of grand achievement and success. The *Life of George Stephenson* shows the Plutarchian method applied to an industrialist who embodies the principle of character in action. Smiles's later work continued this tradition, most notably in his immensely successful *Lives of the Engineers*.

Before discussing that work, however, attention must be given to *Self Help, With Illustrations of Conduct and Perseverance* which appeared in between the two works. This influential text on Victorian morality also has a link to biography in its countless examples of individual success. Compressing the manner of the *Life of George Stephenson*, *Self Help* gives brief, but detailed, examples of personal achievement. Hundreds of figures, including Stephenson, demonstrate the virtue of energy, self-discipline, courage, thrift and character. *Self Help* is a biographical dictionary in reverse; organized by principles or virtues, it gives lives as examples instead of entries.

Organized in 1845 as part of his lectures to working men, *Self Help* was published in 1859 after the success of *Stephenson*, although it quickly outdistanced that work in sales and popularity. Plutarch, cited in the 1866 Preface, stands as a metaphor of the role Smiles played. Through his argument that 'the spirit of self-help is the root of all genuine growth in the individual' and reliance on models rather than rules, Smiles provides an effective moral tract of extraordinary appeal (p. 35). And in the opening chapter, Smiles defines the impulse to write and read biography. After stating that it is 'life rather than literature, action rather than study, and character rather than biography, which tend perpetually to renovate mankind', he corrects himself. 'Biographers of great, but especially of good men', he suddenly states, 'are nevertheless most instructive and useful, as helps, guides, and incentives to others.' Smiles later added that 'the chief use of biography consists in the noble models of character in which it abounds' (p. 350). This declaration of the didactic and moral force of biography, repeated in Chapter 12, shaped innumerable lives in the nineteenth century and demonstrated the continuation of the Plutarchian tradition. In his own work, Smiles tried to be honest, recording the failures or faults of his subjects as well as their successes. This is evident in *Self Help* as well as in the more important, for our purposes, *Lives of the Engineers*.

Smiles labels Chapter 2 of *Self Help* 'Leaders of Industry: Inventors and Producers'. In a host of examples, he summarizes the inventors as simple men who transformed industry and economic life, repeating in his attention to the practical men who have altered the lives of England, the men he would later celebrate in *Lives of the Engineers*. The publication of that series may have been, in fact, Smiles's reaction to an 1857 review of *Stephenson*. Writing in the *Westminster Review*, a critic remarked that Smiles 'has produced a solid, pleasant and useful book. We wish that we had as satisfactory lives of Brindley, Arkwright and the rest of them, as this of the elder Stephenson.'[22] Arkwright did not appear in Smiles's two-volume first edition of the *Lives* but Brindley began the series which included Smeaton, Rennie and Telford, plus shorter biographies of Vermuyde, Perry, Myddelton, Metcalf, Edwards and Meikle. The shorter biographies were supplanted with a social history of inland transportation. Later editions of the *Lives* contained the volume on George and Robert Stephenson (1862) and then one on James Watt and Matthew Boulton. Thematically, Smiles went from inland transportation (vols 1–2) to railways (vol. 3) and then the steam engine (vol. 4).

But what style is this work that prompted Gladstone to write fulsomely to Smiles that you 'have given practical expression to a weighty truth – namely, that the character of our engineers is a most signal and marked expression of British character'?[23] Is there any degree of personality that emerges in the fundamentally adulatory biographies? The short answer is no, but this should not limit our understanding of the contribution of *Lives of the Engineers* to the growth of biography between 1850 and 1918.

Smiles's *Lives of the Engineers* is essentially a model of Victorian collective biography, again in the Plutarchian tradition. Anecdote, digression and achievement characterize his treatment of the lives. A formula soon emerges of an introductory chapter in the tradition of Macaulay, stressing context, followed by a survey of accomplishments and then a summing up of character.

The bulk of the biographies involve the accomplishments of the subjects. Public not private action is the focus and we get detailed but not tedious accounts of construction problems, solutions and reactions. Canals, bridges, roadways and docks become the subject matter of a work subtitled *A History of Inland Communication in Britain.* Supplemented by picturesque engravings of these achievements and often amusing and intriguing footnotes showing how various advances were occurring simultaneously, the collective biography becomes a social history as well as personal account of England's achievements. Visual documentation in the form of reproduced account books, personal notes or even facsimiles of handwriting authenticate Smiles's research[24]. This, in addition to the various engineering drawings, portraits and scenes included, made the edition an expensive purchase (each volume sold for a guinea in 1861). But the frequent quotations from original materials, when available, such as letters by Brindley or notebooks from Telford, furthered the thoroughness of the biographies.

The final chapter of each life concentrates on the death and character of the subject, although the former is treated cursorily, the latter extensively. Smiles is conscious of not evaluating his subject in the body of the life and, in the eighteenth-century tradition of providing a character of his subject, he includes an estimate of his subject at the end. The comments are usually praiseworthy and moral, citing contributions, dutious behaviour and self-improvement. In a sense Smiles has constructed each life until the final chapter when the completed object (bridge, tunnel or canal) can be viewed in its entirety. Smiles seems to have adapted this method from engineering, initially surveying, then mapping or designing with detailed drawings, then overseeing the building and finally evaluating its function and accomplishment. But within the plan, he often varies the structure. Anecdote, such as Brindley's unexpected demonstration in the midst of parliamentary testimony of how he would construct a bridge by using a large cheese (p. 86), or his novelistic description of London in 1785 in his life of Rennie (p. 201), or his lengthy biographical footnote on the painter Skirving (p. 279), illustrates his willingness to depart from any fixed structure for the biographies. A tension emerges in the lives between his determination to stress the products of industrious self-improvement and his interest in conveying something of the personality of those involved with the life of his subject. Indeed, a curious feature of the *Lives* is that one appears to know more about the personality of the secondary figures than that of the major subjects. The Duke of Bridgewater, to whom Smiles devotes several chapters, is an example of this interest in a secondary character who in fact is more attractive than the major figure.

At the end of his life of Rennie, Smiles remarks that Rennie's 'works constitute his biography, overlaying . . . almost his entire life' (p. 274). This statement explains a great deal of the nature of *Lives of the Engineers* as achievements, history, politics and social forces contend with and largely overshadow concern with personal life. Smiles's *Stephenson*, with the additional life of the son, published as volume 3 of the 1862 edition of the *Lives*, balances these two elements more carefully. But in his implicit linking of the lives and their work (see for example, pp. 292 or 405 in 'Telford') through the themes of self-improvement, diligence, discipline and commitment, Smiles creates a unified work of collective biography that shares techniques similar to those used in English Men of Letters and the *Dictionary of National Biography*.

The immensely influential *Lives* demonstrates the importance of biography in dealing with men of action. It assumes a practical, compact form, as the lives achieved practical results. Although Smiles did not heed the anti-heroic thrust of Sir Francis Palgrave's attack on panegyrics, he did react to the voluminous lives that were omnipresent at mid-century. His later works, such as *Industrial Biography: Iron Workers and Tool Makers* (1863), *Lives of Boulton and Watt* (1865) and *Men of Invention and Industry* (1884), underscore his continued attachment to collective biography. The prevalence of this form made the appearance of the biographical series easier and more acceptable by the public. Smiles did not spawn the biographical series but his success with this form demonstrated its wide appeal. It satisfied a demand for biographies with an accessible format and instructive character. Continuing this tradition in nineteenth-century biography is the English Men of Letters series.

According to Harold Nicolson, among the few positive contributions of Victorian biography was what he labelled 'biography for students'.[25] This was a form of short biographical lives which under Leslie Stephen emerged as that great work, *The Dictionary of National Biography* and which earlier, in 1877, inspired John Morley to edit the scarcely less admirable English Men of Letters series. Nicolson's remark is curiously backhanded, criticizing the emergence of jejune textbook biographies, while praising both the *Dictionary of National Biography* and English Men of Letters series. But his ambivalence reflects a larger misunderstanding of the aims and achievements of both enterprises. The *Dictionary of National Biography* and the English Men of Letters series were important stages in the development of biography and epitomize some of the strongest qualities identified in twentieth-century biographical writing. These include illustrative detail, symbolic action, thematic organization, psychological interpretation and character analysis. The English Men of Letters series and *Dictionary of National Biography* confirm the institutional nature of brief biography of the nineteenth century while at the same time indicating some of the more striking features that are to dominate modern life-writing.

Collective biography, biographical dictionaries and biographies in a series had long intermingled but, until John Morley's project for a group of short bio-critical studies of major English writers written by distinguished men of letters, they did not intersect. Other than Johnson's *Lives of the Poets*, there had been no serious effort to present a set of literary lives by prominent writers. Morley, editor of the *Fortnightly Review* and then the *Pall Mall Gazette* (and best remembered perhaps as the editor who insisted on spelling God with a small 'g') was well-suited for the job.[26] Although he later entered politics in 1883, eventually becoming a Cabinet Minister, he continued his interest in literature, publishing a highly successful biography of Gladstone in 1903.

The selection of contributors for the proposed English Men of Letters series, however, was no easy task, as Alexander Macmillan reported to his son in 1877:

Morley has projected a series of *Short Books on Great Writers*. He has got Hutton for Sir Walter Scott, Goldwin Smith for Wordsworth [ultimately written by F. W. H. Myers], Symonds for Shelley, Pattison for Milton, Leslie Stephen for Johnson, Morrison for Gibbon. He tried to get Stanley for Bunyan, and

Matthew Arnold or Seeley for Shakespeare, but neither would accept. He thought if he could get Church to do something he might get the others to come in. So I wrote to the Dean, and in the meantime we got Gladstone to accept Homer and our Garrick dinner. So before I could hear from Church by post, on the morning of Gladstone's acceptance of the dinner I went down to the Deanery to see if Church was disengaged, which he was, and agreed to join us and meet Morley. Thus it all came about. He – the Dean – will do either Dryden or Spenser, he has not fixed quite which. But he will do either well. The idea is a sort of Essay – biographical and critical – on each of the authors about twice as long as a *Quarterly* article, in a little volume to sell at about half-a-crown. I think the series should do and do good. The Primers are all doing well, and I see no reason why such a series should not do also.[27]

The idea of combining the biographical with the critical in the manner of a *Quarterly Review* essay remained the ideal throughout the series, although it was realized with varying success. The quality of contributors included both recognized authorities such as Saintsbury and lesser-known critics such as the young Henry James.

The relationship between Morley and Macmillan, which made the English Men of Letters series such a success, originated in 1866 when the August issue of *Macmillan's Magazine* published Morley's essay on George Eliot. Both Eliot and Macmillan admired the piece and Morley soon became friends with each. By 1867 he was appointed editor of the *Fortnightly Review* (succeeding G. H. Lewes), remaining until 1882 when he became editor of *Macmillan's Magazine*. At the end of June 1877, following publication of his biographies of *Burke* (1867), *Voltaire* (1872), *Rousseau* (1873) and visits to America, Italy and Austria, Morley contemplated several biographical series. He wrote to George Lile Craik, Macmillan associate and author of the earlier and successful collective biography, *The Pursuit of Knowledge*. He described to Craik several schemes, the untitled English Men of Letters and what became Twelve English Statesmen, a series of political biographies he edited from 1888 to 1895. This latter series included Lord Rosebury on Pitt and Morley on Walpole. Craik's own success with collective biography was an incentive and model for Morley who at that time was completing a biographical study of Diderot which appeared in 1878.

A note from this period, however, suggests another influence. The note reads, 'Grove suggests Gladstone for Pitt'[28] and refers to Gladstone as a possible contributor to the Twelve English Statesmen series. The individual first mentioned is George Grove, at that time actively engaged in editing his *Dictionary of Music and Musicians*. Following his resignation as Secretary of the Crystal Palace in the autumn of 1873, Grove spent most of his energy on the dictionary project, contributing, himself, three major biographical entries: Beethoven, Mendelssohn and Schubert. In 1879, the year ten volumes of the English Men of Letters series appeared, parts one to six of the *Dictionary of Music* were also published (the first edition, issued in four volumes, contained twenty-five parts). Grove's earlier publishing experience included some fifteen years as editor of *Macmillan's Magazine* (1868–83), succeeding David Masson, the biographer of Milton, who went to the Chair of English at Edinburgh. Grove was, in turn, succeeded by Morley when the former became the first director of the Royal College of Music in 1883. The point of these details is to indicate the association of Morley with two leading biographical enterprises of his time, *The Pursuit of Knowledge* and Grove's *Dictionary*, the burst of energy during the 1870s in the creation of biographical dictionaries and series, and the small circle of innovative editors and publishers (largely Macmillan) who, together, formulated important elements in the structure, evolution and quality of biographical writing. Craik, Morley, Grove – with Leslie Stephen and later Gosse – shaped the character and continuity of collective and dictionary biography over the last twenty-five years of the nineteenth century.

In his *Recollections*, Morley casually remarks of the English Men of Letters series that 'the long series of short volumes' required 'much discussion as to the title of the series, for to call Milton, Hume, Burke, Bacon men of letters was absurd'. The decision of a title was crucial since it would affect the nature of the entire project. In a letter of 18 November 1877 to Macmillan, Morley reveals something of the debate over the choice of a title and his own preferences:

1. Great Men of Letters.

2. English Men of Letters
3. Short Books on English Authors
4. Masters of Literature.

With any one of them I'll be perfectly content – with preference for 3, and next to 3, and nearly good, I'll like 2. So choose.[29]

Number two appealed to Macmillan and Morley agreed, although not without concern, as the passage in his *Recollections* suggests. But more fundamental than a title for the series were the contributors. And no contributor seemed more important than that for the volume on Shakespeare.

Macmillan reported to his son in October 1877 that Matthew Arnold had turned the volume down, but Macmillan and Morley had other fish for their pond: George Eliot. This possibility Macmillan noted in a letter of 7 November 1877, adding 'If Mrs. Lewes won't do it, perhaps Lewes himself would.' In a postscript he explained why it was so crucial: 'it would be worth much silver and gold to us if she [Mrs Lewes] could start the series – say in April. I'm so afraid of the flatter ones coming first and [making] the impression.'[30] But in a letter two days later, Macmillan narrated the difficulties with such a proposal:

I have just come back from a very pleasant interview with George Eliot. She did not say *no*, and promised to think it over and write to us. She repeated what Lewes told us was her feeling, that she has a dread of coming forward in her own person and passing judgment on authors, and spoke as you, or even I, might speak with aversion of the habit of mind that leads people to pass off as sort of *final utterances* the feelings and thoughts which come to you in reading an author. She quoted a passage from Ste. Beuve which she thought should be the motto of such a series as we propose. I cannot give you the French – she is to send it – but the effect of it was that the business of a true critic was to appreciate, not *fix the doom* of an author. When you see it you will, I have no doubt, at once adopt it – if we can't get her to contribute a book it will be something at least to have a motto from her. But I am by no means hopeless about the book. Lewes came with me to the door and said it was a great thing to have got her to consent to think of it. I asked if I might tell you to write to her, and she said she would be glad to hear from you. But I think it would be well that we should have our talk on Monday before you do write.

On the following day, 10 November 1877, George Eliot wrote to decline the offer. The letter begins with the quotation Macmillan refers to: 'The quotation from Sainte-Beuve which I mentioned to you is on page 11 of his "*Cahiers*": "La critique pour moi (comme pour M. Joubert) c'est le plaisir de connaître les esprits, non de les régenter." '[31] Translated, the motto means 'criticism for me (as for Monsieur Joubert) is the pleasure of appreciating not of governing opinion'. Morley did not adopt it, nor did he succeed in convincing Eliot to participate, despite his offer of an increased fee. Nonetheless, Eliot praised the first three volumes in the series which she read in August 1878, although she refused a second invitation to participate. The series, however, continued and between 1878 and 1892 thirty-nine volumes appeared, including Trollope's *Thackeray* (1879), James's *Hawthorne* (1879), Huxley's *Hume* (1879) and Saintsbury's *Dryden* (1881). A second series started in 1902 with Morley supervising but not editing; twenty-eight volumes appeared including Chesterton's *Browning* (1903).

The correspondence between Morley and Macmillan over the first series, especially in its early years, reflects the variety of problems and challenges facing the enterprise. This sampling illustrates the progress of the undertaking:

5 October 1877. Morley to Macmillan:
Froude will write *Giraldus Cambrisun's*, he says, if I like. If I insist on some other subject, then he would have to take time to reflect on it – but of Giraldus, then he c[ould] do it easily and speedily. His letter is interesting. I will bring it on Tuesday. I hope I have not a true worry in taking a 12th century man: he says it . . . pleasant and amusing. Indeed there is some [argument] in having one far-away man of this sort. It makes the series both more comprehensive and Froude's name is very valuable, of course.

6 June 1878. Morley to Craik on Hutton's *Scott*:
It is good, but entre nous, it rather wants *charm* and that is just what Scott ought to have had – the faithful admirable man.

21 October 1878. Morley to Macmillan:
James is working on the Hawthorne: but he has not yet

answered my questions about biographical material which is a condition since given him. [Notes his refusal of Stafford Brooke for *Keats* because there is little biographical material and adds] strictly between ourselves, I am a *trifle* unhappy about Hume.

16 January 1879. Morley to Macmillan:
I have written to Trollope, and expect his answer today.

20 January 1879. Morley to Macmillan:
Here is Trollope's note about the Thackeray. I *expect* it will be the Dickens after.

27 January 1879. Morley to Macmillan:
PRIVATE / My dear Macmillan
Trollope is to write the 'Thackeray'. It seems that this is to be no full or official life of Thackeray because his family, as T. made his daughters promise, for good reason, I daresay, that no such life should be written. For this reason Stephen says that he would not have done it, if he had been asked. So I believe you will agree with me that we are excellently well off. Trollope says he will be ready by March 31.

17 February 1879. Morley to Macmillan:
Have you thought any more of Dowden for *Dickens*[?] On the whole a literary treatment of C.D. is the best – better than the *Household Words* style of writer, or any of that set. Dowden will follow instructions. I could map the book out. I cannot think of anyone else. If you don't approve, please let me have a line.

21 February 1879. Morley to Macmillan:
Dickens–Dowden may wait by all means.

16 April 1879. Morley to Macmillan:
The Thackeray will be much talked about, and the end of May and opening of June are the time for London talk.

Relations between Morley and Macmillan, however, were not always so congenial. Nearly a year after the series had been underway, Morley learned of a competing and cheaper project Macmillan had approved. A letter of 28 February 1879 expresses his unhappiness. The new series on European authors by John Richard Green, who in 1874 published the successful *Short History of England*, was to include 'eighteen penny books on English authors'. According to Morley, Macmillan could end up publishing two volumes on the same figure, 'one pair for 1/6 each, the other for 2/6 each. It is tolerably plain how utterly inappropriate this must be; and, as I now see the matter, nothing could *be more unfair to me*. For more reasons than one, I am amazed.'[32] Placated by Macmillan, the issue was resolved with new assurances of the continued production of the English Men of Letters series and a de-emphasis on English writers in the Green series.

At the time Morley was planning the English Men of Letters series, he was completing his own biography of Diderot. In it he remarks that the emergence of secular spiritual leaders in eighteenth-century France resulted in the appearance of the man of letters. The test of this new leader was to propagate new philosophies and moral conceptions among the populace. Disseminating ideas became the challenging goal for the man of letters:

> The characteristic of his activity is dispersiveness. Its distinction is to popularise such detached ideas as society is in a condition to assimilate; to interest men in these ideas by dressing them up in varied forms of the literary art; to guide men through them by judging, empirically and unconnectedly, each case of conduct, of policy, or of new opinion as it arises.[33]

The passage is a virtual prospectus for contributors to the English Men of Letters and a rationale for its existence.

An 1870 essay on Byron makes the link between biography and criticism even clearer:

> There is a sense in which biographical detail gives light to criticism, but not the sense in which the prurient moralist uses or seeks it. The life of the poet may help to explain the growth and prominence of a characteristic sentiment or peculiar idea. Knowledge of this is that fact in his life may uncover the roots of something that strikes, or unravel something that perplexes us. Considering the relations between a man's character and circumstances, and what he produces, we can . . . hardly know too much as to the personality of a great writer.

The life and work are, however, separate: 'each of these manifestations is to be judged independently of the other'.[34] Biography can aid criticism if the critic is not a narrow moralizer. In the series, and in his own criticism, Morley sought to correct the distortions resulting from moralizing that restricted the understanding of both the life of the author and his work.[35]

Not only was the series to provide the public with well-written biographical/critical studies of figures who were, in their own right, heroic, but it allowed intellectuals, statesmen and writers to fulfil their roles as secular leaders of a new humanism where the writer's work as well as life becomes a spiritual guide and historical centre for the reader. The series also provided recognition of the writer in his time and his importance for the age, past and present. It is not surprising, then, that the first man of letters selected by both Carlyle and Morley is Dr Johnson. In Carlyle's 1840 lecture, 'The Hero as a Man of Letters', he is the first figure extensively discussed while the first volume of the English Men of Letters is *The Life of Johnson* by Leslie Stephen, published in February 1878.

Another influence on the series, in addition to the French Enlightenment and Carlyle, is positivism. Emphasizing the unity of historical fact and critical interpretation, Morley extends Auguste Comte's idea that the lives of the great benefactors of humanity must always remain before us. Hence, the series concentrates on the contributions of a life and its achievements, rather than on a mere chronicle of activities. Despite the limitations of size – each volume normally had only 180 pages or approximately 45 000 words – the subjects are presented as representative of their time. Shelley, for example, is part of a tragic triumvirate of Romantic poets who died young, and J. A. Symonds's 'gloomy' prelude to the life dramatically places Shelley within such a dominating context. As Mark Pattison wrote in his *Milton*, establishing a guideline for the series, 'the study of Milton's poetry compels the study of his time'.[36] The key to this approach is Comte.

Introduced to the work of Comte at Oxford by J. Cotter Morison and friendly with such English Positivists as Frederick Harrison, G. H. Lewes and Richard Congreve, as well as Pierre Laffiete, friend and literary executor of Comte, Morley was long attached, if not, at times, devoted to the Positivist movement. John Stuart Mill strongly influenced Morley's involvement with Comte, which was intensified by the publication of Mill's *Auguste Comte and Positivism* in 1865. 'True positivism' for Morley became 'the habit of seeking explanations of all phenomena in experience'. In Comte, Morley also found the *raison d'être* of the biographical enterprise, the usefulness of 'deep and perpetual recollection'; biography became the literary manifestation of such remembrance.[37] In 1876, the year before he organized the English Men of Letters, Morley wrote the biographical entry on Comte for the *Encyclopaedia Britannica*. The historical and social dimension of the series reflects the positivist orientation of Morley to the 'social element in every part of conduct'.[38] The overriding pattern that controls the English Men of Letters series is positivism and the entire series might legitimately be called 'positivist biography'.

The desire to present representative men, representative of great social, historical or philosophical forces, expresses a central positivist goal. One selects the subjects because they illustrate the effect of literature on learning or life; they reach beyond the study to the street. The seeming eclecticism of the series is actually the application of his principle. Consequently, as English Men of Letters, we find politicians, poets and historians united with novelists, philosophers and dramatists. Collectively, they embody progress, change in society through literature. Burke and Coleridge, Byron and Gibbon, Hume and Milton – the link between these figures is their impact upon their time. It is fitting, then, that so important a moral, social and literary figure as Samuel Johnson should initiate the series and Carlyle end it.

The subject of 'positivist biography' must be a synthesizer, in Comtian terms, of science and society or revolution and continuity. Consequently, to understand how various men attain this it is necessary to maintain an historical perspective which explains why the English Men of Letters stresses the context of its subjects. Morley's biographies of Burke, Voltaire, Rousseau and Diderot, which preceded the series, emulated such goals of 'positivist biography' – to see the subject in and of his time, related to history and conscious of the effect of social and economic forces. These early, distinguished biographies by Morley also established the method he sought in the writing and shaping of lives in the series which a passage from *Voltaire* expresses clearly. Objecting to the *impedimenta* of details, Morley writes that Voltaire had the gift of

throwing rapid glances over a wide field on the suggestion of a minor fact . . . and of converting what to others would be the

mere unconsidered trifles of narrative into something possessed
of its due measure of vitality and significance.

In the limited frame of the English Men of Letters, Morley
expected no less from his contributors. In a later review of
Frederick Harrison's *A New Calendar of Great Men*, Morley further
justified the method of the short life, arguing that such an exercise
required a concentrated effort and critical mind.[39]

Morley's 1870 essay on 'Byron' most concisely describes his
positivist approach and view that art is 'only the transformation
into ideal and imaginative shapes of a predominant system and
philosophy of life'. Poets and artists represent 'the hope and
energies, the dreams and the consummation, of the human
intelligence in its most enormous movements'. In the essay
Morley outlines a three-stage method that parallels the positivist
condition Comte outlined. The critical method for Morley begins
with analysis, moves to the coherence of the 'poet's mental figure'
and ends with tracing 'the relations of the poet's ideas, either
direct or indirect, through the central currents of thought, to the
visible tendencies of an existing age'. This is the ideal of positivist
criticism, the result of transcending the scientific (analytic) and
moral ('mental figure'). For biography it means the relation of
individual facts to general concepts, and the application of
analysis and observation to literary lives seen in relation to their
times. The articulation of the homogeneous system of Comte and
Morley's method of criticism finds expression in the unity of the
English Men of Letters and its attempt to do for literary
biography what Comte did for social and moral thought – the
condensation of knowledge into a workable system. What Morley
later wrote of Pater, that he associates art with 'the actual moods
and purposes of men in life', is also a statement of his ideas as a
biographer.[40] Morley transfers the positivist impulse to link life
and art to the lives of writers; Samuel Smiles preceded him in making the association with engineers; Leslie Stephen followed him
recording those lives that advanced the well-being of the nation.

Competing with the practicality of the series was Morley's
concern in his 1877 essay, 'Harriet Martineau', with what he calls
'the true maker of literature, the sense of proportion, the
modulated sentence, the compact and suggestive phrase'
(p. 258). In the same paragraph describing the qualities of
Martineau's biographic sketches, Morley praises

their conciseness, their clearness in fact, their definiteness in
judgment, and above all, the rightly-graduated impression of
the writer's own personality in the background . . . There is no
fretting away of the portrait in over-multiplicity of lines and
strokes . . . There is a happy precision, a pithy brevity, a
condensed argumentativeness.[41] (p. 258)

Such qualities best summarize the compositional goals of the
English Men of Letters series – in advance of such later
biographers as Stephen and Edmund Gosse who will propose
similar values.

At first, reaction to the English Men of Letters was sceptical,
with critics objecting to the appearance of 'literary cooks . . .
mincing and seasoning such familiar viands as the works of
Bunyan, Defoe, Goldsmith, Scott and Dickens'. The idea of an
intermediary between the works and the reader upset the
Athenaeum reviewer because it suggested readers of the original
works were diminishing: 'we are drifting', he complained, 'into an
age of literary middlemen.' Nonetheless, the first English Men of
Letters volume, Leslie Stephen's *Johnson*, received high praise.
Reviews of *Shelley*, however, were even more positive, remarking
that the volume presents the 'essential facts and a variety of
appropriate details in a compact shape, perfectly readable both
from its choice subject matter and from its literary form'. But the
reviewer of Hutton's *Scott* was upset that the age had become one
of competitive examinations where readers were 'losing all sense
of the charm of literature as literature, and wish to secure the
greatest quality of information in the smallest possible space'. The
English Men of Letters was designed, as the reviewer of *Johnson*
noted, for 'those who have to run as they read'. Nonetheless, he
admitted it did its job well, encouraging all readers to turn to the
original works of each subject, extending, not limiting, the
readership of the English classics.[42]

Judgements in the English Men of Letters on its subjects,
however, especially the near contemporaries, often reflect some of
the strongest limitations of the Victorian mind. Virtues such as
the family are upheld, vices such as unfaithfulness criticized.
Kindliness, manliness and wholesomeness bring praise; selfishness, effeminacy and immorality bring blame. The focus remains
on the unexceptional elements of a man's life, on those Plutarchian details of everyday existence that, in their seeming lack of

significance, reveal elements of the self. Several examples indicate
the overall pattern and structure of the English Men of Letters but
I shall limit myself to two representative works: Leslie Stephen's
Johnson (1878) and Edmund Gosse's *Gray* (1882). The former was
the first volume published in the series; the latter, the twenty-
sixth. Both were written by men who became professional
biographers and went on to make major contributions to the
writing and study of life-narratives.

Leslie Stephen was to contribute five lives to the English Men of
Letters, having the distinction of publishing the original volumes
in both the first (1878–92) and second series (1902–19). *George
Eliot* by Stephen was the first volume of the second series, the very
figure Morley and Macmillan sought in vain to contribute and
who praised the first three volumes. On the success of the first
volume, *Johnson*, Stephen wrote Morley the following on the
anniversary of its publication: 'it has been the cause of more
compliments to me than anything, perhaps everything that I have
ever done before. My vanity has been tickled.' A year previous
Morley was also delighted, writing to Macmillan on 5 February
1878 that 'I have got Stephen's *Johnson*, and I think you will agree
with me, when you have read it, that it is charmingly done. If the
rest are as readable and workmanlike, I shall be well pleased.' In
August 1877, Stephen accepted Morley's invitation: 'So be it!', he
began his reply: 'Put me down for Johnson, if you please',
although he added a caveat: 'I have a kind of sneaking feeling that
"Swift" would have made a better life and he has had no Boswell.'
The existence of a Boswell worried Stephen, and by December,
that year, his enthusiasm became embarrassment as he explained
to C. E. Norton:

> My chief employment at this time is doing a little book on Sam.
> Johnson, for a series of which Morley is editor . . . I am half
> ashamed of the business in one way, for it seems wicked to pick
> the plums out of poor old Bozzy, and yet that is all that is to be
> done; and the plums are very fine ones. I don't fancy I am much
> like S.J. in any way and guess that he would have hardly
> attracted me very much in his life-time; but I don't know any
> one whom I enjoy so much in 'the subjective stage of existence,'
> as the positivists say. His unreason is so incomparably better to
> my taste than Macaulay's good sense.

Morley was not as disturbed by Stephen's work, although he was upset by the visual look of the page. To Craik he complained that thirty-three lines to a page made it look 'too long. I think it ought not to be more than thirty-two.'[43] Nonetheless, on 4 February 1878, the work appeared, at a particularly happy time for Stephen; on 5 January he had become engaged to Mrs Herbert Duckworth and on 26 March he married her.

Johnson more or less set the pattern for the English Men of Letters series, as Stephen's first biographer, F. W. Maitland noted, adding that it also became 'a model for many a series in England and elsewhere; with . . . the Life of Samuel Johnson came a model among models'.[44] The style of the biography, however, partly reflects Stephen's own limitations. 'I am very short winded and provokingly argumentative. My fault is to be always logic chopping, and I can never keep at a high level of rhetoric for two sentences together', he once wrote. The opening sentence of *Johnson* illustrates this difficulty:

> Samuel Johnson was born in Lichfield in 1709. His father, Michael Johnson, was a bookseller, highly respected by the cathedral clergy, and for a time sufficiently prosperous to be magistrate of the town, and, in the year of his son's birth, sheriff of the county.[45]

Respectability, social position, religion and economic success – not tone, point of view or style – are Stephen's focus. The remainder of the paragraph deals with the problems of a bookseller's career, the hypochondria Johnson inherited from his father, an apocryphal visit by Queen Anne, as well as disease, superstition and Boswell. Here the themes of the biography become clear, as well as the major problem for Stephen: Boswell's *Life of Johnson*.

No subject could have been more problematic for Stephen than Samuel Johnson because of Boswell. The final three chapters of the biography dangerously become 'extracts from Boswell's reports' Stephen notes (p. 140) and when Chapter 4 opens, Stephen discusses the problem because the last twenty years of Johnson's life are better told in Boswell. Independence from, yet attention to, Boswell creates a singular difficulty for Stephen; at worst, Stephen presents a Victorian re-writing of Boswell; at best, a Victorian engagement with the dominating figure of English biography. Taken from their setting, the gems of Boswell's life lose their glitter in Stephen's narrative, but inevitably, and almost uncontrollably, Stephen borrows from Boswell. The final chapters of *Johnson* become an account of the former biography intertwined with new extracts of conversation, incident or anecdote. What precedes them, however, is a more legitimate example of the English Men of Letters approach.

Accompanying the economic interest is the continual sense of historical change in the status of literature and the rise of Johnson from Grub Street hack to literary dictator. This sense of achievement is a literary example of those engineers Smiles celebrates. Success in any field, especially with adequate remuneration, remains a focus of Victorian biographical writing, forming its most consistent theme. Stephen also analyses the changing social scene, commenting in several places on how his age would not permit the existence of such an autocrat as Johnson. Today, no monarch of literature could reign: 'the world of literature has become too large for such authority' (p. 47). In the 1870s no conversationalist could rule. But throughout the contextual and comparative representation of Johnson, Stephen also displays a powerful analytic ability. He analyses as well as summarizes Johnson's career, although, like other volumes in the series, the analysis centres on the literature rather than the life.

In particular, Stephen concentrates on Johnson's style. In the tradition of Morley who in 'Byron' linked style and the times, Stephen repeatedly unites the way Johnson wrote with his type of mind and character. Language provides or reveals personality: 'Johnson's sentences seem to be contorted, as his gigantic limbs used to twitch, by a kind of mechanical spasmodic action . . . Johnson's style is characteristic of the individual and the epoch' (pp. 167–8, 170). With his predilection for the philosophic, Stephen then provides a stimulating analysis of the how the shift from self-satisfaction and common sense to discontent and dissent (following optimism) are reflected in Johnson's style. 'The substance corresponds to the style', he maintains, and 'Johnson has some thing in common with the fashionable pessimism of modern times' (pp. 173–4). This linking of the individual with his age through particulars like style, this sense of the unity of history and the individual effort, reflect the positivist attitude uniting with the tradition of the Plutarchian anecdote. Paradoxically, because limitations of size and the shape of the series dictate the biographical nature of the text, more comments on the historical or universal qualities of the subject and his writing need to be made. The shorter or more restrictive the life, the broader the statements about that life in its time.

In his comments on *Lives of the Poets*, Stephen reveals his preference for the brief life, anticipating some of the principles he will develop some three years later in the *Dictionary of National Biography*. With little effort, one can 'swell volumes ... by industriously sweeping together all the rubbish which is in any way connected with the great man' and by 'elaborately discussing the possible significance of infinitesimal bits of evidence' (p. 186). The real goal, however, is seen in Johnson's aim: 'simply to give a vigorous summary of the main facts of his heroes' lives, a pithy analysis of their character, and a short criticism of their productions' (p. 186). This Stephen was to do in his own contributions and guidelines for the soon-to-be-launched *Dictionary of National Biography*. But in his life of Johnson, hamstrung by Boswell's great work, he could not freely dispense with 'the extraneous'.

In *Johnson*, Stephen furthermore exhibits the Victorian morality that constrained the biographical freedom of the series – reflecting in part Morley's own preference (see 'Byron', pp. 26–7). Most noticeably, he emphasizes domestic sovereignty and family reverence, especially for departed wives (see his personal comment on the death of Johnson's wife – a reflection of his own loss, p. 41). His admiration for Johnson's manliness balances his disgust with Mrs Thrale's behaviour with Piozzi (cf. pp. 164 and 168 with 153–7). But beyond these shortcomings, Stephen displays a critical approach and interpretative awareness joined to an important sense of the problems of biographical structure and style which anticipate his later concerns and principles. His engagement with Johnson is an encounter with biography at large and a significant introduction to its formal as well as thematic difficulties. Auspiciously appearing as volume one of the English Men of Letters and as Stephen's first extended effort at biography, the volume clarified Stephen's own conception of biographical writing and, by extension, the development of biography in the late nineteenth century.

Stephen continued to find satisfaction in his contributions to the English Men of Letters. In January 1882 he accepted Swift, comically commiserating with Gosse that 'we are both victims to Morley's seductions'. Swift 'absorbed' him and he reproached himself: 'if I cannot make an interesting book out of such a hero, I deserve to be excommunicated.' Six months later, however, he was finished, as he told C. E. Norton. *George Eliot*, published in 1902, was next, although he considered writing on Browning and Froude. He did not favour all of Eliot's works but was gratified by Morley's comments praising the volume as 'a masterpiece . . . The criticism is to my mind, the best the world has seen for many a day, and I owe to you my first comprehension of "Middlemarch".'[46] Stephen's last contribution, and his last published volume written in his final illness, was *Hobbes*, published in 1904, the year he died. Collectively, his contributions to the English Men of Letters not only provided a distinguished name to introduce and sustain the series but his *Johnson* and *Eliot* were major contributions. In addition, his experience with the series no doubt aided in organizing, administering and executing the apex of Victorian series biography, the *Dictionary of National Biography* which began to establish itself in December 1882, the year his *Swift* appeared.

Another contributor to the English Men of Letters was the professional biographer Edmund Gosse, who was principally known by 1880 as the author of *Studies in the Literature of Northern Europe* (1879). His biography of Gray appeared in June 1882, and was the first of his critical biographies. Gosse's contribution to biography is exceeded only by his astute criticisms of the form which he continued to make throughout his life in works that highlight changes in biographical method and in numerous essays. Gosse's *Life and Letters of John Donne* (1899), the first scholarly study of the poet, his life of Swinburne (1917), a remarkable union of literary criticism and biographical detail, plus his critical biography of his father, *Father and Son* (1907), are his most accomplished biographical efforts. However, his biographies of Browning, Patmore and Ibsen are equally important for their originality and introduction of certain 'distant' literary figures to the English public. His entry, 'Biography', for the eleventh edition of the *Encyclopaedia Britannica*, remains a cogent assessment of the genre. Emerging as the leading biographer between Froude and Strachey, Gosse plays an important role in the course of biography in the later nineteenth century. Indeed, in the development of biography as an institution, Gosse has a pivotal position because he links the Victorians to the early moderns, marking a crucial change in perspective that will influence later biographers. In 1882, however, Gosse was just beginning to formulate his approach to biographical writing. He was, in fact, the second choice for the Gray volume; it was first offered to Stafford Brooke who refused.

Gosse's English Men of Letters experience prepared him for his own support of brief biography which his *Encyclopaedia Britannica* essay endorses:

> Broad views are entirely out of place in biography, and there is perhaps no greater literary mistake than to attempt what is called the 'Life and Times' of a man. In an adequate record of the 'times,' the man is bound to sink into [in]significance. (III, 953)[47]

Gosse alters the emphasis on context in the English Men of Letters to fact, to correct detail. The biography of Gray also assumes a didactic character as it revises previous lives and establishes the record at the same time as it interprets the work. By the time Gosse writes the 'Biography' entry, his ideas have become more refined, centring on the importance of conciseness and brevity. However, interceding between the principles of the English Men of Letters and Gosse's 'Biography' statement, and acting as a bridge between the two similar but not identical views, is the quintessential example of brief biography in the nineteenth century, the *Dictionary of National Biography*. Under the direction of Leslie Stephen, it formalized a style and approach to writing lives that Gosse elaborated and Strachey confirmed.

From 1835 until the end of the century, dictionaries of national biography appeared in a variety of European countries beginning with Sweden's twenty-three volume series published between 1835 and 1857. The Dutch, Austrians and Germans followed, the latter publishing a forty-five volume work between 1875 and 1900. At Oxford in 1864 Matthew Arnold complained about the inadequacy of any English biographical dictionary and his remarks spurred the interest and concern of various publishers. But until George Smith in 1881, no one took up the cause despite frequent expressions of need.[48] George Smith, the chief partner of Smith and Elder, initiated the idea of a national biography in the spring of 1881 as the circulation of the *Cornhill*, edited by Leslie Stephen, was slipping. The coincidence was fortuitous; as Stephen was becoming more disenchanted with his editorship of the magazine, Smith recognized the benefits of having him take over the new project. Coupled with his disappointment at the unpopular reception of his six-year labour, *The Science of Ethics* (1882), Stephen welcomed the challenge of the *Dictionary of National Biography*, although the scale of the enterprise often scared him.[49]

Two statements from the *Athenaeum* publicly record the evolution of the *Dictionary*. The first, appearing in the 'Literary Gossip' section for 11 November 1882, welcomes the news of the proposed quarterly-published volumes of national biography and celebrates the appointment of Stephen to 'the arduous duty of editing this important work'.[50] There is, of course, no suggestion of the delicate negotiations between Smith and Stephen so that the latter would not be hurt by his removal from the *Cornhill* while the former would benefit from Stephen's taking on the large-scale effort. By October 1882, Stephen was committed to the new project, backed by Smith's finances and the cooperation which the November *Athenaeum* summarizes.

Five weeks later, 23 December 1882, Stephen published a two-column statement outlining the guidelines of the dictionary which he refers to as 'a new Biographia Britannica', alluding to the 1747 publication based on Bayle's dictionary. But the *Biographia Britannica* was 'commonly dull, without force of character, and without adequate discrimination', while few articles 'rise above compilation' according to Sir Egerton Brydges, author of the four-volume *Biographical Peerage of the Empire of Great Britain* (1808–17).[51] Stephen sought something different: the biographies were, first, to be selective, both in the choice of entries and nature of information, and were to be presented in a full but 'business-like form'. Second, condensation was essential: 'Philosophical and critical disquisition, picturesque description and so forth', are obviously out of place. There would be no room for 'elaborate analysis' although authenticated, characteristic anecdotes should be included; all contributions, however, 'must be strictly biographical' (p. 850).

On the matter of literary style, Stephen is firm. 'Superfluous ornament' is to be expunged, but he recognizes that 'style, and even high literary ability, is required for lucid and condensed narrative, and of such style I shall be anxious to get as much as I can'. Almost unwillingly, however, Stephen allows for the artistic element of brief biography: 'A biography written with a single eye to giving all the information presumably desirable by an intelligent reader may be not only useful, but intensely interesting, and even a model of literary art' (p. 850). Accurate condensation based on authorities is the primary concern; aesthetic unity or proportion a welcomed but not necessary element. Stephen's declaration ends with a notice that lists of names for inclusion and comment will be published, that contributors 'who have made a special study of any particular period or class of biographies' will be 'peculiarly welcome', that specimen lives will be available and that by necessity he must be 'autocratic' although he will 'do his best to be a considerate autocrat' (p. 850). (Later difficulties with such contributors as E. A. Freeman and A. B. Grosart made this statement prophetic. Freeman never accepted editorial policy concerning Ae spellings; his insistence on Anglo-Saxon rather than common forms led to his withdrawal over Athelstan spelt with an A. Grosart, a seventeenth-century specialist, borrowed so fully from his articles in the *Encyclopaedia Britannica* that he violated copyright and, increasing his culpability, manufactured sources.) Once the editorial procedures were established, a printed circular was sent to prospective contributors outlining the nature of the contributions to the dictionary.

'Addison' was the specimen life Stephen began in 1883 which was circulated to contributors as an example of balance and concision. The published version (*Dictionary of National Biography* [1885], vol. I) represents the confident tone and critical judgements Stephen sought in other entries. Running for nearly nine, double-columned pages, it is a major entry acting as a model for the project in terms of its structure, detail and style. Revising certain facts and dates regarding Addison, the entry also displays the corrective impulse of biography and the *Dictionary of National Biography*, documenting its new details with a variety of primary sources such as legal papers and letters. Sources are always given, as Stephen, for example, clarifies the authentic anecdote of Addison putting a £1000 lien on a new home built by Richard Steele, cited in Johnson's life of Addison. Evidence in a letter by an actor, B. Victor, to Garrick shows that Addison executed an agreement between himself and Steele and that it was not, in Stephen's words, 'a case of a friend suddenly converted by anger into a severe creditor, but a deliberate plan from the first to give a serious lesson'.[52] Stephen also provides humour in his account including, but discounting, gossip about Addison and his wife, or defending Addison's pleasure with drink as 'not intemperate according to the standard of his time' (I: 125A).

The Addison entry has charm and conveys the affability of the subject. Stephen achieves this by blending the literary and political careers of Addison via his social attributes, love of good company and wit. The organization of the life is by stages of growth, not chronology. The opening paragraph quickly moves from parents to youth and education and then to its main purpose: the impression Addison made as a Latin poet of unequalled skill upon the writers of his time. The prose itself reflects the activity and interests of Addison as in this summary of his trip to Italy: 'He sailed from Marseilles; was driven by a storm into Savona; thence crossed the Mts. to Genoa, and travelled through Milan to Venice, where his fancy was struck by a grotesque play upon the death of Cato' (I: 123B). The final clause surprises the reader by its attachment to the travel narrative but prepares one for Addison's later dramatic success, *Cato*. Stephen is concise with his detail and interpretation.

It is the critical voice that responds most clearly to Addison, and which gives the entry its force. Stephen is personal and at times blunt, unafraid to identify a puzzle or express a broad opinion: 'Addison's finances are a mystery', begins one paragraph; 'Addison's social qualities helped his rise', states another (I: 124A, 125A). Supplementing politics as a theme in the entry is patronage, life in the coffee houses (identified by Stephen as 'the resort of the wits'), the literary nature of the *Tatler* and *Spectator* and an evaluation of Addison's best writing (the essays on Roger de Coverley) and his weakest ('The Pleasures of the Imagination'). 'Addison' possesses a directness that is refreshing in its evaluative statements, honest citation of sources, confident yet corrective tone. Stephen does not hide Addison's lack of high social position, or inadequacies as a 'vigorous debater' as he describes his personal popularity or his political success. In a short span we get a complete sense of Addison as writer, politician, traveller and journalist. The entry also maintains an aesthetic unity through its constant evaluation of its subject. The reader's confidence grows as more and more facts are substantiated and impressions disappear. Integrating Johnson's life of Addison and Macaulay's review essay of him, Stephen gives a balanced picture of the man in a manner he hoped other *Dictionary of National Biography* contributors would emulate.

For one critic the specimen life became the starting point of a full assessment of biographical dictionaries and the need for an English version. R. C. Christie, scholar and bibliophile, reviewed the specimen life plus the *Biographie Universelle* and the *Nouvelle Biographie General* in the January 1884 issue of the *Quarterly Review*. The essay, however, becomes a detailed historical survey of biographical dictionaries in general and ends with tempered encouragement for Stephen and his project while restating the importance of an English biographical dictionary. With facts and examples, Christie highlights the virtues of a biographical dictionary, the strengths of the *Biographie Universelle* and the qualities he believes the *Dictionary of National Biography* should possess. Echoing Stephen in his 1882 statement from the *Athenaeum*, Christie writes that 'what is wanted are commonplace biographical details illustrated by personal character concisely stated, duly marshalled in order, and accompanied by dates and authorities'.[53] 'We do not go', he adds, to biographical dictionaries for narratives of military campaigns or political history but 'to have the *men* and their lives and characters brought before us' (p. 229). In 1887 Christie will provide a full estimate of volumes one to ten of the *Dictionary of National Biography*. In this essay, however, the fullest survey in English of biographical dictionaries published in the nineteenth century, he provides a history of the form and the context for the proposed dictionary. One year later, the first volume appeared.

Beginning 1 January 1885 and every quarter afterwards, a volume of the *Dictionary of National Biography* was published until the midsummer of 1900 when volume sixty-three completed the work. Starting with volume twenty-two (1890) through volume twenty-six, Sidney Lee's name appeared as joint editor on the title page; by May 1891, Lee became sole editor since Stephen's health forced his resignation. Lee, a graduate of Balliol and recommended by F. J. Furnivall, had been sub-editor since the start. Lee took his work seriously; he was thorough, workmanlike and conscientious. Like Stephen, he tended to overwork and after Lee took on sole responsibility for the dictionary, he received notes such as the following from Stephen in St Ives, Cornwall:

I am sorry that you should think of being in doubt about a holiday. Do not let the Dictionary overpower you as it did me . . . The danger of dictionarying is like the danger of walking –

one finds out suddenly that one has been overdoing it, though no warning appeared at the moment.[54]

Nonetheless, Lee continued to devote himself to the dictionary while developing a career as an independent biographer. In 1898 he published a life of Shakespeare (revised 1915) and the official biography of Edward vii (1925). But the *Dictionary of National Biography* was for him, as it was for Stephen, his principal occupation.

'No flowers by request', Alfred Ainger's phrase, became the watchword of the dictionary entries, which had to be completed within six months, contain few irrelevancies and eliminate any element of eulogy. However, choosing entries was a difficulty and only the unique step of publishing names considered for inclusion and inviting commentary avoided the problem of editorial prejudice. The response was often overwhelming; 'one specialist', wrote Stephen to Gosse, 'offers me the lives of 1,400 hymnwriters alone.'[55] The editorial staff was deluged with suggestions and the difficult task of selection commenced at once.

Work on the dictionary was drudgery and Stephen repeatedly complained of the task. This was not because of an aversion to research nor his commitment to other activities, such as a life of his friend the politician Henry Fawcett, but because of Stephen's resistance to the antiquarian bias for useless data, the relentless job of double-checking facts, and the fear of being incorrect. 'That damned Dictionary is about my bed and about my path and spies out all my ways, as the psalms puts it', he wrote in November 1884. Almost a year and a half earlier, he wrote that 'Reading MS. lives is my chief occupation of a serious kind and that is stupid enough. The infernal Dictionary must be kept going though I begin to long for the day when it will appear, and have its fate decided one way or other.' But impatience never replaced accuracy and in both his letters and late memoir, *Some Early Impressions* (1903), he records the discrepancies and misdoings of various contributors. Ironically, it was his assiduous sub-editor, Lee, who discovered the possible breach of copyright which nearly halted publication of volume one.[56] But in his insistence on, attention to, and publication of, all sources for an entry, Stephen set new standards for biographical writing. The achievement of the *Dictionary of National Biography* is not only the artful condensation of lives but the condensing of lives accurately.

The *Dictionary of National Biography* represents the apex of the Victorian belief in, and commitment to, fact, reflecting the importance of science and history in the age. The translation of scientific fact into experience, such as the geological proofs of Lyle or the discoveries of Darwin, equalled the historical researches of Lecky or Trevelyan. For Stephen, this meant that any research must be professionally and thoroughly, if not scientifically, done. Or, as Sidney Lee summarized in 1911, 'The object of national as of all collective biography is Priestley's object in scientific exposition – "to comprise as much knowledge as possible in the smallest compass." ' Even a study of morality could be carried out in this fashion as Stephen attempted in *The Science of Ethics*. In that work, he argued for the universal obligation to responsible conduct and precision of detail. Furthermore, *The Science of Ethics* reveals Stephen's belief in unification and synthesis, the lynchpins of both individually written lives and the dictionary as a whole. Consistency of presentation was a persistent goal of the project. And in his quest for 'the scientific form of morality', Stephen outlines a theory of character implicitly transferred to the dictionary. Each man, he writes, possesses 'a certain unity of character in spite of the complex condition of his nature . . . There is a causal connection underlying the apparently arbitrary movements of the individual.'[57] This theory of unity and the belief in the link between moral judgement and aesthetic interpretation make *The Science of Ethics* a necessary theoretical introduction to the principles, if not the methods, of the *Dictionary of National Biography*.

Codification of masses of information and detail into 29 120 entries meant the formalization of the ideas expressed in *The Science of Ethics*, resulting in the largest national dictionary published in the century. The product is a natural history of man in England providing, in Sidney Lee's words, a 'greater mass of accurate information respecting the past achievements of the British and Irish race than has been put at the disposal of the English-speaking peoples in any previous literary undertaking'.[58] Nowhere is the Victorian devotion to fact better exhibited than in the ideals of the *Dictionary of National Biography*. Coupling the private enterprise aspect of the project (although Smith figured he would lose approximately £70 000 on an expenditure of £150 000), with the punctuality of its appearance, and the professionalism of its research, the dictionary may represent, with singular force, the finest example of the Victorian spirit at work.

But fact requires language for expression and in the particular style Stephen demanded of his contributors he furthered the literary quality of the brief biography. Condensation summarizes the Stephen method which he continuously reiterated to his contributors: 'If the book was ever to be completed, wordiness must be sternly excised . . . The sweating of articles was certainly the most trying of my duties . . . it was clearly our business to be sternly concise.' 'I learnt to think', he added, 'that the whole art of writing consists in making one word suffice where other ordinary men use two.' As work got underway on the dictionary, he complained to C. E. Norton that 'My greatest worry is in struggling against the insane verbosity of the average contributor. I never knew before how many words might be used to express a given fact.'[59]

Sidney Lee described Stephen's approach as an 'energetic style' which 'set his comrades a stimulating example of terseness, perspicuity, thoroughness and independence'. Maitland, Stephen's biographer, used more graphic language to articulate the style: it is Stephen's 'very self on one of his "going days"': making a bee-line across country, with no ounce of flesh to spare, and with that terrible step which looked so short and was so long'. In his 1911 Leslie Stephen Lecture at Cambridge, Sidney Lee again outlined the Stephen method for the *Dictionary of National Biography*: 'Rigid selection and lavish rejection of available records are processes which the biographer has often to practise in the sternest temper . . . Personality is not transmitted on the biographic canvas through overcrowded detail.' Combined with his directness of opinion – 'Portraiture is black and white' – and his determination to be accurate, Stephen and the dictionary set new standards of biographical authority and research.[60]

As an example of this new precision and standard, one may take the entry on Shakespeare, also the longest single entry in the dictionary. Written by Sidney Lee for volume fifty-one (seventeen in the reprint), it appeared in 1897 when the *Dictionary of National Biography* was edited by Lee alone. Long a student of sixteenth-century literature, beginning at public school under the direction of Dr Edwin Abbott, Lee had already written entries on Lyly, Lord Herbert of Cherbury and Marlowe for earlier volumes. As an undergraduate at Oxford, Lee published two essays on

Shakespeare in *The Gentleman's Magazine* which brought him to the attention of Furnivall who, in turn, recommended him to Stephen for the sub-editorship of the dictionary. In March 1883, for £300 a year, Lee joined the dictionary staff, remaining until 1917. But work on the dictionary, as Stephen's principal aide, did not prevent Lee from other research. In 1885 he published a history, *Stratford on Avon, from the Earliest Times to the Death of Shakespeare*, while contributing individual lives, often enlarged and republished, to the dictionary. These include a biography of Queen Victoria, reprinted in 1902. Lee also edited the autobiography of Lord Herbert of Cherbury (1886), a reproduction of Shakespeare's first folio (1902), a two-volume edition of Elizabethan sonnets (1904) and Methuen's Standard Library (forty volumes, 1905–6).

Two lectures on biography by Lee, in 1911 and 1918, provide the ideas that, retrospectively, shaped his life of Shakespeare in the *Dictionary of National Biography*. Summarized, they include the view that biography has a national, institutional function, transmitting to a new generation the achievements of individuals from another – a clear echo of positivism according to Morley. Discriminating brevity is the only technique in writing a life, and hero worship or historical context should not subvert the biographer from his major task: conveying the personality of the subject. The purpose of the biographer is limited to fact and detail: 'discovery, not invention. Fundamentally, [the biographer's] work is a compilation, an industriously elaborated composition, a mosaic.'[61] Following this principle, his 'Shakespeare' became, in the words of Samuel Schoenbaum, 'the most solid, condensed treatment of the subject yet published: unrivalled in amplitude and in richness of documentation'. The facts and achievement are united while important appendices focus on portraits, bibliography and reputation. The writing is lucid and concise, as in this brief example which also reveals Lee's tone and use of sources:

To London Shakespeare naturally drifted, doubtless trudging thither on foot during 1586, by way of Oxford and High Wycombe (cf. Halles, *Notes on Shakespeare*, 1884, pp. 1–24). Tradition points to that as Shakespeare's favourite route, rather than to the road by Banbury and Aylesbury. Aurey asserts that at Grendon, near Oxford, 'he happened to take the humor of the constable in "Midsummer Night's Dream" –' by which he meant, we may suppose, 'Much Ado About Nothing' – but there were watchmen of the Dogberry type all over England and probably at Stratford itself. The Crown Inn (formerly 3 Cornmarket Street) near Carfax, at Oxford, was long pointed out as one of his resting-places.

The correction of myth, attention to detail – 'formerly 3 Corn-market Street' – the conscious employment of research dis-tinguish Lee's contribution. Although Schoenbaum, writing some seventy-three years after Lee, points out inconsistencies and several minor errors of fact, there is little dispute that the entry was, for its time, the most accurate, informed and concise presentation of Shakespeare's life. Maintaining certain traditions, such as Shakespeare holding the horses of patrons attending London playhouses, Lee's entry nonetheless does not over-dramatize, fictionalize or idolize the subject. Stressing perhaps too much of the prosaic quality of Shakespeare as a man, Lee nevertheless recognized the greatness of his subject without re-inventing the man, achieving what the dictionary continually sought: authority. The acceptance of this interpretation of Shakespeare was in part demonstrated by the fourteen editions of Lee's *Life of William Shakespeare*, first published in 1898, an expanded version of the *Dictionary of National Biography* entry.[62]

'I prefer to have all lives written by persons who sympathise with the subjects, what ever my personal feeling may be', wrote Leslie Stephen to Dr Norman Moore in 1884 and in general he succeeded. To obtain competent contributors was his first goal and his method was to draw on established scholars as well as reputable men of letters, politicians, or other specialists. But they had to be men who 'would take an interest in the work for its own sake and discharge minds already full of the required knowledge'. A contributor must have enthusiasm, historical knowledge and literary skill. Information must be sought from first-hand sources, 'often from unpublished papers and records'. And when a contributor did not follow the guidelines, Stephen dealt with him forcefully, as a letter from 3 March 1889 shows:

My Dear Mr. X – Many thanks for your articles. I have been forced to take liberties with one or two. Unless I make a firm stand against the amount of MS. which comes in, we shall be

crushed. Everybody thinks his own case exceptional and takes
advantage of every precedent – What I most hold to is the scale
. . . I am really driven to bay, and can only say for your comfort
that the mangling process is the most painful part of my duties.

In turn, contributors found Stephen exacting and critical but,
after gaining his confidence, they were given freedom within the
limits of his project. In the words of Professor Tout, 'While
insisting on brevity, scholarship, punctuality, and businesslike
precision, he never worried his contributors by fussy insistence or
trivialities.'[63] Of the 653 contributors to the *Dictionary of National
Biography*, approximately 100 were regulars who wrote nearly
three-quarters of the work. Some would specialize, such as Joseph
Knight, who composed the majority of actors' and actresses'
entries, or Richard Garnett who specialized in nineteenth-century
lives such as Rossetti and Shelley. By number of pages, however,
Sidney Lee contributed the most articles (820), while Leslie
Stephen contributed 378. Interestingly, a number of contributors
to the English Men of Letters also appeared as entries in the
dictionary, including Sidney Colvin, Alfred Ainger, Edmund
Gosse, R. H. Hutton, Richard Jebb, John Morley, Edward
Dowden, A. W. Ward, John Nichol and Thomas F. Fowler.

Reaction to the dictionary from its earliest appearance was
mixed. The *Athenaeum*, reviewing volume one, Abbadie–Annie,
admired the scholarship and fulfilment, at last, of the need for 'an
exhaustive work on English biography'. But it also noted certain
errors – in proportion (why should Anne of Denmark, wife of
James I, rate ten pages while Anne Boleyn receive only four?); in
the use of abbreviations, especially in the bibliographies which
would confuse the unlearned reader; in the absence of special
American figures who had unique ties with England. Nonetheless, 'in fulness, in thoroughness and general accuracy it leaves
little or nothing to be desired'. Leslie Stephen's 'Addison' was
singled out for praise for showing that a biographical essay 'need
not be "dry" because it is compact and impersonal'; similarly,
those entries that clarify earlier but minor figures are com-
plimented. The consistency of publication, reference to sources
and support by private rather than public finance are all
commended. Reviewing volume four, Beal–Biber, in October
1885, the *Athenaeum* continues its enthusiastic support. Noting
that the treatment of minor lives is often the test of any

biographical dictionary, the journal admires the accuracy and authority of the *Dictionary of National Biography*. Again, Stephen is praised, this time for the Berkeley entry; also, the re-evaluation of figures is seen as a positive feature, as in Edmund Gosse's 'Aphra Behn'. Quibbles, however, included overdocumentation, as in J. R. Rounds's entry for 'Roger Bertram', or comic false judgements, such as Professor Laughton's statement that ' "Admiral Basil Beaumont (d. 1703) might," to judge by his portrait, "have become stout if he had lived!" '[64]

By February 1887, however, criticism of the dictionary was less approving. A commentary in *Blackwood's* used satire to express its unsympathetic reaction:

> It is to the outside spectator a goodly and inspiring sight to behold Mr. Stephen and his many men gathering in the Reading-room of the British Museum, poring over catalogues with a zeal and enthusiasm which do equal honour to their heads and hearts, and wrestling with mightly tomes even until evening. The fare provided by these literary bees is no doubt nourishing food but it is not always appetising.

On the whole, for *Blackwood's*, the work is too pedantic and uninteresting, although a few essays have 'undeniable merit from a literary point of view'. Stephen's on Carlyle is praised as well as the work of James Gardiner. The problem, however, is how to be entertaining and exact. Dr S. R. Gardiner, for example, is a historian 'far too ponderous to be inaccurate'. The reviewer cites the E. A. Freeman controversy over spelling Anglo-Saxon names and concludes that in general there are too many obscure lives in the work which will become 'a very ordinary book of reference with a good article here and there'.[65]

The *Quarterly Review* responded differently. The longest and most detailed survey to appear by 1887, the review-essay examined volumes one to ten. R. C. Christie was the author, himself a later contributor to the project and, after his death, an entry-subject. The essay is, again, a wide-ranging survey of biographical dictionaries in English, with preferences clearly stated. In such a dictionary we want only, he explains, those details that 'exhibit or illustrate the character of the Man . . . general views are wholly out of place'. A biographical dictionary should be, for Christie, borrowing Carlyle's phrase, ' "the essence

of innumerable biographies" '. Outlining his own ideas, Christie
then examines the first ten volumes of the *Dictionary of National
Biography* in detail. Stephen is again favoured, his 'Byron' cited as
perhaps the best entry in the work because it is readable, factual
and full of character. Biographies in the same field by the same
contributor also meet with Christie's approval, as do those by
Sidney Lee whose entries are always of correct if not portentous
length. But there are also criticisms: entries on those recently
deceased tend to be panegyrics; too many minor lives are
excluded; ranks and titles appear confused; the E. A. Freeman
contretemps should not have occurred. But despite these shortcomings, the dictionary 'bids fair to be one of the most important – we
would be disposed to consider it *the* most important of the literary
undertakings of the nineteenth century'.[66] Such approval resulted
from its unity of conception, number of entries, accuracy of detail,
care of citation and bibliographical information, surpassing
anything else attempted in England or Europe.

In 1893, two years after he resigned as editor of the dictionary,
Leslie Stephen wrote in his essay 'Biography' that 'in these days,
when we have decided, as it seems, that nothing is to be forgotten,
two things are rapidly becoming essential – some literary
condensing machine, and a system of indexing'. Discounting
Stephen's satiric tone, the dictionary became the very 'condensing machine' he desired through its massive survey and condensation of English lives. Stephen could afford to be ironic about the
work, calling it 'the most amusing book in the language', because
he knew it stood as his greatest literary accomplishment and a
fitting capstone to nineteenth-century biographical writing.[67] Its
importance in providing reliable, brief lives as a model for
twentieth-century life-writing is equal in significance to the
impact of Boswell's *Johnson* on the conception of early nineteenth-
century biography.

In the midsummer of 1900 the first series of the *Dictionary of
National Biography* ended and a gala dinner was held by the Lord
Mayor of London on 30 June. John Morley proposed the chief
toast. The Prince of Wales sponsored the inaugural dinner of 1885
(and Max Beerbohm provides a comic account of the preparation
for the dinner including the uninformed decision by the Prince to
cut Leslie Stephen from the guest list!).[68] The intervening years
saw the development of brief biography which continued after the
dictionary concluded. In spite of the appearance of such massive

works as Trevelyan's two-volume *Life and Letters of Lord Macaulay* (1876) and Morley's three-volume account of Gladstone (1903), the importance of brief lives remained, often under the new biographical designation of literary portrait or biography in miniature. Edmund Gosse is again important for sustaining this approach, preparing the way for Lytton Strachey who would publish, almost at the culmination of his career, a work entitled *Portraits in Miniature*.

The attraction to biography in miniature in the late nineteenth and early twentieth century is not only the continued reaction to the monumental life and times form or a response to the new interest in psychological interpretation which a concentrated style enhanced. Nor is it a greater interest by readers in the meaning rather than the mere compilation of a subject's life, despite Sidney Lee's 1911 statement that a biographer creates an 'industriously elaborated composition'. The principal reason for the continuation of the brief biography is aesthetic and analytic, for in the reversal of scale from the monumental to the miniature there is a greater degree of comprehension on the part of the reader. Anecdote rather than history teaches us more about the subject, as Plutarch and Boswell demonstrated. Claude Levi-Strauss has clarified the significance of the miniature by explaining that

> To understand a real object in its totality we always tend to work from its parts. The resistance it offers us is overcome by dividing it. Reduction in scale reverses this situation. Being smaller, the object as a whole seems less formidable. By being quantitatively diminished, it seems to us qualitatively simplified.

Reduction may create the illusion of simplicity but it is also a method of conquering the subject more easily. Furthermore, reduction in scale suggests room only for the essential elements – or as Lee analogized, 'Biography may be compared to chemistry, the science which analyzes substances and resolves them into their constituent elements.' In biography there should be no extraneous parts; all is essential. For biography, this means replacing the impossibility of knowing everything about the subject's life with 'the acquisition of intelligible dimensions' of the subject's life. The aesthetic demands on the biographer increase as the size of his form reduces, although the effect on the reader is a broader grasp of the subject because the interpretation is more concentrated. The 'vast majority of works of art', adds Levi-Strauss, 'are small-scale'.[69]

The Victorians lacked such a vocabulary but not an understanding of this process and Gosse most clearly articulated this 'theory'. In the Preface to his 1896 collection, dedicated to Thomas Hardy, *Critical Kit-Kats*, he writes

> In an age when studies multiply, and our shelves groan with books, it is not every interesting and original figure to whom the space of a full-length or even a half-length portrait can be spared. For the low comfortable rooms where people died in the last century, there was invented the shorter and still less obtrusive picture called a Kit-Kat, and some of our most skilful painters have delighted in this modest form of portraiture, which emphasizes the head, yet does not quite exclude the hand of the sitter. I have ventured to borrow from the graphic art this title for my little volume, since these are condensed portraits, each less than half-length, and each accommodated to suit limited leisure and a crowded space.

The head and the hand of the sitter reveal all; the condensed technique and approach of painting provides Gosse with a method to write biography which will outline the personality as well as the character of the sitter which his essays on Whitman, Pater and Swinburne in the volume demonstrate. And associated with this approach is the continued effort to combine biography and criticism:

> We are familiar with pure criticism and with pure biography, but what I have here tried to produce is a combination of the two, the life illustrated by the work, the work relieved by the life . . . What is here essayed is of the analytical, comparative, and descriptive order; it hopes to add something to historical knowledge and something to aesthetic appreciation.

The fascination with the interrelationship between personal character and the work finds elaboration in Gosse's later effort in condensed biography, *Portraits and Sketches*. 'I have tried', he writes, 'to concentrate attention . . . on such traits of character as throw light on the man's intellect and imagination and are calculated to help us in the enjoyment of his work.'[70]

The use of artistic metaphors by Gosse to express the new view of biography (the 'Kit-Kat'; 'the life illustrated by the work') reflects a general tendency in the first two decades of the twentieth century to think of biography in the critical terms of art. Echoing Plutarch's comparison of biography and painting in 'Alexander I', Sidney Lee in 'The Perspective of Biography' expands the terminology through his adaptation of Ruskin's language. Lytton Strachey applies the ideas through his use of portraiture in *Eminent Victorians* (1918), while Geoffrey Scott demonstrates the sustained technique of the artist as biographer in *Portrait of Zélide* (1925). Beginning with a comparison of La Tour's painting of Zélide (Isabella van Tuyll) and Houdon's bust of her, Scott proceeds to present a biography striking in its refined style and delicate irony. The detachment, however, was difficult to sustain because of parallels between the life of the subject and that of the biographer. Understated tone and modulated imagery combine with a narrative that often slips into an expression of the subject's thoughts to create an absorbing but relatively brief – 216 pages – life. Tact and amusement, befitting this elegant woman of the eighteenth century admired by both Boswell and Benjamin Constant, characterize this example of elegant, aesthetic biography which Scott describes in terms of art: 'All I have done is to catch an image of her in a single light, and to make from a single angle the best drawing I can of Zélide, as I believe her to have been.'[71] The inner life and the scenes that depict it indicate the importance of portraiture which affected biography at this time.

By 1925 the concept of biography in miniature had been defined not only in Scott's biography but in an Oxford lecture entitled *Tallemant des Réaux or the Art of Miniature Biography* given by Edmund Gosse. A kind of French John Aubrey, Gédéon Tallemant's seventeenth-century *Historiettes* were discovered between 1834 and 1846 when publication of the 798-page manuscript folio, purchased at auction in 1803, appeared. These miniature biographies of eminent members of seventeenth-century French society anecdotally revealed extraordinary details of myth-breaking behaviour. No longer were the grand figures so grand in Tallemant's opposition to the marmoreal school of French biography. In Gosse's words, biography for Tallemant became 'not as a set-piece on a grand scale but as "*l'arrangement de*

petitesses.'' Tallemant is a miniaturist and a realist . . .' 'The
miniature biographer' is 'interested in persons but indifferent to
events' states Gosse. But he also possesses detachment: 'What
gives unique value to the testimony of Tallemant is that he is
never astonished and never indignant.'

Tallemant was furthermore little concerned with dates or facts;
he had no plan on which to build up his figures but plunges into
the story, giving 'a string of diverting instances of the follies and
the vices' of a subject. The stamp of conversation is everywhere as
Tallemant avoids the use of printed material. 'He was the wax on
which the stamp of gossip descended', although in Tallemant's
own words, he says his goal was 'to set down good and evil alike,
without tampering with truth'. From witnessing the events and
conversations at the Hôtel de Rambouillet, Tallemant becomes a
precursor of what is now commonplace: 'He was the first person to
assert, for his own entertainment, the value of little things, *petitesses*,
in the building up of a literary portrait.' Plutarch, amiably, and
Seutonius, maliciously, preceded him, but Tallemant for the
nineteenth century is central. He helped to redirect the movement
of biography so that it should not be 'a philosophical treatise' or
'sermon in religion or morals'. No longer should the biographer
need to 'produce a grandiouse moral effect' but reveal the
'*petitesses* of human experience'.[72]

The admiration of Gosse for Tallemant is an expression of his
own attitude towards the writing of biography and is the
culmination of the approach he sought to demonstrate not only in
his late biographical essays but in his earliest publications, as
Robert Louis Stevenson noted in a letter of 16 April 1879. The
subject is Gosse's first publication, *Studies in the Literature of
Northern Europe*:

> The book is good reading. Your personal notes of those you saw
> struck me as perhaps most sharp and 'best held.' See as many
> people as you can and make a book of them before you die. That
> will be a living book upon my word. You have the touch
> required.[73]

For a 'living book' Gosse extended the movement towards brief
lives originating in nineteenth-century biographical dictionaries
and collective lives, translating the method into a viable technique for individual lives by twentieth-century biographers who

found the biographical essay-portrait a congenial and authoritative form of literary expression.

Paralleling the ideas of Gosse were the works of the scholar-journalist and friend of W. E. Henley, Charles Whibley. In a series of books published between 1897 and 1917, with titles like *A Book of Scoundrels*, *Studies in Frankness*, *Literary Portraits* and *Essays in Biography*, Whibley displayed the virtues and popularity of the brief, often critical, but also reticent life. Emphasizing the dramatic moment and visualized scene, as well as the foibles rather than the virtues of his subjects, Whibley anticipated the style and approach of Lytton Strachey and later imitators. True biography, he wrote, was an 'imagined portrait stripped of all that is unessential, into which no detail is introduced without a deliberate choice and a definite intention'. His direct style and use of invective made him a predecessor of Strachey's method. But in contrast to Gosse, Whibley was unsympathetic to total biographical freedom: 'It is irrelevant to plead love of truth in excuse for betrayal.' And in contrast to Strachey, he objected to the use of psychology: 'the worst foe to biography that has yet appeared is the disciple of Freud who crawls like a snail over all that is comely in life and art.' Imaginative treatment of the subject seemed more crucial than fact: 'the biographer's first necessity is invention rather than knowledge'.[74] T. S. Eliot's 1931 memorial essay on Whibley implicitly indicates agreement with this approach: 'He [Whibley] gives always the impression of fearless sincerity, and that is more important than being always right.'[75] Nevertheless, Whibley was recognized as a major biographer for his life of Lord John Manners (1925) and at his death Eliot praised his style and integrity as a writer.

Lytton Strachey reflects the interest in brief lives I have been outlining in his decision to title one of his last publications *Portraits in Miniature*. The choice was not accidental, but an expression of a long-standing tradition originating in Plutarch, Aubrey and Johnson, as well as in the more immediate nineteenth-century lives in series. For Strachey, brief biographical portraits and concentrated biographical essays had almost become his hallmark, from the early *Landmarks in French Literature* to *Eminent Victorians*, originally titled *Victorian Silhouettes*. But in *Portraits*, he excels in the miniature life. Dedicated to Max Beerbohm, himself a practitioner of visual miniatures through his caricatures, *Portraits* becomes a kind of prose equivalent of the Beerbohm style:

brief, clear and telling. Beerbohm in fact, explains the relationship of the miniature to character through caricature: 'The most perfect caricature is that which, on a small surface, with the simplest means, most accurately exaggerates, to the highest point, the peculiarities of a human being, at his most characteristic moment, in the most beautiful manner.'[76] Strachey displayed these qualities to their fullest.

The epigraph on the title page of *Portraits* from Horaces's tenth Satire expresses these concerns with terseness: *Est brevitate opus, ut currat sententia, nue se / Impediat verbis lassas onerantibus aures*. This was not so much a declaration of a new direction but a summation of Strachey's earliest goals as a writer seen in the Preface to *Eminent Victorians* where his admiration for French biographers who can compress 'into a few shining pages the manifold existences of men' is made clear. Compression and brevity had long been qualities of Strachey's biographical and critical writing. Among the titles Strachey considered for *Portraits* was *Little Lives* and 'Jewels five words long'. The eighteen studies that make up *Portraits*, including the six devoted to historians, demonstrate the fruition of a biographical technique Michael Holroyd summarizes as 'the split-second focus'.[77]

With penetrating detail, crisp style and emphasis on the compression of facts, *Portraits in Miniature* stands as a kind of climax to a long tradition in biographical writing, the embodiment of those qualities Strachey identifies in his essay on Aubrey in *Portraits*: 'The pure essentials – a vivid image, on a page or two, without explanations, transitions, commentaries or padding' (p. 28). In his section on historians, he continues his argument that history must be well written before anything else; only this way will it last. Three qualities make an historian, qualities that also characterize the biographer: 'a capacity for absorbing facts, a capacity for stating them and a point of view' (pp. 169–70). Strachey added, however, that 'a point of view . . . by no means implies sympathy. One might almost say that it implies the reverse' (p. 170). United with the determination to condense, these statements form a biographical 'programme' which has continued a tradition of nineteenth-century biographical writing originating in collective lives, both classical and Victorian. In the last few years, Louis Kronenberger's edition of *Atlantic Brief Lives* (1971) and William Pritchard's *Lives of the Modern Poets* (1980) have maintained the tradition.

The institutionalizing of biography in the nineteenth century occurred not in the monumental or 'marmoreal' (the term is Gosse's) life-and-times biographies but in the more prevalent and influential forms associated with brief lives. The idea of biography in miniature is its culmination, a response to the new interpretative demands of psychological analysis forcing a more concentrated life-story as well as a reaction to things Victorian. (Even satire has registered the appeal of brief lives. See Samuel Nisenson and Alfred Parker, *Minute Biographies* (1931), *More Minute Biographies* (1933) and Howard Moss, *Instant Lives* (1974).) This latter response is a misunderstanding of the nature of Victorian biography for it had a side other than the large, unfocused, factual account which over time became distrusted as much for its factual errors as for its lack of literary design. But in reaction to those short lives that at times possessed more psychological fancy than unity in the 1920s and 1930s came a return to factual and scholarly biographies which began to dominate life-writing in the 1940s through the 1960s. Stressing relentless adherence to factual detail in an objective manner with limited interpretation, they appeared constantly. Replacements for the more extreme Freudian or post-Stracheyan lives, these academic biographies emphasized narrative objectivity and factual accuracy at the expense of analysis and aesthetic wholeness. More recently they have been challenged by experimental methods and new forms such as group biography. But this anticipates what follows. The next stage is to examine the emergence of the professional biographer whose appearance coincided with the institutionalization of biography in the nineteenth century.

2 Biography as a Profession

The popular idea seems to be that no one is too great a fool or too complete an amateur, or too thoroughly ignorant of the modes of composition, to undertake the 'life' of an eminent person.

Edmund Gosse, 'The Custom of Biography'

In 1750 Dr Johnson complained that biography was a journeyman's task, distinctly unprofessional. Those who wrote it, he commented, 'seem very little acquainted with the nature of their task, or very negligent about the performance'. Their sense of composition was at worst uninformed, at best slapdash as they 'imagine themselves writing a life when they exhibit a chronological series of actions or preferments'. So little do they

> regard the manners or behaviour of their heroes, that more knowledge may be gained of a man's real character, by a short conversation with one of his servants, than from a formal and studied narrative, begun with his pedigree, and ended with his funeral.[1]

Edmund Gosse, 151 years later, echoed Johnson, although in the intervening years the stature of those who seriously wrote biography changed. Most importantly, in the nineteenth century the professional biographer emerged as a respected if not admired figure in the literary landscape. With his studious approach to his subject, comprehensive search for facts and careful reporting of details, plus his proven economic power – biographies, as publishers quickly learned, sold well – the biographer commanded and received fees and royalties commensurate with his position. In an age of investigation and personality, biography attained popular and commercial prominence. For the biographer this meant high fees, good sales and social importance. John Forster (1812–76) is representative of this change; his development from journalist-editor to professional biographer is symptomatic of the new respect for biography. His career is the focus of this chapter; its consequences for later biographers and biography its theme.

It is largely true that throughout the nineteenth century writers treated biography as a second career. Traditionally, such biographers had other occupations, from clergymen to professors, from doctors to politicians. Many were journalists and editors such as Lockhart and Leigh Hunt; others might be poets or novelists like Southey, Scott or Mrs Gaskell. Still others were civil servants or academics such as Austin Dobson or David Masson. But gradually there appeared individuals who treated biography as their primary occupation. They were professional in their attitude and approach to writing lives, a professionalism marked by their assiduous gathering of data, care in the composition of narrative, precision in the documentation of evidence and worry over the preservation of their material. They wrote not to commemorate lives but to record them, as accurately and truthfully as possible – while being as well paid for their work as they could demand. In the nineteenth century, biography did not remain another task for the busy man of letters, one of his innumerable writing assignments; it became a serious undertaking requiring a major commitment.

The decision to write a biography became a responsibility and obligation not only to a family, public or publisher, but to a genre. A renewed awareness of the value of biography paralleled a stronger interest in the lives of others for the Victorians. Assisting in this new consciousness was the successful reissue of Boswell's imposing *Life of Johnson* in 1831, edited by J. W. Croker, and the appearance of Lockhart's model life of Scott in 1836–7. A compelling force for biographers became the tradition as much as the popularity of a career in biography, while the seriousness of being a biographer grew in proportion to its status as a profession. The result, reflecting the period's absorption with detail, accuracy and objectivity, continues in the biographical practices of today. What the professionalization of biography accomplished was not only the rise of the biographer, but the establishment of a contract of responsibility between the work of the biographer and the reader of the life.[2]

Literary confidant, adviser, historian, journalist and biographer, John Forster represents the acceptance and prominence of the biographer as a professional in the nineteenth century.

Through his admired, although criticized, lives of Goldsmith, Landor, Dickens and Swift, as well as his political biographies, historical essays and literary reviews, Forster commanded a position in the literary world of mid-Victorian society equalled by few. His editorship of *The Foreign Quarterly Review*, *Daily News* (succeeding Dickens) and *Examiner* capped an active and meteoric rise in journalism highlighted by important friendships. In 1847 G. H. Lewes satirized Forster as 'Pungent, the editor of the "Exterminator"' in *Ranthorpe* and wrote of him 'though overflowing with kindness, he unfortunately mistook asperity for wit'. But Dickens dedicated the 1858 Library Edition of his works to Forster, while Wilkie Collins dedicated *Armadale* (1866). Landor dedicated his *Works*, Browning both his three-volume 1863 edition of *Poems* and his six-volume 1868 *Works*. Charles Lamb, Leigh Hunt and Landor were all appreciative friends who valued his assistance. Forster publically celebrated Lamb's criticism, defended his personal mannerisms, and emphasized his humanism. For Leigh Hunt, he organized a subscription and guided through publication his collected poems; for Landor, he assumed financial and moral responsibility for Landor's care and comfort in Italy. In such dealings with these and other literary figures, Forster was clearheaded and sensitive – a fact recognized by Landor, Dickens and Carlyle in their individual appointments of him as their literary executor.[3] Forster's stature and respect resulted as much from his dignified and responsible treatment of the lives and careers of others as from his own literary abilities.

In addition to his business acumen, social stature and literary influence, signified by his role as drama critic, journalist and editor, Forster displayed another talent of the professional biographer: versatility. Beginning with seventeenth-century political biographies in the *Lives of Eminent British Statesmen* series, 1836–9 (in 1840 his contributions were separately reprinted in five volumes as *Statesmen of the Commonwealth*), Forster then wrote a literary biography in the popular tradition: *Oliver Goldsmith* (1848; revised 1854). This was followed by documentary lives of two contemporaries: Landor (1869) and Dickens (1872–4). At the end of his career, Forster completed the first part of what was recognized as the most scholarly life of Swift yet attempted. During this period of writing literary lives, he expanded his earlier political biographies, publishing a new version of Charles Churchill in 1855 and Sir John Eliot in 1865 while revising five biographical essays – those of Cromwell, Defoe, Steele, Churchill and Foote from the *Edinburgh* and *Quarterly Reviews*. They appeared in 1858 – revised and enlarged in 1860 – as *Historical and Biographical Essays*.

Supplementing Forster's versatility was a strong sense of the popular tradition in literature which continuously shaped the character of his writing. Sensitive to the need for maintaining public interest in the lives of others, whether historical or contemporary, a consequence of his study of history and experience as a journalist, Forster strove to sustain the involvement of the reader in the biography through narrative, style and structure. He may have learned this awareness from Dickens, who continuously revelled in his identification with his audience; furthermore, Dickens did not believe being a popular novelist prevented one from being a great artist. Forster shares this view of the importance of popularity and begins his life of Landor with an expression of this concern: 'I am not insensible to what is generally taken to be expressed, in matters of literature as in many other things, by great popularity.' The opening sentence of *The Life of Charles Dickens* similarly refers to popularity. To Forster, greatness and popularity were not in conflict, although in criticizing the vicissitudes of popular taste, he favours those writers who have 'purified, enlarged and refined the language; who have gathered to it new possessions, extending its power and variety'.[4] To that group who combine the talent of a popular writer with the learning and attention to detail of the scholar, Forster belongs.

In the pursuit of his various biographical subjects, Forster, who until December 1855 was active in other journalistic endeavours, always isolated his work as a biographer. From Saturday morning until Tuesday evening he cut himself off from any journalistic activities to research and write biography. His inclination was continually for biographies 'which required elaborate research' as his close friend Reverend Whitwell Elwin remarked (Elwin, in fact, was asked by Carlyle to write Forster's life but refused). After Forster resigned from the *Examiner* to become Secretary and then a Commissioner of the Lunacy Commission, Forster used virtually every morning and evening to write biography.[5] A reason for accepting the administrative post was actually the greater availability of time to write and the assurance of a steady income, a fact not to be overlooked in a discussion of Forster's career.

John Forster's father was a butcher who could ill afford to send his son to school. A wealthy, or at least well-off, uncle could and did, paying for Forster's grammar school education in Newcastle and, later, his education at University College, London where, after an unsuccessful month at Cambridge, Forster began to read law in 1828. That same year his keen interest in the theatre resulted in his play, *Charles at Tunbridge*, being performed at Newcastle. During his student days, however, he began to seek ways of earning income through writing and started to contribute drama reviews to the *True Sun*. His undergraduate contributions to several school publications caught the eye of Professor Dionysus Lardner, then preparing a multi-volume encyclopedia. He immediately commissioned Forster to write a series of biographical articles on statesmen of the Commonwealth. For Forster, interested in seventeenth-century Commonwealth history, this was a welcome assignment and his enthusiasm for research and desire to uncover new details led to his well-received lives of Sir John Eliot, John Pym, Oliver Cromwell and others that appeared in *Lives of Eminent British Statesmen*, five volumes in Lardner's *The Cabinet Cyclopedia*.[6]

The idea of being commissioned to write these lives, combined with his determination to succeed in the literary, not legal, world of London initiated Forster's long-term consciousness of writing and money. In an early essay on Dryden, Forster commented, in language applicable to himself, 'literature was his trade: he not only lived upon its wages, but was never ashamed to own it . . . It was a man's own fault, after this, if he was thought disreputable because he wrote for bread.'[7] Forster always thought of himself as a professional and was proud of his literary calling and its authority – critically, to shape literary reputations, such as those of Browning or Tennyson, or socially as he gained increasing prominence as editor, literary friend and biographer. Each stage in Forster's career led to greater financial security. From his early editorship of the *Daily News* in 1846 to that of the *Examiner*, 1847–55, from his appointment as Secretary of the Lunacy Commission in late 1855, with its secure £800 per annum, to that of a Lunacy Commissioner in November 1861 receiving £1500, Forster improved his finances. And he never hid his professional success.

By 1863 Forster had built an imposing home at Palace Gate, Kensington and, by the accumulation of 18 000 volumes, includ-

ing a first Folio and a first edition of *Gulliver's Travels* with notes by
Swift, he left an inestimable legacy to the nation through his
bequest to the South Kensington Museum, now the Victoria and
Albert. Earlier, his marriage in September 1856 to the widow of
the publisher Henry Colburn increased his financial security
while starting what many have called his 'Podsnap phase' as seen
in his secure, blustery and occasionally pompous manner. In 1835
he was briefly engaged to 'LEL', Letitia Landon, but this
attachment of the young journalist and poetess did not last. These
details of financial success, however, are not intended to emphasize the materialism or philistinism of Forster but to show how his
awareness of the relation between money and literature shaped
his sense of being a biographer. As a professional biographer,
Forster was not unaware, as sales of his *Life of Goldsmith* proved, of
the value of writing biography. And as a study of his publisher's
agreements show, the profit to be had from writing the lives of
historical as well as contemporary figures did not escape him.

Ever since his earliest writing projects, Forster appears to have
considered himself a professional and his agreements record a
dramatic increase in payment. The earliest in his Deed Box, dated
17 February 1835, between Forster and a group of booksellers
(including Thomas Longman) for 'a series of short Biographical
Sketches of the most eminent British Statesmen from the reign of
Elizabeth to the present day', specifies payment of 10 shillings and
6 pence per page. Forster was to produce 'not less than 600 pages
per annum'.[8] The resulting lives of Defoe, Cromwell, Eliot and
others satisfied this requirement and brought adequate, although
by no means excessive, remuneration.

By August 1838, Forster had placed more value on his
biographical writing. Having just completed a contract on 22
August 1838 with Richard Bentley for a two-volume edition of
Landor's work, with an equal division of profits, Forster drafted
an agreement the next day for a new project. Tentatively called
Memoirs of the Court and Times of Queen Anne, this was to be a
three-volume work, with each volume approximately 400 pages.
For this work Forster proposed payment of 500 guineas, payable
in the form of promissory notes coinciding with the completion of
each volume. Optimistically, he believed he could finish volumes
1 and 2 in eight months and the third in the following two.
Bentley, responding with his own draft, dated the same day, 23
August 1838, surprisingly does not dispute Forster's claim to 500

guineas, an extraordinary sum for so inexperienced a biographer. The project, perhaps for this reason, never got beyond this stage.

Later agreements between Forster and his publishers mark the increasing value of his work as his fees dramatically increased. An 1843 agreement with Chapman and Hall for a twelve-volume series on English history, each volume 350 pages, was to bring £350 per volume and an additional £50 if sales reached 5000 copies. But this project also failed to materialize. An 1862 agreement between Forster and Frederick Longman for Forster's contribution to the Life of Sir John Eliot stipulated a 1/3–2/3 split between Forster and Longman for the first 1000 copies with profits from a second edition to be divided in two equal parts. By 1871, however, renegotiating with Frederick Chapman for a popular edition of his *Life of Sir John Eliot*, Forster received £200 upon acceptance plus a further £50 if 750 copies of the 1000 printed were sold and another £50 if 850 copies were sold. The biography would be offered at 14 shillings and published in December 1871. This agreement, dated 8 November 1871, follows, by one day, Forster's largest fee, that established for volume I of his *Life of Dickens*.

Dated 7 November 1871, the agreement between Forster and Chapman and Hall stipulates 5000 copies of volume I of *The Life of Charles Dickens* to be printed, not to exceed five impressions. The size, format and price (12 shillings) are all specified, as well as payment: £1000. No cheap edition was to appear for two years, and then only with the written consent of Chapman and Hall, while Forster retained all rights of reproduction or translation in countries other than America. Five hundred pounds were to be paid to Forster at publication, the balance to be given six months later. One year later, 6 November 1872, the agreement for volume II reveals some extraordinary changes: 10 000 copies are to be printed with a new price of 14 shillings. Forster has doubled his fee (reflecting the increase in printing), receiving £2000 in five payments, plus £250 from J. P. Lippincott in Philadelphia for transmittal of plates and publication. Additional printings would give Forster £225 per 1000 copies. The agreement also notes that further printings of volume I resulted in 13 000 copies in all with a separate agreement covering payment. Any impression beyond 13 000 for volume I would bring Forster £200 per 1000 copies.

On 28 January 1874 the agreement for volume III of the Dickens life increased Forster's payment still further. At 16 shillings a

copy, 10 000 would be printed and Forster would receive £2350 in
five instalments plus £250 from Lippincott, for transmittal of
plates in preparation for American publication. For additional
impressions of volume III Forster was to receive £250 per 1000
copies. Chapman's letter to Forster, elatedly celebrating the
burgeoning sales, makes clear that the biography was a bestseller:

21 November 1872

My dear Forster,
  I have nothing to report but what is good. The demand keeps
coming in steadily and I hope that we shall be ready with the
New Edition by the end of the Month.

Three weeks later Chapman writes to Forster that the eleventh
printing has sold out (16 December 1872). *The Life of Dickens* made
Forster a wealthy man; the agreements show a total of £5850
guaranteed. Forster's youthful hope of 500 guineas for the
proposed biography of Queen Anne was more than realized at the
end of his career.[9] Ironically, one reaction to volumes II and III of
The Life of Dickens centred on Forster's emphasis on money in
Dickens's career and the suggestion that Dickens drove himself to
death in pursuit of enlarging his already ample fortune. Nonetheless, Forster's agreements show him establishing a precedent for
biography that later biographers such as Morley and Gosse
sought to emulate. And such an awareness of financial matters
Forster also imparted to his friends.
  Much has been written about Forster and his friendships but
rarely in any critical manner.[10] An important sourcebook,
however, is the diary of William Macready, an intimate associate
not above criticizing Forster's gruff personality but generous
character. At one moment a helpful and loving associate of
Macready, Forster can almost instantly become a bitter enemy.
An entry in the diary for 16 June 1848 records Macready's
frustration over Forster: 'His caprice is beyond all management. I
have done my utmost to show him my regard and desire to be a
friend to him. I can do no more.' But the next day Macready
writes that he has a letter 'from Forster with account that the
Queen will command a night for me (Thank God!)'. 'This is very
gratifying', he adds on the 21st in response to further details from
Forster.[11]

Impatient but sociable, Forster was alternately feared and admired, as R. C. Lehmann, son of Frederic Lehmann, noted:

> a very big, square beetle-browed, black haired piece of solid humanity, with a voice that made the glasses jingle on the table . . . he could roar you (on paper) as gently as any sucking dove, for with all his arbitrariness and resolute roughness he had one of the kindest hearts that ever beat in the breast of a literary dictator.[12]

The reference is to Forster as editor as well as arbiter of literary taste but the paradox of the final phrase captures the ambiguity of Forster as colleague and counsellor to innumerable Victorian men of letters. His rudeness was legendary but acceptable only because of his genuine affection for his friends.

Forster used his friendships to generate other associations. His early assistance to Leigh Hunt led to his meeting B. W. Proctor, which, in turn, led to meeting Charles Lamb. His close association with Lamb resulted in the nervous concern of Lamb's executors that the ambitious Forster might be a serious contender to write Lamb's biography. Through his work as drama critic of the *True Sun* he met Macready in May 1833; in 1834 he met and befriended Bulwer-Lytton; Ainsworth introduced him to Dickens; Macready introduced him to Browning. Advancing the reputations of Browning, Patmore and Tennyson in the pages of the *Examiner*, of which Forster became drama critic in 1833 and shortly after literary editor and then sub-editor (1835), led to friendships of varying intensity with these men. But his patronizing air offended some. His failure, for example, to give proper recognition of Dickens's friendship with Ainsworth and Collins in his biography of Dickens led Ainsworth caustically to remark at Forster's death that he 'was *not* the friend of men of letters unless they could serve him'.[13] But through his activities as literary critic, editor, confidant and promoter, Forster became, in the late 1830s and throughout the 1840s, 'the most important personality of literary London', or, in the telling phrase of Leigh Hunt's son, 'the Beadle of the Universe'. It was Forster's activity as 'beadle', as witness and recorder of the lives of his time, that produced his distinguished group of biographies which has led historians of biography to identify him as perhaps the first professional biographer of the nineteenth century.[14]

With his training in law, love of English history, and skill at research as well as writing, Forster brought to biography discrimination, a quest for authority and determination. His biographical practice, however, requires some comment because it became, and to some extent remains, controversial. The problem is his distortion or misrepresentation of material, whether it is the conflation of letters by Dickens, the misrepresentation of his own importance, as in the life of Landor, or praise of subjects at the expense of their bad habits, as in his account of Thomas Wentworth, the first Earl of Strafford (1593–1641).[15] An explanation of this must begin with Forster's own sense of self-importance. With Landor and Dickens, Forster was clearly instrumental in the conduct of their lives and he does not hesitate to stress this at the expense or prominence of others – Mrs Linton in the case of Landor, Wilkie Collins and Ainsworth in the life of Dickens (Collins's refusal to lend Forster his letters from Dickens, however, might have prompted his minor role in volume III). Forster thought himself equal to his contemporaries, believing his part as friend and counsellor justified his claim to biographical freedom and self-importance. His presence is a defence of the roles he performed and enjoyed.

Secondly, Forster's distortions resulted from his desire to present a portrait, not simply a chronicle of his subjects. Individual details must blend into an overall image or theme. By shifting dates, figures, locations or even facts, not actually contradicting but altering them, Forster is able to present the dramatized life he envisions for his subjects – often matching the life to the image created by the subject's writings. And if aesthetic demands overrule the historical record, the result may be inaccurate but not, strictly speaking, false. This approach is in accord with the practice of Romantic biography as identified by Francis R. Hart. Allegiance to the image rather than the facts is evident in the work of Lockhart and his use of fictional methods to present the life of Scott. Working through the voluminous material led Lockhart to an intuitive vision of Scott which sometimes meant altering the record. This method of rearranging data to provide an organic form anticipates the practice of Forster who enlarges this style in his conflation of letters, alteration of dates, changes in language and shifts of scene. But his defence is the imaginative integrity required for a coherent portrait of his subject. J. W. Croker, editor of the popular 1831 edition of Boswell's *Johnson*, explains the problem and solution:

In the voluminous memoirs dictated by Buonaparte to his followers at St. Helena, many of the facts are notoriously false, and most of the commentaries are studiously delusive; but the memoirs are not, on that account, less characteristic of the author, less entertaining to the casual reader, or less important to the critical history of the man.[16]

Supplementing the adaptation of material is Forster's strong sense of the Victorian audience. Often, he alters material and its presentation to provide them with a picture of the subject they themselves imagine. Truth to the conception of the figure takes precedence over the absolute record. Consequently, Forster omits the coarseness of Goldsmith, the temper of Defoe, the drinking habits of Steele or his own role in exiling Landor to Italy. Such avoidance or alteration of material creates 'authorized fictions' which combine the Romantic drive for coherence adjusted to a Victorian determination to be copious. This challenges the moral obligation of the Victorian biographer who must now compete with aesthetic claims on his subject's life. The image rather than the fact appears to dominate the work or, at least, battle for control in the presentation of the life. Hazlitt expressed this ideal in his fictional monologue, 'Boswell Redivivus':

My goal was to catch the tone and manner, rather than to repeat the exact expressions, or even opinions; just as it is possible to recognize the voice of an acquaintance without distinguishing the particular words he uses.

The individualizing characteristics rather than the specificity of the record is primary. The change is from objective, biographical fact to the experience of the biographer envisioning his subject. For Forster this also means maintaining the mythical dimension of his subject and the need to equate the record of the life with an ideal often established in the writing. Hence his comment in *Dickens* that the novels 'formed the whole of that inner life which essentially constituted the man . . .'[17] Paradoxically, distortion of the record encouraged a more artistic development of biography while at the same time altering its reliance on the historical past. The 'freedom' from fact in biographies by Mrs Kingsley, J. W. Cross or Lytton Strachey, partially defended by Virginia Woolf as 'creative fact', has recently become celebrated by contemporary biographers as a new methodology. However, its roots are in how Lockhart, initially, and Forster, repeatedly, (mis)treated fact.

Forster's university study of the seventeenth century and his pleasure in seeking out detail led to his appointment and successful completion of a series of lives in the *Eminent British Statesmen* series. Varying in length from the brief, 74-page life of John Hampden, in volume 3, to the two-volume, 798-page life of Cromwell, Forster displays an early understanding of political biography, research and literary narrative. Not above moralizing his subjects, Forster writes in the opening of the Hampden biography of his concern with the public context of his subject's life:

> So little, after the most extensive researches, is known of the man, that all may, unfortunately, be very briefly told: his history is written in the great public actions he forwarded through life, and in the assertion and defence of which he died.[18]

Conscious of disputes and confusions regarding facts, Forster carefully clarifies rumours and hearsay such as London being the actual birthplace of Hampden or the controversy surrounding Hampden's speech in response to the impeachment of five members of Parliament (p. 343). Forster provides an assessment of Hampden's character four pages into the life, not at the end, and quotes liberally from documents and letters that give a sense of his personality. A detailed evaluation of Hampden's trial for refusal to pay the 'ship-money levied on gentry in Autumn of 1635' is based on passages from Clarendon and Lord Nugent to supplement Hampden's action. Forster presents a heroic defence of a patriotic parliamentarian (pp. 333–6), correcting earlier evaluations.[19] 'No one of that age', writes Forster, 'looked at the great question of resistance to tyranny on a larger or more extended ground, or in a more philosophic spirit' than Hampden (p. 337). This attitude towards the hero is more evident only in Forster's life of Hampden's cousin, Oliver Cromwell. Decisive in its interpretation and dramatic in its descriptions, 'Hampden' suggests the qualities of narrative and accuracy, as well as admiring tone, that characterize Forster's later biographies. And shaping the biography is a coherent pattern which distinguishes all of Forster's biographical efforts. Here, Hampden is a representative of the laws and liberties of England; Cromwell, its symbol.

Until Forster's 1838–9 life of Cromwell, there had been the usual celebratory but inaccurate lives by such writers as Oliver Cromwell (1742–1821), great grandson of Henry Cromwell, fourth son of the Protector, and Bishop Michael Russell, whose popular two-volume life appeared in 1829. Forster's was the first to research carefully and investigate as many aspects of Cromwell's life as possible. He first projected the life as early as 1830. Footnotes pepper the pages, giving original sources, correcting errors and providing references for various events. Volume 1 of the life covers the period 1599–1658 and begins with parentage and youth. But, again, Forster is keen to separate myth from reality, although not so eager to reject the myth completely. What he seeks is its firm foundation in actuality to make it more convincing. The stories of Cromwell's youth have an instructive dimension because 'the fables of biography may show us, at all events, in what various ways the celebrity of their object has wrought upon his countrymen'.[20] Forster then repeats various tales for their fictional charm as much as their use in revealing Cromwell's character. Forster continues to correct previous biographers, from the Royalist Heath's *Flagellum*, the first biography of Cromwell after the Restoration, to Russell. Whether he details Cromwell's school behaviour, his conduct at St Ives or the idea that in the 1630s Cromwell thought of going to America, Forster revises. The American journey, writes Forster, is 'utterly incredible, and supported by no worthy evidence. Elsewhere, in these lives, it has been refuted' (I: 54). Fact proves Forster's interpretation of Cromwell's life as he repeatedly tells the reader (re I: 61), citing letters, memoranda and personal accounts whenever available.

As the biography progresses, Forster summarizes for the reader moments of change or development, making Cromwell's ascendancy clear and understandable, as well as narratively dramatic (I: 148–9). The shift from military commander to political leader highlights the organization of material. And generating the reader's confidence is Forster's willingness to admit his own occasional perplexity over Cromwell's character, despite his thorough research (I: 184). This sense of limitation that characterizes the biographer's task establishes a rapport with the reader which unites the biographer with his audience. Forster employs this personalizing element in such later works as Goldsmith and Landor. If something appears uninteresting, Forster tells the reader so and removes it from his narrative (i: 227), generating belief that one reads the best or at least the most important of the details.

The attempt at drama in many passages of *Cromwell* suggests Forster's strongest habit as a biographer, which sections of *Goldsmith, Landor, Dickens* and *Swift* repeat: his attempt to convey a sense of the contemporary or immediate experience of the subject to the reader. This stylistic and structural feature dominates his biographical writing whether it is his judicious selection of letters in Landor or his use, *verbatim*, of actual reviews he wrote of Dickens's novels in the *Examiner* as literary criticism in his *Life of Dickens*. To give a sense of the actual – whether consciously in the reconstruction of a life through letters, narrative pattern or dramatic scene, or critically through contemporaneous commentary of texts – is the overriding quality of Forster as a biographer. It not only defines his appeal to readers but, coupled with his determined research, furthers his claim to being one of the most widely read and professional biographers in the period. Contemporaneousness provides the narrative and literary excitement for his audience, while the facts and research provide the historical basis which legitimize his effort.

Forster wants his readers to experience directly and completely the lives of his subjects. In each of his biographies he consciously strives for a blend of stylistic power and historical detail. In this way he unites his love of drama – his earliest composition was an essay in defence of the theatre – with his devotion to collecting and scholarship. The result is professional biography – biography that is knowledgeably written, carefully structured, thoroughly researched and lively in its style. Forster is always conscious of his audience.

Another feature of Forster's biographical method is hero worship or reverence for his subject. As early as 1813 James Stanfield in his *Essay on . . . Biography* described the importance of this quality and by 1834 Carlyle confirmed it when Teufelsdrockh announced that 'Thought without Reverence is barren, perhaps poisonous.' This indirect means of morally approving the act of biography because of its positive treatment of the subject found new significance in Lockhart's life of Scott through the admiring tone and treatment of detail in the work. Forster recognized the value of this approach early in his career. His 1844 review of Stanley's *Life of Thomas Arnold* stressed the 'reverence for the character' by the author as a positive feature of a just account. But in his own biographies, Forster tended to overemphasize this quality, as Carlyle, whom he admired, often noted. A letter from Carlyle of 18 November 1847 concerning the first three books of *Goldsmith* praises the life for its 'artistic Picture of the 18th Century and . . . moral Dis-course on it', but questions the excessive amount of praise for the subject. He suggests Forster is too good natured and should look more completely at his subject's character: 'mind the *per-contra* of it too, which is here urged'.[21]

Eighteen years later, Carlyle still recommends a more balanced presentation to Forster. Admiring his expanded life of Sir John Eliot, Carlyle writes 'we expect more from the same hand (Strafford, for instance, and a *per-contra* side of things?) – this of Eliot being the *best* we have had from him'. In 1854 Dickens also told Forster that he probably exaggerated his praise of Strafford in a recent lecture; though Strafford was a man of great abilities, he was also 'a proud, ill-tempered arrogant man'.[22] Forster always had difficulty in distancing himself from his subjects although he was not uncritical of them. Indeed, Dickens goes on to make the following generality which clearly offended Forster: 'I know the old rule that when you write Mr. Smith's biography you are to conceive a violent affection for Mr. Smith and invest him with all the old cardinal virtues and several new ones.' A letter to Forster two days later begins with an apology about the Smith reference and closes with this plea: 'As to Smith he was merely a stupid illustration and may be put into the limbo of all bad jokes.' Forster's response to Dickens's remark does not exist but his obvious sensitivity suggests his belief in the integrity and objectivity of his biographical writing. Offended by Dickens's suggestion, Forster no doubt believed he wrote honestly and candidly. This problem of sympathy for his heroes persisted throughout his work; as his close friend Whitwell Elwin stated, Forster 'could scarcely bring himself to recognize that moral meanness could co-exist with majesty of intellect'.[23]

The life of Cromwell balanced biography with political history. The life of Goldsmith achieved a similar unity although between history and a literary career. The popular reception of the book and its qualities attests to its success. To Forster, Dickens wrote

'I have never liked Johnson half so well . . . to read the book, is to
be in the time', while Carlyle praised the work excessively:
'Except *Boswell*'s there is no Biography in the English language
worth naming beside it.'[24] The expanded *Life and Times of Oliver
Goldsmith* (1854), however, met with less approval because it
blurred the focus on the author in giving an elaborate and rousing
account of eighteenth-century life. But Forster again exhibited his
concern with fact and accuracy, actually working on and off the
text for five years before it appeared. Nevertheless, his heroizing of
the subject led to a recurrent charge of puffery, enthusiasm and
inflation. Edward Fitzgerald critically expressed this view in
January 1869, when he complained that 'it astonishes me to see
the best English Brains, like old Spedding, go the whole hog so
with any hero they take up'. Anticipating some of the reaction to
Forster's next major biography, that of Landor, Fitzgerald noted
in November of that year that

> I have not seen Forster's Landor: not caring much for either
> party. Forster seems to me a genuine Cockney: be-heroing
> Goldsmith, Landor, etc. *a outrance*. I remember so well his being
> red-hot in admiration of Coventry Patmore's first Poems: 'By
> God, they came up to Tennyson's, etc.'

Yet Forster's heroism for his subjects was a necessity, as Samuel
R. Gardiner explained in his 1876 memorial article on Forster:

> He had almost a feminine need for a personal attachment in his
> literary work; of some hero with whose cause he could
> thoroughly identify himself, and whose faults and mistakes
> could, if they were acknowledged at all, be covered with loving
> tendencies . . . His portraits have in them the life which springs
> from sympathy.[25]

This need for personal attachment is nowhere better illustrated
than in Forster's life of *Landor*, his first life of a contemporary, his
first official biography and his first literary biography after giving
up his post as editor of the *Examiner*. By this time (1856–66),
Forster was very much a respectable figure, married to a
well-to-do widow, living in a Kensington mansion, and satisfied
with a Podsnapian existence. Landor was to him slightly bo-
hemian, scandalous and impulsive. But the life typifies the pro-

fessional attitude of Forster towards biography as he gathered original documents and prepared an accurate and critical view of his subject. In practice, however, the work is Romantic, since it selects, manipulates and even alters original documents to accord with Forster's intuitive sense of the subject. But the conception is Victorian, providing a critical, demythologizing, but also discrete account.

Moving away from the essentially popular conception of biography as seen in *Goldsmith*, Forster attempts in *Landor* to resolve the paradox of nineteenth-century biography – being honest without being libellous. Offended by Landor's improprieties such as his seduction of Nancy Jones and his later relationship with the sixteen-year-old Geraldine Harper, Forster nonetheless only hints at these associations. But to equate details with his sense of Landor's character, he needs to alter, conflate and even misquote his sources. Rather than criticize these changes as biographical weaknesses, they can be defended as the effort to solve a continual dilemma for biographers: the unity of factual accuracy with organic form creating a consistent characterization. Forster not only extends the tradition of Romantic biography but alters it in his more focused narrative style, stronger sense of composition and greater freedom of prose than his predecessors. Furthermore, having to write the life of a contemporary, and a controversial one as well, required greater detachment and impersonality. But that was to be balanced with a sympathetic portrait of the character of one known for his irascibility and impatience.

Despite the alterations of letters and mixing of dates, *Landor*, appearing only five years after the subject's death, remained for nearly 75 years 'the unchallenged authority on Landor's life'.[26] Neglecting his own illness and the burden of other work, Forster compiled one of the most complete and detailed lives so far published in the century. Having met Landor in 1836 at the age of 24 (Landor was 61), there was an immediate liking between the young but influential writer and the old, difficult poet (although in the biography Forster neglects his role in the exile of Landor to Italy). Appointed literary executor at Landor's death, Forster began the life in 1865 but the peculiarities of Landor embarrassed Forster, according to his close friend Whitwell Elwin, and he did not finish volume I until 1867; volume II was completed in 1869. Severe criticism greeted the life, largely by those who felt left out of the account, such as Mrs Lynn Linton. Offended by her lack of prominence in the life and her belief that Forster displayed little loyalty to the dead writer whom he revered when alive, she wrote a vitriolic review. The biography, she said, was 'a book eminently wanting in magnanimity . . . so pitiless a dissection and so cold and "candid" an analysis have come with a singularly bad grace under all the circumstances of their friendship from the hand of the present biographer; who would have done better to have rebuked Landor in his lifetime for the faults and weaknesses of which he has told the world so much after his death'.[27]

Mrs Linton's objections to the realistic portrayal of Landor, the deflation of such myths as Landor's fine lineage, athletic prowess or profligate life in Bath echoes the call for the ethically correct in biography – lives of piety and conscience not criticism and truth. Such 'bits of ill-natured "honesty" ' result in an unfair and dishonest life (p. 292). Ironically, it was Forster's very determination to be truthful that led to such a reaction, anticipating the controversy Froude's *Thomas Carlyle* later generated. Interestingly, Forster would probably have written Carlyle's life since he was appointed Carlyle's literary executor. Fifteen years his junior, Forster nonetheless predeceased him. In his quest for honesty regarding Landor, criticizing Landor's desertion of his family, and his failure to educate his children, Forster generated hostility, although he made his purpose clear on the second page of the biography: 'It is not my intention to speak otherwise than frankly of his character and of his books . . . [although] his faults lie more upon the surface than is usual with writers of this high order.'[28]

For Landor, writing was an indulgence and in him Forster confronts the undermining of his traditional theme of the writer's dignity. Southey, whose correspondence appears in the work, becomes the figure who upholds that role in the life. But such candour and criticism seemed too strong for Victorian readers, who reacted strongly against the life. Nevertheless, the biography is a model of research and evaluation, a combination of Baconian fact-gathering and Boswellian interjection combined with dramatic portrayal. Such features anticipate what will become both the attraction and objection to Forster's life of Dickens.

Literary criticism is also very much a part of Forster's life of Landor. More so than in any of his previous biographies, Forster analyses the literature he describes: *Gebir* he evaluates for its style, 'richness of detail and descriptive power'; *Imaginary Conversations*

he scrutinizes for their method; the *Hellenics* he discusses for their
theme (I: 83; 502–4; II: 514). Among his readers, Dickens especially appreciated this dimension of the biography. Literary
reaction to Landor's compositions, as well as the problems of
writing, form a good part of the narrative, making the work an
important model of literary biography. Almost all of the fifth book
of the biography, over 100 pages, concerns itself with *Imaginary
Conversations*, from conception to critical reaction. Personal details
and literary life blend together providing an example for later
literary biographers. There is even the revelation of literary
history as Forster relates how Landor was the model for Lawrence
Boythorn of *Bleak House*, which Dickens confirmed in his review of
the biography (II: 394). Dickens admired *Landor* as 'a generous
and yet conscientious picture of one life . . .', adding that 'It is
essentially a sad book, and herein lies proof of its truth and worth.
The life of almost any man possessing great gifts would be a sad
book to himself; and this book enables us not only to see its
subject, but to be its subject if we will.'[29] Here, Dickens senses an
identity with a fellow writer that goes beyond the superficial and
historical to the core of his character. And that writer is Forster.

Despite the objections of later biographers – Sidney Colvin in
his *Landor* for the English Men of Letters series is representative
when he says the life was written 'with knowledge, industry,
affection and loyalty, of purpose' but is 'cumbrous in comment,
inconclusive in criticism and vague on vital points, especially on
. . . bibliography' – despite the limitations of characterization –
Malcolm Elwin says inaccurately that Forster saw Landor 'always
as Boythorn, the caricature' making Landor 'bluster his turbul-
ent, headlong way' – Forster's biography remained (until the
1940s) the standard life. His confidence that his attempt had been
'honestly made . . . to estimate with fairness and candour'
Landor's life and work (II: 594) deserves greater sympathy of
understanding because the life actually presents, in the words of
Dickens, a figure 'with the dignity of generosity: with a noble
scorn of all littleness, all cruelty, oppression, fraud and false
pretence'. It furthermore confirms, as James A. Davies has
shown, that when drawn to contemporaries, Forster did not
preimpose ideas upon his material as he did with those of the past,
but presented 'honest revelation' bordering on explicitness.[30]

The second volume of *Landor* appeared in 1869, the year the
health of Forster's close friend, Charles Dickens, began to fail.

Forster worried over the strain of Dickens's extensive public readings but could not curb the strenuous activity. The sudden death of Dickens on 9 June 1870 led Forster again to take up the role of official biographer, a task he could not refuse in spite of his planned life of Swift which had been gestating since 1855. Of the friendship between Dickens and Forster a great deal has been written.[31] From their early meeting in 1836, they remained intimate until the early 1850s when Wilkie Collins, W. H. Wills, Frank Stone and other young men began to supplant Forster as Dickens's companions. But Forster's role as critic, adviser (both legal and personal), investment counsellor and travel companion was essential. From 1837 on, Forster read in manuscript or proof everything Dickens wrote. In the earliest days of their friendship, Forster introduced Dickens to Macready, Talford, Bulwer-Lytton and Leigh Hunt, expanding his social circle. And at various crises, Dickens turned only to Forster. During the difficult negotiations between himself and his wife at their separation in the spring of 1858, Dickens chose Forster to represent him. In planning for Ellen Ternan's possible trip to America in 1867 to join him on his reading tour, Dickens informed Wills that Forster alone could be trusted to act in the best interests of Ellen and Dickens. In appreciation of Forster's help, particularly with his marriage problems, Dickens dedicated the Library Edition of his works to Forster, bequeathed the remaining manuscripts of his books to him and, in 1869, made him, with Georgina Hogarth, his executor. There was never any question that Forster, 'the only person who has the material – the knowledge and the power' would write his life.[32] Undertaking the biography was a task Forster performed out of obligation to their friendship and because of his superb collection of personal documents. Furthermore the life permitted Forster to reaffirm his central role in Dickens's career.

In his July 1869 review of *Landor* in *All the Year Round*, Dickens summarized Forster's method and achievement in this manner:

> Mr. Forster step by step builds up the evidence on which he writes this life and states this character. In like manner he gives the evidence for his high estimation of Landor's works, and – it may be added for their recompense against some neglect, in finding so sympathetic, acute, and devoted a champion . . . It rarely befalls an author to have such a commentator: to become

the subject of so much artistic skill and knowledge, combined with such infinite and loving pains. Alike as a piece of Biography, and as a commentary upon the beauties of a great writer, the book is a massive book, as the man and the writer were massive too. (p. 185)

Implicitly, Dickens is approving the form of his own biography and indicating his sympathy with his unofficially designated biographer. What he would hope for he sees in Forster's *Landor*: a balanced, judious and accurate life aided by insightful and full analyses of his writing. Forster's subsequent biography fulfils this prescription which Dickens, in the year before his death, approves.

The form of Dickens's biography is the source of its popularity as well as its criticism. Relying on the numerous letters in his possession, Forster based his narrative on personal record. But his very presence in the life, especially volume I, prompted many to agree with the assessment of the *Saturday Review*: the book should 'not be called the Life of Dickens but the History of Dickens's Relations to Mr. Forster'. (Similar comments were made, however, about Boswell's *Johnson*.) To Sara Hennell, George Eliot wrote that the book should be read for the story of Dickens's early life but that the work is 'ill-organized, and stuffed with criticism and other matter which would be better in limbo'. Wilkie Collins referred to the work as 'The Life of John Forster with occasional anecdotes of Charles Dickens.' But the response of George Gissing, as that of Carlyle and Edward Fitzgerald, signals the more genuine and appreciative reception of the biography:

much fault has been found with Forster's *Biography* which is generally blamed as giving undue prominence to the figure of the biographer. I cannot join in this censure . . . I should say, indeed, that there exists no book more immediately helpful to a young man beginning his struggle in the world of letters (especially, of course, to the young novelist) than this of Forster's. And simply because it exhibits in such rich detail the story and the manner of Dickens' work.[33]

Praise of the life reveals two important qualities: the first is Forster's repeated insistence on factual detail in presenting his subject. In showing Dickens, in Gissing's words 'at his desk day by day, recounting his hidden difficulties, his secret triumphs; in short, making the man live over again before us the noblest portion of his life', Forster provides the authenticity necessary for his subject and his immediacy (pp. 59–60). And supplementing this detail is a feature Forster's other biographies display: the theme of success against difficult odds. The subject of biographies diverse as Smiles's *Lives of the Engineers* or Stephen's *Johnson*, success in *Dickens* reveals the essentially moral appeal of nineteenth-century biography and its underlying archetype: overcoming adversity, whether it be ignorance, poverty or illness. This emerges as the constant force that unites the biographies of disparate lives. Labour, productivity and reward do not remain abstractions but, in biographies, the actual accomplishments of individuals. The method most used to express this advance, in keeping with a nineteenth-century attraction to history and documentation, is the letter. In those records that personalize achievement and reveal the past, the biographer and reader enter the spirit of the subject; or, as R. H. Horne commented, 'You are thus, through their aspirations, let into the secret of the noblest part of their characters.'[34]

But in *Dickens*, Forster questions the theme of success by suggesting that it became overconfidence resulting in determined, single-minded achievement created by a deprived childhood. Contradicting those who have stressed the uncritical nature of *Dickens*, Forster's analysis of Dickens's character honestly balances 'the restless and resistless energy, which opened to him opportunities of escape' with 'a too great confidence in himself, a sense that everything was possible to the will that would make it so'. 'In that direction', Forster explains, 'there was in him, at such times, something even hard and aggressive' (I: 34). Through his analysis of success and its cost, Forster provides a biography more critical than any he had so far written. This realistic, as opposed to idealistic, aspect of Dickens is especially manifest in Forster's account of Dickens's unhappiness preceding and following his separation from his wife. There, Forster compassionately feels for Dickens's loss of security and dignity: 'There was for him no "city of the mind" against outward ills, for inner consolation and shelter' (II: 200). In showing Dickens's failings as well as failures in life, Forster gives an honest account of his close friend beyond praise and admiration.

The epitome of middle-class social ascendancy, Forster

embodies Victorian middle-class virtues throughout his biographies, but most especially in *Dickens*. However, his concern in the life with Dickens's loss of dignity and security represents his own anxiety over the stability of these verities. His defence is constant attention to the theme of the socially acceptable literary man, a consequence of the stature accorded the widely respected professional writer. And accompanying such a reputation are the habits of discipline, domestic happiness and a common-sense way of dealing with the world. That Dickens should oppose these qualities in his private life after 1858 was no small challenge to the principles Forster upheld. Emphasis on the continued acceptance of Dickens as a popular writer whose fictional characters largely maintained domestic values and correct behaviour (although figures of personal unhappiness and unfulfilled love began to appear with some consistency in his later fiction) was the means Forster applied to mitigate the shortcomings of Dickens's private behaviour. And parallel to the account of society's acceptance of Dickens as a writer is the increasing stature of Forster as literary colleague, intimate and man of letters. Implicitly and explicitly joining his own life to that of Dickens (compare their poor backgrounds, attraction to literature, desire for recognition and achievement of success), Forster writes his most personal biography. The theme of the biography becomes the integration of the writer with society and what the narrative records is the simultaneous triumph of novelist and biographer.

In telling the story of Dickens's life, Forster reached his largest audience through his most popular work. Volume I went through twelve impressions within the first three months of its appearance. What the *Life of Dickens* reveals is how the biographer becomes both a subject in, and the creator of, the biography. In reconstructing the life of another, he constructs his own. The biography is dualistic, self-confirming as it creates, historical as it narrates. To read biography adequately is to recognize the presence and function of the biographer/narrator in the text, an unavoidable subject in *Life of Dickens*.

Not surprisingly, the *Life of Dickens* follows the Romantic mode of biography, characterized as the commitment to image rather than fact, with imagination more dominant than record. As the editors of volume I of the Pilgrim edition of *The Letters of Charles Dickens* state, Forster was not concerned with the public image of

Dickens 'but with the truth, as he conceived it. The *Life* contains
numerous small distortions of fact, but paradoxically these
distortions were in the interest of a larger or ideal truth.'[35] This is
the essential style of Romantic biography as Francis R. Hart has
shown and J. G. Lockhart practised. In the 1870s Forster re-read
the life of Scott and an 1871 edition of the life is heavily
underlined. Forster no doubt reviewed Lockhart's method,
especially his use of letters. Yet the reliance on letters created a
dilemma for Forster which highlights one of the difficulties of the
professional biographer, especially when he has had a personal
attachment to his subject.

Fundamentally, the problem for Forster was how to sustain and
make convincing his importance and involvement with Dickens
while presenting an honest portrait. This was not a difficulty in
volumes I and II of the *Life* because he had numerous letters
addressed to him by Dickens which confirmed Dickens's dependence on Forster's judgement, advice and friendship. But as
Dickens turned to others, Forster had to alter texts in order to
maintain the appearance of Dickens's continued reliance on him.
The result was not only falsified letters but a change in narrative
point of view as Forster became less prominent in the *Life*.

Lacking first-hand, daily knowledge or a cache of letters
detailing Dickens's activities diminished the presence of Forster.
The result was a more objective but less personal narrative. When
the intrusions did occur, however, the texts were more corrupt.
For example, a long letter by Dickens to Lord Lytton on *A Tale of
Two Cities* implies that it was sent to Forster and that it was
Forster who made the criticisms of the novel which prompted
Dickens's lengthy reply. The actual letter, reprinted twice in the
Nonesuch edition – first as written to Forster (August 1859) and
then as to Lytton (5 June 1860) – contains no reference to Forster,
although its appearance and context in the *Life* is to compensate
for the few letters from Dickens to Forster concerning the later
novels. In volume II of the three-volume original edition, Forster
printed a letter to Maclise as though it were to him. Dated 22 July
1844, the letter is printed as Dickens's 'second letter from Albara'
to Forster with 'an outbreak of whimsical enthusiasm . . ., meant
especially for Maclise'.[36]

Altered texts, italicized passages, misdated letters, corrected
originals – Forster committed all these misdeeds in an effort to
maintain his conception of Dickens and their association, extend-

ing the continued dependence of the novelist on the advice of the
friend. Such manipulation is indefensible on scholarly and factual
grounds but is understandable if one is to absorb the powerful
nature of Romantic biography as practised in the Victorian
period. Where allegiance to the portrait or vision of a subject takes
precedence over fact, the life must alter, as in Lockhart's *Scott* or,
later, J. W. Cross's *George Eliot's Life*. But it also shows the
powerful, personal control the biographer has over his subject, a
control that manipulates, shapes and even realigns the life. As
many have noted, the subject of the *Life of Dickens* is as much
Forster as it is Dickens.

A disheartening postscript to the matter of sources in Forster's
account of Dickens is that of the nearly 1000 letters from Dickens
at Forster's disposal, only fifty-five survive and all but two of them
are early letters. Forster himself contributed to the paucity of
material by destroying, as early as 1864, those letters he felt were
too private for inclusion in the *Life* – and his literary executors, W.
J. Chitty, Lord (Robert) Lytton and Reverend Whitwell Elwin,
followed his orders and destroyed the majority of what remained.
In 1864, according to his account book, Forster had six bound
volumes of Dickens's letters in addition to 173 packets of letters and
papers. Many of Dickens's most important letters exist only in the
Life where, from volume II on, Forster cut up most of the originals
and pasted them in the manuscript. At that period Forster was ill
and his health worsened; the effort of transcription was perhaps
too strenuous, as the editors of the Pilgrim edition of Dickens's
letters suggest (p. xi). However, the falsification or 'improvement' of texts began with letters dated as early as 1837 and
continued throughout the life; and in some cases Forster intensified Dickens's affections, as in his continual substitution of
'Kate' for Dickens's 'Mrs. D'. Yet, there was never any question
that Forster should be the author of Dickens's biography.

Forster titles his concluding chapter of the eleventh book of the
biography, 'Personal Characteristics'. In these pages, however,
he expresses his rationale and method for the entire biography,
which is to narrate the life via the works. Dickens's books become
the source material and proof of his existence: 'they formed the
whole of that inner life which essentially constituted the man . . .
The story of his books, therefore, at all stages of their progress,
and of the hopes or designs connected with them, was my first
care' (II: 376–7). This statement echoes Dickens's own wish,

expressed in his will of May 1869, not to have 'any monument, memorial or testimonial whatever. I rest my claims to the remembrance of my country upon my published works . . .' (II: 422). The result is a phenomenological biography, one where the works define the life, and are the experience of the life. Or, in different terms, where each fiction becomes a stage of fact, each novel (fiction) a factual experience. The interaction of the two establish a life (the biography) via art (the novels). Fact becomes the source of fiction; fiction for the biographer the substance of the author's life.

Using letters in the life provided intimacy for the reader and seeming objectivity for the narrator. They also clarified the major subject and theme, while making Forster ubiquitous, since the majority of the letters were addressed to him. His statement has an ironic undertone: 'The purpose here was to make Dickens the sole central figure in the scenes revived, narrator as well as principal actor; and only by the means employed could consistency or unity be given to the self-revelation, and the picture made definite and clear' (II: 377). The final phrase defines the importance of integrating the factual with the fictional; incorporating letters provides evidence for the fiction, giving it reality as the subject assumed a dual role: that of narrator and actor. The life of Dickens is a biography of process revealing how fiction unites with fact and the ways fiction can illuminate the experience of the author. However, including letters to others by Dickens alters the focus gained from the central concentration on a single, long-term recipient who was both an adviser and collaborator (II: 377). But shaping the structure of the three-volume biography, revised into two in 1876, is the development of Dickens as an artist and the use of literature to tell the story of his life. Following the pattern of *Goldsmith* and *Landor*, Forster joins life with literature in providing an integrated narrative.

But what distracts the reader and affects the quality of the biography are its digressions, personal asides and changes of subjects, according to Sylvère Monod. Monod gives, but does not develop, however, his own defence of this technique, when he notes that the yearly publication of the life meant that each volume was reviewed, commented on and criticized before its successor appeared.[37] Naturally, Forster felt compelled to reply to the criticisms and, rather than suspend direct addresses to his detractors and forge ahead with his narrative, he digressed to explore, explain, justify or restate his method or organizational procedure. Each volume required a new defence. The opening of volume III (1874), dealing with the serial publication of *Bleak House*, reflects some of the problems generally associated with the plethora of available documents and the personal involvement of Forster in the narrative (II: 114–15, 1876). But his drawing back from the narrative, in response to charges of overinvolvement in the preceding volumes, creates an imbalance of narrative design and shift in tone. The cause is his wish to provide an honest and, at the same time, personal portrait of his subject. 'Of the charge of obtruding myself to which their publication [the letters] has exposed me, I can only say that I studied nothing so hard as to suppress my own personality', declared Forster in Chapter III of Book I (II: 377, 1876). The statement echoes Lockhart and his method in the *Life of Scott*.

Written during illness, old age and with Dickens's wife and other family members still alive (note the dedication to the daughters of Dickens), the *Life of Charles Dickens* is an accomplishment. Despite such omissions as Dickens's vulgarisms, dandyism, pessimism over the future of England and antagonism towards the church, it embodies Forster's professional attitude of accuracy, completeness and truth (II: 206, 247). Yet certain ironies emerge.

The first is the way the theme of dignity for the artist–gentleman is undercut by Dickens's behaviour towards the end of his life. In his striving for greater public acceptance, larger fortune and more public acknowledgement of his personal unhappiness, Dickens undid the tradition Forster emphasized concerning the nobleness of England's most professional and popular writer. The crass motives of Dickens regarding his numerous public readings, which Forster honestly presents through letters, is only one example of how the life and the image of that life begin to divide at the end of the biography. Unlike Dryden, Goldsmith or Southey, subjects of earlier biographical writing by Forster, Dickens appears to contradict the traditional virtues of a Victorian writer. Furthermore, Forster candidly and ironically shows that for all his intimacy with Dickens and importance as adviser and friend, Dickens repeatedly rejected his advice. Forster counselled Dickens not to take the editorship of the *Daily News*, not to separate from his wife, not to print a public statement of the separation, not to give public readings and not to tour America. Dickens refused

every request. Increasingly, Forster's disappointment complicated his affection for his subject and intensified the conflict
between success versus fierce determination in the book. There
emerges, despite Forster's involvement and self-defence, a clear
disassociation from Dickens. Yet Forster includes all, showing the
paradoxes of Dickens's life and the ambivalency of his own
relationship to him. He could have chosen silence but he tells
much and implies more. The *Life* does not, as one critic wrote, put
'a halo around Dickens' head, a harp in his hand, and make wings
sprout from his shoulders'. Carlyle, in his letter on the biography,
provides a more just assessment when he notes the wonder at
Forster's even writing the life considering his illness, age and
relation with the subject. What the *Life of Dickens* remarkably
accomplishes, as Dickens himself said of *Goldsmith*, is to present in
an 'admirable manner . . . the case of the literary man'.[38] Such a
concern is fundamental in all of Forster's biographies, not the
least his final biography, the incomplete *Life of Jonathan Swift*.

Surveying the lives of Swift at the beginning of the twentieth
century, Leslie Stephen noted that Sir Walter Scott's life,
published in 1814, was 'defective in point of accuracy. Scott . . .
liked a good story too well to be very particular about its
authenticity.' By contrast John Forster's 1875 life 'contains the
results of patient and thorough inquiry' but 'was unfortunately
interrupted by Mr. Forster's death and ends at the beginning of
1711'. Echoing Stephen's remarks are those of Henry Craik,
author of a comprehensive *Life of Jonathan Swift*. Of Forster he
writes that his objective was 'to apply a clearer light and a more
sympathetic criticism to the intricacies of Swift's career' than had
otherwise been done. Death prevented the completion of such a
task but

> not before Mr. Forster had accomplished enough to lay any
> fresh biographer under a heavy debt. Not only did he gather
> much new material, but he entered so minutely into the earlier
> part of Swift's career, as to leave but few points undiscussed – or
> we might even say, undecided.[39]

These views and others indicate the reception and importance of
Forster's last biography, a work of prolonged scholarship and of
bibliographical exactness as well as of textual significance. It
stands as an appropriate capstone to his career, summarizing his

professional habits in both researching and writing political and literary lives.

The *Life of Swift* accompanied a planned edition of Swift's writing suggested to Forster by John Murray in November 1854. Initially to be moderately longer than a *Quarterly Review* essay, the biography grew in importance and size as Forster began to collect manuscript materials and information. Six years after beginning the project, an announcement of the '*Life, Journals* and *Letters*' appeared in Forster's *Arrest of Five Members of Parliament* (1860). Forster's move to Palace Gate, Kensington, in December 1863 initiated a decade of intense biographical activity with other writing taking precedence over *Swift*, although he continued to collect materials, including early editions of the works, torn apart and pasted up to make a new working text (a method he later employed when working with his Dickens letters). An expanded life of *Sir John Eliot* appeared in 1864 (2nd edition, 1874); the biography of Landor (1869), research for a life of Strafford, composition of the *Life of Dickens* and editing eight of Dyce's nine-volume edition of Shakespeare's works intervened. During this period until 1872, Forster continued his work for the Lunacy Commission although he resigned because of ill health in that year. By March 1875, however, Forster was telling his publisher John Murray that he hoped for an edition of 3000 copies of *Swift* by the middle of June. Two thousand copies of the volume were published by mid October 1875.[40]

Reverend Whitwell Elwin, friend of Forster's, adviser to Murray, editor, from 1853–60, of the *Quarterly Review* and literary executor of Forster's estate (the man in fact responsible for destroying so many of Forster's letters) wrote this account of the writing of *Swift* some three weeks after Forster's death:

> With the exception of a few pages he did not write a line of it till after he had completed his Life of Dickens. He was always rather impatient to get his works before the world. This impatience increased latterly from the fear that he should not live to utilize his materials, and he printed as he wrote . . . The marvel is that he could attempt to do anything, and his determination to defy pain, and lassitude and failing perceptions must have been truly heroic. If he had lingered he could not possibly have continued Swift to any purpose.

Suffering from illness and overwork, Forster nonetheless managed to complete two more books of volume II before he died suddenly on 1 February 1876.

The day after Elwin described the impatience and illness of Forster and his concentrated composition of the life, he added that 'Forster's scheme was to republish the whole of Swift's Diaries and Letters with connecting comments. He had allowed himself so much lattitudes of disquisition in the first volume that there would have been small space for a commentary in the second volume and the third.'[41] The actual form of volume I, however, displays not the excessive reliance on letters nor first person narrative characteristic of *Dickens*. There is by contrast a firm narrative, carefully and fully documented, that establishes 'a new standard and pattern for detailed investigation of Swift's life and close comment on his writing'. Passages like the following make this clear in Forster's decisive style. After quoting from a previously incomplete letter to Lady Gifford, Forster says 'All this is proof that Swift did not live idle days at Moor Park; and his own memorandum of one year of his reading, from 7th January 1696–7 to the 7th January 1697–8, shows a strenuous employment of his leisure.'[42] A detailed list of what Swift read follows. At the end of the section on Temple, Forster confidently asserts that the death of William Temple 'closed what without doubt may be called Swift's quietest and happiest time': 'In the three peaceful years of that second residence he had made full acquaintance with his own powers, unconscious yet of anything but felicity and freshness in their exercise; and the kindliest side of his nature had found growth and encouragement' (p. 102). Analysis joins with description here, displaying the ability of the biographer to assess as he reports. The entire section examines the financial as well as moral and literary value of the period for Swift.

Forster begins the Preface to the *Life of Swift* by noting how little is known, although much is rumoured, about his subject. His job is to dispel myths through fact and link the life to the literature as he did in *Dickens*, and earlier, in *Landor* and *Goldsmith*. The biography has a purpose – the correction of error and demythologizing of its subject, a quality that will unite many of the most successful biographies. Forster is to prove that Swift was not 'an apostate in politics, infidel or indifferent in religion, a defamer of humanity, the slanderer of statesmen who had served him, and destroyer of the women who loved him' (p. v). Through 'minute examination' Forster will eradicate these falsehoods in a style that is direct, in a narrative that is critical and in a tone that is objective (p. v). *Swift* is unlike *Goldsmith*, *Landor* or even *Dickens* in its method; it possesses not a Romantic but a scholarly-objective style that has a clear-cut theme. Characterized by thorough research and a distinct point of view, this corrective biography sets a pattern for generations of literary biographers freed from prejudice or methodological biases. Its successors might be Newman Ivy White's *Shelley*, Richard Ellmann's *Joyce* or Gordon Haight's *George Eliot*.

For Forster, his focus is on the whole career of his subject, 'to get at the proper comprehension of single parts of it', a quality shared with his earlier biographies (p. v). And it is this determination to see the entire life and work of the subject united that is Forster's greatest contribution to the writing of biography. Reflecting a Romantic ethos rather than practice based on the concept of an organic, unified life, Forster strives, as he did in his own life, to unite the life with the work; literature for Forster was life, as his life was literature. Dickens noted this in reading *Goldsmith* as did Fitzgerald in reading *Dickens*. In *Swift* Forster sought his most intense linking of these qualities. The result is his best professional biography, reflecting years of research and thought. Like his biography of *Dickens*, he has his subject in perspective, although unlike that work, it is not based on personal acquaintance. *Swift* is a greater test of Forster's ability, as were his historical biographies, because only through sustained research could he finally establish an understanding of the subject. The inclusion of more than 150 letters in the *Life* represents a good part of that research, although these letters remain generally untouched by Forster's reshaping hand.

A survey of the varied biographical writings of John Forster between 1836 and 1875 reveals certain patterns which unite his work. The desire for accuracy, completeness and research is obvious; less clear is his effort to unite a Romantic tradition of biographical writing which stresses the image or portrait of the figure with a positivist drive towards integration, of seeing the life of the subject whole. The first method may require the modification of texts to fit the image the author has of his subject, the second, the development of a coherent pattern in the life. The Victorian success story remains the general theme of Forster's literary biographies, the acceptance by society of the writer the more limited focus, while the integration of the life and the work supply the particular method for Forster of joining the Romantic attitude with positivist ideals.

In his predilection for literary lives, Forster finds an easy conjunction between the work and the life, as well as confirmation of his own integrity as a writer. In showing how the lives of other writers are harmonious, he implicitly provides an estimate of his own. Self-perception derives from objective analysis. Choosing as subjects friends – Landor, Dyce, Dickens – Forster demonstrates his own unity with their lives just as he shows how his subjects have successfully united with their age – sometimes in contrast to the facts. The integration of the writer and his dignity in society is a constant theme in the lives, a projection of Forster's own desire for self-respect and recognition. And he shows each of his figures to be part of their world: *Swift* ends in 1710 as he becomes an integral part of English politics; *Dickens* emphasizes the unprecedented acceptance of the author by society and his veneration by an admiring public. *Landor* defends the sociability of the writer despite his impatience and irascibility. *Goldsmith* narrates the union of the man of letters with all aspects of eighteenth-century life, making a hero out of a ne'er-do-well. The political-historical biographies display a similar drive towards integration as Eliot, Cromwell and others are shown to be necessary figures in the political landscape of England.

The unified life is the continual theme of Forster's biographies and in showing that the literary man gains recognition through a career defined by his writing which society values, Forster in turn redefines the role of the biographer. It is the biographer alone who articulates and creates this cohesiveness. His vocation defines itself by the demonstration of exactly how the subject achieves his integration and respect, establishing, by extension, the same for himself. The professional status Forster creates for the biographer is more than social or financial recognition; it is the realization that the identity and even existence of the subject is solely with and through what the biography has created, the organic union of the subject and his work, or of history and the individual. Hence, the obligation to correct inaccuracies, or discover new material in order to prove the responsibility of the genre and the sincerity of the biographer. No longer can the biographer be thought of as a casual journeyman, indifferent to his task and irresponsible in his art. As Forster shows, biography is a consuming social and moral occupation, requiring both commitment and dedication.

The heirs of Forster include John Morley, Leslie Stephen and Edmund Gosse, biographers who shared his sense of obligation to accuracy and completeness. Morley, editor of the English Men of Letters series, was professionally involved with the production of more individual biographies than any other figure save, perhaps, Leslie Stephen. In addition to his contributions to the *Dictionary of National Biography*, Stephen published five lives in the English Men of Letters series, a life of Henry Fawcett, a biography of his brother Fitzjames Stephen plus numerous individual essays of a biographical nature. Stephen, as well as Morley, made biography an institution and a dignified profession in late Victorian England, choosing to write lives that were neither blatantly panegyric nor repositories of unassimilated fact. Stephen, with his love of the eighteenth century (the age that saw the appearance of the first professional writer, Pope), extended its rationalism in his own biographical enterprises which became separately and collectively his principal literary pursuit, especially after resigning the editorship of the *Cornhill* in 1882.

Successors to the professional biographers of the late nineteenth and early twentieth centuries include Lytton Strachey, Emil Ludwig, Gamaliel Bradford, Philip Guedella, Hesketh Pearson, Leon Edel, Michael Holroyd, Elizabeth Longford and Victoria Glendenning. The contemporaries in this list sustain the profession of biography through innovative as well as authoritative presentations of material, whether through Edel's masterly use of psychology and imaginative sense of structure, or Holroyd's blend of social context, individual character and literary analysis. But there consistently remains the problem of adequate remuneration for the biographer, a cold but useful measure of his professionalism.

In his autobiography, Hesketh Pearson provides a useful account of a biographer's financial life. Although he writes that up to the 1960 publication of his life of Charles ii, *Merry Monarch*, he 'had never written simply to make money', his autobiography constantly appraises his financial gain or loss. His early life of Erasmus Darwin brought in no money but established his commitment to biography. His life of Sydney Smith brought negligible royalties, possibly £300, while his account of Hazlitt 'did not sell enough copies to cover the £100 advance on royalties'.

Lives of Gilbert and Sullivan, Henry Labouchere and Thomas Paine all disappointed. Not until his life of Shaw did Pearson become prosperous and properly compensated. His £1500 advance from Collins created such pleasant confusion that he could not resist telling Shaw as soon as possible. Shaw's remark was appropriately understated: 'Well, you've got to live.'[43] Only Pearson's *Oscar Wilde* brought similar prosperity and healthy sales. For the professional biographer, the past century improved his social status but only marginally his financial condition. (No doubt biographers of popular figures do better; reported advances and royalties for lives of rock stars, politicians and the like parallel the inflated reputations of their subjects.) The serious biographer remains committed to a task of modest financial reward, although sales of biographies have constantly increased.

Biography, as Harold Nicolson declared, 'was invented to satisfy the commemorative instinct'.[44] But over time the didactic combined with the ethical and then the psychological to shape a modern approach. The emergence of the professional biographer in the nineteenth century advanced these changes and paralleled a renewed interest in scholarly fact-finding and scientific analysis marked by a detached interpretation of the subject. This, in part, reflected the historical impulse of the age. But there also grew a new awareness of style on the part of the reader who demanded art as well as information, pleasure as well as truth. The fundamental achievement of biography as a profession is the establishment of the biographer as a writer of integrity and discipline. His work, as John Forster demonstrated, was responsible and important for its accurate description of its subject's life which also redefined the role of the biographer from casual historian to reliable narrator. The result was authenticity and authority. And literary art, in the form of narrative style, structure, characterization and figurative language provided the facts with an aesthetic form.

In many ways, however, the completeness of biography, the achievement of its professionalization, is an ironic fiction, since no life can ever be known completely, nor would we want to know every fact about an individual. Similarly, no life is ever lived according to aesthetic proportions. The 'plot' of a biography is superficially based on the birth, life and death of the subject; 'character', on the vision of the author. Both are as much creations of the biographer, as they are of a novelist. We content ourselves with 'authorized fictions'. Following the conception of his subject, the biographer chooses the most workable strategies for presenting the life. But despite the most strenuous efforts at comprehensiveness by the professional biographer, no final or definitive life can ever be written. A consequence of the professionalization of biography is the intensification of a set of formal and thematic problems which the following chapters discuss.

3 Versions of the Life: George Eliot and her Biographers

> How would it be if the life we had already lived were, so to speak, the first draft of which the second would be the fair copy! Every one of us, I think, would try above all not to repeat himself . . .
>
> Chekhov, *The Three Sisters*

Every biography is in one sense a failure because it cannot duplicate the life of its subject nor recreate its character on the page. The myriad of facts, incidents, relationships and settings that a biographer encounters frequently overwhelms his effort at reconstruction. Forced to select, balance, evaluate and at times suppress aspects of his subject's life, the biographer is often frustrated in his attempt to unify individual experiences in an artistic fashion. He must condense, eliminate and even forget in the process of writing the life. His goal is to convey something of the personality or identity of his subject; but when this cannot be done, or when his artistic sense is thwarted by a mass of facts, he often compensates by writing an inclusive, encyclopaedic life that emphasizes the newly-gathered materials. But increasingly, this traditional and current practice of biographers, the chronological and comprehensive life, is incommensurate with what we know about the complexity of individual lives. Today, new demands are placed on biography from psychology, anthropology and history; as a literary enterprise, biography must respond by registering in its form and content new means of expressing human experience.

These comments are preparatory to examining the need for various lives of a single figure. Dissatisfaction with previous biographies of an individual seems endemic to readers and biographers alike. Consequently, multiple lives of both major and minor figures are not uncommon. Of Johnson there are over 225 biographical studies, of Dickens over 57 and of Joyce more than 71. Why should we need so many? What prompts our compulsion to rewrite? Initially it might be the discovery of new information requiring a new interpretation. The discovery of the Boswell papers in 1924 prompted reassessments of both Boswell and Johnson; publication of the Arnold–Clough letters in 1932 called for a new account of Arnold's love affair in Switzerland. But as each age redefines itself, it asks new questions that former biographies cannot answer. Epistemological or moral changes generate new concerns, stimulated by developments in science that revise our sense of time and space, or in morals that alter our notion of sexual freedom. As a genre, biography continually unsettles the past, maintaining its vitality through its continual correction, revision and interpretation of individual lives. Each new life is a provocation to reassess all past lives of that subject. Versions of a life are necessary stages in the evolution of the genre as well as in the understanding of the subject.

A literary reason for the appearance of multiple lives of the same individual relates more directly to the nature of biography. Versions of a life exist not because the facts may differ but because of differing conceptions of what form of story-telling, of narrative, is best suited to the facts. The configuration of the life, not the facts, alters. Shifting ideological, psychological or aesthetic imperatives prefigure the form of plotting to be followed, which changes with each 'reading' of the life by a biographer. Through alternate plots, each biography of the same person demonstrates the multiple meanings and interpretations possible which the form (biography) does not limit. Versions of a life actually record the discovery of how various plot structures can be applied to provide sets of events with different meanings but with no loss of factual value.[1] Through literary tropes, the constituted life transfers the symbolic significance of a comprehensible plot structure to the events. Each biography of the same individual has a different story to tell not because the facts differ but because the plot structures available to, and employed by, the biographer differ. The ways of telling a life-story are not numbered.

Of course, new data or new theories bring about fresh evaluations. Coupled with the impulse to correct, there emerges in biography the desire to revise. A remark of Francis Bacon's that 'truth emerges more readily from error than confusion' summarizes the causes for the various accounts of a single life. As more facts and details become known, a new, corrected record must be established. Thomas S. Kuhn has described the process of scientific revolution in terms which are applicable to multiple lives in biography. A new theory of interpretation, the result of new evidence, explains Kuhn, is 'seldom or never just an increment to what is already known. Its assimilation requires the reconstruction of prior theory and the re-evaluation of prior fact, an intrinsically revolutionary process . . .'[2] For biography, this means a reassessment of earlier lives resulting in a fresh presentation of the new life.

Kuhn based his interpretation of the structure of scientific revolution on the notion of paradigms, shared examples, that unified the scientific community. Biographers have a similar set of paradigms that organize the representation of lives. Three dominant paradigms are (1) the idea that a biography is the history of an individual, functioning as a record or commemoration of a life; (2) the idea that a biography presents an example, a model of moral and didactic value for readers; (3) the idea that biography is discovery, revealing previously unknown aspects of the subject often through detail or anecdote. These paradigms have themselves been altered so that biographies are written for aesthetic as well as historical reasons, and may be about failures or reprobates as well as heroes. Furthermore, discovery in biography now exists equally in what the biographer reveals about himself as well as in what he uncovers about his subject. But such modifications do not invalidate the continuation of these paradigms; rather, they suggest that new emphases and approaches create new demands on the way lives have been previously written.

New ways of presenting character provide a single example of change that affects biography and causes multiple lives of a single figure. The failure of early biographies to provide a complete picture of their subjects because of the suppression, distortion or ignorance of detail clearly necessitates new lives. A shift from a chronological to developmental form of representing character, a change seen in fiction rather than history, also necessitates adjustment to the presentation of character in biography. This coincides with the impact of psychology on understanding lives. However the greatest stimulus to the re-presentation of lives in biographies is the novel, with character forming the most important point of intersection between the two genres. But, where fiction borrowed from biography in the eighteenth century for the presentation of character, the reverse appears to be true for the twentieth. Absorbing the developments in character portrayal from such writers as George Eliot, James or Woolf, as well as Beckett, Barth or Nabokov, biographers have been confronted with challenging ways to represent individuals in non-fiction. Not all, however, are prepared, or have the capacity, to adopt new fictional ways to biographical technique but, as Leon Edel has suggested, Proust, rather than Boswell, may be 'a better guide to modern biography'.[3]

The difficulty of establishing the reality of character in fiction and biography, what critics have traditionally and vaguely referred to as the 'life' of the work, is problematic for biographer and novelist alike. Boswell relied on dramatic techniques and conversation; Lockhart on copious quotation from letters; Strachey on a remarkably fluid and vivid prose style. But contemporary biographers cannot neglect advances in the novel and many seem ready to borrow freely from their techniques, as Andre Maurois and, more recently, Margaret Drabble have shown. The web of relationships and variety of perspectives fiction presents in displaying character find expression in a variety of new methods, replacing earlier, largely chronological accounts. The goal is for readers of biography to *experience* as well as understand the character of their subjects. Where the novel and biography differ, however, is in the limited range of character in biography – there is principally a single character at the centre of the biographical work while a novel may have many. But conversely, a biography traverses a lifetime from birth to death, while the time-frame of a novel is often more limited, sometimes to a single day such as 16 June 1904. Such distinctions, however, do not mitigate the interaction between these two forms in ways less consciously fictional and more methodological. How to represent character convincingly is the issue for the biographer as well as the novelist.

As new influences shape our perceptions of past figures, we need to redefine them. Earlier biographies become inadequate because what we want to know does not equal what we have been told – nor how we want to say it. As new means from various disciplines become available to the biographer, he discovers new ways of reading old materials. Writing biography is always a relative exercise, bounded by cultural and historical forces which alter, as do the personal conditions of the biographer, who may have known the subject or never had any contact with him.

Examples of biography as rewriting or revision are innumerable. Among contemporary illustrations there is Ronald W. Clark's *Freud: The Man and the Cause* (1980), a one-volume life which alters and updates Ernest Jones's three-volume life (1953–7). Using the archive Jones amassed for his biography, Clark re-examines documents used by Jones and queries as well as revises their significance and meaning. The result is a more critical and uncompromising biography, in part reflecting Clark's experience and approach as a professional biographer; he is not a disciple, Viennese associate or psychoanalyst. The professionalism of Clark replaces the piety of Jones. Two recent lives of W. H. Auden reveal a similar situation. Well known for his opposition to biography, Auden has nonetheless been the subject of two lives within eight years of his death – the first by Auden's friend, the writer Charles Olson, the second by the biographer, Humphrey Carpenter.[4] Olson's is conventionally admiring, personal, anecdotal and at times indiscriminate in its use of materials and statements. Carpenter's is more exact in its presentation, analysis and documentation without foregoing any aspect of Auden's character. Its goal is critical, not appreciative.

A further example is Bernard Berenson. In 1979 two biographies of him appeared, one by Meryle Secrest, the other by Ernest Samuels. A journalist, Secrest presents a vivid narrative, creating a remarkable portrait, although occasionally committing factual errors in the midst of her energetic re-telling. Samuels, an academic with access to the archives at I Tatti, is more accurate although less exciting in his style. His concern is with analysing the writings of Berenson and the intellectual development of his subject. Secrest focuses on Berenson's personal, psychological development. An indication of the differences between the two biographies is Secrest's psychological reading of Berenson's early story, 'The Death and Burial of Israel Koppel', which she relates to his sense of guilt at renouncing his Jewishness. By contrast, Samuels stresses the literary and historical quality of the work, relating it to Berenson's personal experiences in Lithuania and his study of Russian and French realists. Whereas Secrest views the writing of the story as the expiation of guilt, Samuels understands it as a justification of Berenson's escape from 'an oppressively ritualized life' of Judaism.[5] Samuels is reluctant to assign motives to the writing of the story, however, preferring to identify historical detail and literary allusions. The example briefly shows how different concerns by biographers create varying but often complimentary readings of a life. But what remains constant is the effort of the biographer to uncover the truth of his subject.

Lytton Strachey wrote that 'History is not the accumulation of facts, but the relation of them.' For biographers the recognition of this shift parallels the self-consciousness that has overtaken modern fiction. More importantly, however, it marks the modern concern with process rather than product, Whitehead declaring in 1925 that 'reality is . . . process'. Consequently, biographies that concentrate on the process of writing the life, such as A. J. A. Symonds's *Quest for Corvo*, appear more central to the form. No life is ever complete; no biography ever completed, as modern biographers are learning. The need to rewrite a life when previous biographies exist is actually the recovery of one's freedom, for in the act of rewriting the biographer learns that he is not a passive victim of history or circumstance but is free to redefine them and rediscover new ways to tell the story. By linking oneself anew with the lives of others, each generation of biographers frees itself both to 'imitate' the experiences of the subjects and, through that process, to re-create them. For biographers and readers, to experience 'character forming' may be what most clearly expresses the persistent need of each period to recast the lives of its predecessors and contemporaries.[6]

For George Eliot the numerous biographical approaches applied to her life – there have been roughly twenty-six book-length accounts – significantly parallel the unsettled history and theory of biography. Furthermore, they indicate the effort of the biographer in recent times to locate a form appropriate to his subject. An early example is the 1883 life by the minor English poetess, Mathilde Blind, entitled *George Eliot*, and published in London by W. H. Allen. It appeared in the Eminent Women Series edited by John H. Ingram and marks the influence of the serial life, the introductory record following a specific format. Blind's approach anticipates the volume by Leslie Stephen in the English Men of Letters series. The author of *The Prophecy of Saint Oran and Other Poems*, Blind (a writer the *Athenaeum* praised as being one of 'the few contemporary poets who could have done so much dramatic business in so few lines'[7]) attempts to be thorough and accurate. Like John Walter Cross in his later biography,

Blind cites the aid of Mr Isaac Evans in addition to Mr and Mrs
Charles Bray, Miss Sara Hennell and 'contemporaries of . . . Mr.
Robert Evans' (p. iii). Previously unpublished letters coupled
with an emphasis on the feminist accomplishments of Eliot give
the biography a detailed and distinctive outlook. One of its
distinctions is that it provides, for the first time, the correct
birthplace and date of Mary Ann Evans. (But *Coton* is misspelt
Colton.) The enthusiasm of Blind, however, fashions numerous
overstatements such as the claim that George Eliot is 'the greatest
realist . . . of her sex' (in contrast to George Sand who is 'the
greatest idealist of her sex' [p. 67]), or that Eliot combines in
extraordinary ways intellectual power and 'an unparalleled vision
for the homely details of life' (p. 5). Although limited by a lack of
extensive data, Blind's well-researched life shows that the supposedly uniform and uneventful life of Eliot was a myth,
contradicting early, memorial accounts of her life shortly after her
death.[8] By contrast, Blind suggests a stressful, troubled existence
for George Eliot, but one that had a heroic if not transcendent
quality.

   John Walter Cross's three-volume life of Eliot appeared two
years after Blind's and, of course, for many years remained the
standard life. Unlike his predecessor, Cross knew the subject
intimately yet strove to preserve a distance between his role as
biographer and his subject. This resulted, of course, in the
well-known truncation of the letters, the resistance to commentary on various events in Eliot's life and the general avoidance of a
conclusion. But Cross conceived of his life as an *'autobiography'* of
Eliot, as he announced in the opening sentence, and it may be
unfair to judge his work exclusively as a biography.[9] With its
prejudicial and protective attitude, Cross's life remains a
memorial to Victorian biographical practice with its emphasis on
letters to tell the story, its chronological, day-to-day narrative
structure and with its stress on accuracy ('everything depends on
accuracy', he wrote [p. vi]).

   The detail, arrangement and precision of Cross's life of Eliot
anticipate the very shape of Gordon Haight's biography eighty-
three years later. Cross's life, in fact, sets a pattern that Eliot's
most authoritative biographer has followed. Both emphasize the
daily life, liberally quote from the letters (which are similarly the
principal sources of information) and resist interpretation of the
life and the literature. In addition, Cross and Haight deal

extensively with sources, emphasize Eliot's sensitivity to criticism as well as diffident behaviour, and concentrate on what Cross calls 'the development of her intellect and character' (p. v). They differ drastically, of course, in the full disclosure of facts and complete citation of material found in Haight and absent in Cross. Joining a series of Victorian widow or widower biographers such as Mrs Kingsley or Mrs Clough, Cross's life stands as an example of the Victorian passion for remembrance, protection and selective accuracy.

'No flowers by request' was the unofficial motto of the *Dictionary of National Biography*, and Leslie Stephen in his 1902 life of George Eliot in the English Men of Letters Series clearly follows the spirit of the phrase. Author of an earlier, 1881 tribute to Eliot in the *Cornhill*, Stephen was eminently suited to deal with her life and work. Like Cross, Stephen favoured the use of letters in telling the life, but he also recognized the need to condense: 'To write a life is to collect the particular heap of rubbish in which his [the biographer's] material is contained, to sift the relevant from the superincumbent mass and then try to smelt it and cast it into its natural mold.' In another passage from this same essay on biography, Stephen anticipates Strachey, as well as his own life of Eliot, when he writes 'we have to learn the art of forgetting – of suppressing all the multitudinous details which threaten to overburden the human memory. Our aim should be to present the human soul, not all its irrelevant bodily trappings.'[10]

The desire to condense, however, overrides the possibility of conveying a soul in Stephen's life of Eliot. The style is abrupt, rigid and cold, as in this commentary on Eliot's sense of duty expressed in a letter while she stayed in Geneva in 1850. Says Stephen: 'The phrase is significant. She was now thirty years old, and her outlook was sufficiently vague. She had grown to her full intellectual stature. She had read widely and intelligently.'[11] More directly than either Blind or Cross, however, Stephen provides a criticism of Eliot's literary works and indulges in some theorizing about literature as in his commentary on subjectivism in fiction in relation to *The Mill on the Floss* or on morality in art (pp. 87–8, 117). He is also unafraid to criticize her characters, calling Stephen Guest, for example, 'a mere hairdresser's block' (p. 104). Stephen also marks his debt to earlier biographies of Eliot, notably Blind (pp. 105–6). A healthy contextualism emerges in the life so that we see Eliot in a European framework, especially in relation to French nineteenth-century writing (p. 111). Overall, a welcomed irreverence appears in Stephen's life, refreshingly engaging for the reader and author alike.

Not all, however, welcomed the life. In October 1902 Stephen received an emotional note from a Jessie Lawrence expressing indignation at various passages in the biography dealing with the private life of Eliot and G. H. Lewes. In particular, she asked Stephen to remove this upsetting sentence referring to an illicit relationship: 'Mrs. Lewes [Agnes Jervis] preferred Thornton Hunt to her husband, to whom she had already borne children' (pp. 46–7). Mrs Lawrence cites the passage from the most sensitive (and one of the longest) paragraphs in the biography where Stephen clearly but discretely deals with Lewes's ideal of free love and Eliot's defence of a union with Lewes she 'considered as equivalent to a legitimate marriage' (p. 47). Stephen's own position is that he does not have enough knowledge to judge the situation fully, declaring that he would not 'argue the ethical question, raised by George Eliot's conduct' (p. 47). However, he then goes on to analyse Eliot's opposition to the indissoluble nature of marriage and describes the close and lasting domestic relationship between Eliot and Lewes.

Mrs Lawrence, however, discloses that she has not actually read the offending section and has no intention of doing so because

> if I were to bring it [the biography] into this house much unhappiness would be caused to a younger generation of the family who are in complete ignorance on the subject, – and a state of painful inquiry would be raised of which you can have not the smallest conception.[12]

Iconoclastic and potentially immoral biography was definitely not welcomed by certain readers at the turn of the century, although as the father of three daughters, Stephen might, himself, have had an idea of the potentially 'painful inquiry' Mrs Lawrence alludes to.

Stephen's account of Eliot, extending the critical tone and approach found in the *Dictionary of National Biography*, is a reaction to the adulation expressed by Cross. A sensitivity of response challenges the narrative which involves the reader in the biographer's unfolding estimate of his subject. This sense of the puzzle and confusions of the life and their recognition as such by the biographer who, in turn, avoids predisposed or preformulated opinions characterizes some of the most recent suggestions about biographical writing, as Robert Gittings has noted.[13] Although Stephen, writing the biography late in his life – he died two years later – appears distant from his subject, partly because he had little sympathy with fiction, the book is a healthy critique of Eliot's life and career, an antidote to the uncritical and voluminous life Cross complied. The value of her novels, Stephen concludes, again anticipating several more recent biographers, is that they are 'implicit autobiographies' and manifest a sympathetic nature united with 'a large and tolerant intellect' (p. 201). The scepticism of Stephen, particularly when dealing with the philosophic aspects of Eliot's work, is in part a reaction against what he felt to be idolizing tendencies in her reputation. His biography is a corrective, limited but honest in its appraisal; it may be thought of as the first critical biography of Eliot and her work.

The Freudian domination of biography lasted roughly from 1920 to 1935 and might be epitomized by Lewis Mumford's 1929 life of Herman Melville. The psychic significance of ordinary and extraordinary events were consistently analysed as the unconscious, repressed, sublimated or compulsive aspects of human behaviour and compelled the biographer to speculate and interpret. Anne Fremantle's 1933 life of Eliot in the 'Great Lives' series published by Duckworth illustrates many of these preoccupations. De-emphasizing the early life and religious conflict (to be stressed by Gordon Haight and then Ruby Redinger), Fremantle concentrates on London, the *Westminster Review* and, tangentially, the literary works of Eliot. It is perhaps the first biography to make use of the diaries of John Chapman. Context, however, merges with psychological overstatement to produce a biography that has as its theme the interaction of retribution and tradition.

Unlike Stephen's discrete and even unconnected remarks, Fremantle's account is unified by her themes. There is also greater candour in detailing the emotional life of Eliot in contrast to the objective assessment of Stephen. Of Lewes's commitment to Eliot, for example, Fremantle writes that 'there was a great risk that he might quickly tire of the ponderous, middle-aged, priggish and high minded but humorless woman who was giving up everything for him'.[14] This 'storm-tired matron', however, is subject to excessive speculative analysis in a neo-Freudian manner. We are told, for example, that Griff was Marian's secret garden, and that the real reason for Hetty's punishment was that

> Marian's whole creed, first as an Evangelical, then as a disciple of Mr. Bray's, later still as a Positivist, was that the wages of sin are paid C.O.D.; her whole philosophy was a spiritual accepting of absolutely inevitable consequences. (p. 87)

This law of consequence, of guilt, Fremantle proposes as the key to understanding the action of Eliot and her heroines: 'As, when a child, she had driven into her wooden doll's head the nails her wicked aunts should have endured, so now she made her books what her dolls had once been: the sublimation of her vision of retributive justice' (p. 88).

Near the end of her account, Fremantle tells us that Eliot suffered from a 'deepening earnestness of gloom' but that her marriage to Cross was her attainment of at least tradition and the entry into a world of 'regularity' (pp. 100, 136). Anticipating a later and better argued case by Ruby Redinger, Fremantle avoids evidence or detail in her assertions. In her enthusiasm for psychological interpretation, she overstates her position. Reflecting the absorption with the psychological that highlighted biographical writing in the 1930s, Fremantle paradoxically simplifies the life of Eliot while overinterpreting it. A curious counterreaction merges within the biography so that the moral psychology of Eliot is found to be antithetical to the Freudian concerns of the day: 'her psychology', writes Fremantle, 'is abhorrent to our psychoanalytical generation' (p. 140). We are also told that Eliot 'had no sense of form, and no love of, nor gift for handling, words' (p. 142). But admirably for Fremantle, George Eliot was a rebel, reacting against the inhibiting conventions of Victorian life while providing 'invaluable guides to the Victorian attitude of mind' (p. 141). Distrustful of Victorian earnestness, supportive of psychological interpretation, Fremantle's opinionated life stimulates our impression of Eliot by its directness, suggestion of human foibles and presentation of weaknesses.

To counter the prejudices and errors of earlier lives and to incorporate his own magisterial scholarship, Gordon Haight published his biography of George Eliot in 1968. It immediately superseded all others. A work of outstanding research, it nonetheless might be seen as the apotheosis of the scholarly, academic biography, in dramatic contrast both in form and substance to a biography that appeared the following year: Erik Erikson's *Gandhi's Truth*. From the perspective of the evolving form of modern biographical writing, the two works stand in absolute opposition to one another, the former displaying the best of the academic approach, the latter exhibiting the new direction of psychobiography that has characterized a great deal of recent work. For Haight it is the accumulation of evidence that determines his form, establishing a narrative of contiguity; for Erikson, it is the identity of significant configurations in a life fusing it into a whole that determines his form, or narrative of substitutions.[15]

George Eliot, A Biography by Gordon Haight reflects a stage in the writing of literary lives by academics. These lives are meticulous in their detail and scrupulous in their documentation. They also, however, tend to avoid any analysis of the writer's work, fail to establish any theoretical connections between individual experience and the literary text and concentrate on influence rather than interpretation. Other lives that appeared in the 1960s which exhibit these qualities include Mark Schorer's *Sinclair Lewis* (1961), Herschel Baker's *Hazlitt* (1962), Arthur and Barbara Gelb's *O'Neill* (1962), William Riley Parker's *Milton* (1966), R. W. Stallman's *Stephen Crane* (1968) and Carlos Baker's *Hemingway* (1969). These biographies are inclusive, archival and comprehensive in detail, acting as records rather than responses to the life. A minor example of the contrast between this approach and, say, Erikson's is the absence of any statement about method at the beginning of Haight's life of Eliot and the several pages devoted to procedure in Erikson's life of Gandhi. While Haight's life of Eliot remains an outstanding contribution to Eliot scholarship, it is unadventurous and conservative in approach, like a large number of scholarly biographies in the 1960s.

More particularly, Haight is hesitant to judge. This clearly balances the excesses of the Fremantle approach but still disappoints the expectations of a reader. 'Speculations are futile; one can tell only the facts', Haight announces on page twenty-two, yet his account of important events in the life of Eliot demands interpretation.[16] Haight's sympathies lie elsewhere and he patronizes those 'Freudians' and others who might elaborate, for example, the meaning of Marian Evans's forgetting her brooch containing a lock of her father's hair in her haste to return to London from Rosehill to meet Lewes (p. 135).

Fact alone cannot determine a life nor can it fashion a narrative. In his account of Eliot, Haight provides a surfeit of fact, reaching such lengths as to name the mountains Herbert Spencer climbed in a summer 1853 tour of Switzerland or specifying the precise dates John Chapman went to bed with his mistress, Elisabeth Tilley (pp. 118, 87, 93). This concern with detail derives from an attachment to letters to tell the story for Haight, but it also illustrates the influence or effect of a biographer's subject upon the text. The paramount place of domestic detail in the fiction of Eliot appears to be echoed in Haight's accumulation of important domestic facts.

In his lengthy life of Eliot, Haight offers only tenuous interpretations of events and none of the work (see pp. 52, 79, 86). He shies away from analysis and confuses the issue, as when in a single sentence censuring the John Chapman relationship, he momentarily presents a theory but then rejects it. After quoting from Chapman's diary, Haight writes: 'There can be little doubt that Marian was guilty of some indiscretion, probably more serious than holding hands. Her over-ready expansiveness, her incapability of practising the required conventionalism, her unfortunately balanced moral and animal regions – all come to mind' (p. 86). But interpretative reticence replaces the anticipated conclusion. The passage shifts suddenly to Chapman's reputation as a philanderer, Marian's susceptibility to affection, and the detail of Chapman relating to a friend in the 1890s that Eliot was once very fond of him. Haight's tone is defensive, but his innuendos are troublesome and the absence of a knowledgeable interpretation is dangerously left to the reader. A suppressed hostility to psychologizing about her life appears throughout the biography.

Acting to unite the facts, however, is a muted metaphor found in the repeated references to George Eliot's need for someone to lean on. Haight first refers to this when citing a passage from Charles Bray's *Autobiography* dealing with George Combe's analysis of Eliot's phrenological cast made in 1842. Chapter 4 in the biography borrows the image for its title. Most interestingly, Haight first employed this image in 1940 in his study *George Eliot and John Chapman*. There, Haight declared:

In that phrase lies the key to an understanding of that
extraordinary life. All the strange contradictions in her career
from the passionate childhood dependence on her brother . . .
to her marriage with John W. Cross a few months before her
death are explained by her 'always requiring some one to lean
on.'[17]

In the 1968 biography Haight applies the same 'key', only
enlarging its application to the entire life. Conceptually, Haight's
earliest perception of Eliot's life remained unchanged between
1940 and 1968 and one might ungenerously remark that in this
approach to Eliot we have the only major biographical study of a
nineteenth-century writer with its interpretative foundation
embedded in phrenology. Furthermore, the determinancy of fact
in the narrative structure and language of the biography has
devalued the application of other figurative language in the life
and made insufficient use of the posturing image for analysing or
harmonizing the life. Additional difficulties in the biography
include the minimal sense of prolepsis as the life-narrative unfolds
and the absence of any sense of Eliot's development as a writer.
The singular, and let me emphasize, significant accomplishment
of the biography is the establishment of the record, but the result
is ultimately unsatisfying because a series of crucial questions
concerning personality and creative development remain after we
complete a reading of the book.

In part a response to this factual life and in part a desire to
present an integrated life-account, Ruby Redinger published
George Eliot: The Emergent Self in 1975. Supplementing these
reasons and explaining a great deal of the importance of
Redinger's work is an awareness in the text of the difficulty of
writing biography. The work is an example of psychobiography,
equivalent in nature to two other biographies published the same
year: Bruce Mazlish's *James and John Stuart Mill, Father and Son in the
19th Century* and Karl Miller's *Cockburn's Millennium*, a biography
of the Scottish jurist and writer Henry Cockburn. What these
works have in common is a concern with a fundamental portrait of
the subject's inner world, organized around either significant
moments in that life or probing questions concerning that life. For
Redinger, the central issue is why did Eliot begin to write
creatively only in middle age? The very centre of her biography is
the formation of the imaginative life of the subject, the essential

interest in the life of any artist. Psychobiography attempts to see
the life of the subject in its totality, discovering or inventing 'the
organic unity that links all the aspects of his [the subject's] life
together'.[18] By definition and intent, this form of biography
demands interpretation, originality and analysis. Redinger
accepts this challenge and creates what is to date our most
imaginative life of Eliot.

Redinger's biography exhibits Todorov's narrative as substitution theory, refreshingly adhering to no rigid chronological
structure. It begins with a sympathetic analysis of Cross's
biography and the context in which it was completed. The
biography then becomes a kind of Freudian 'family romance' but
without the doctrinaire emphasis a Freudian would impose. Its
structure is proleptic, forming an advancing spiral that thrusts
characters and events forward and then returns to an original
point until the next thrust. This 'cyclical construction of substitutions', as Todorov might call it, provides an involving narrative
that unites moment and sequence. But in her pursuit of a
psychological interpretation, Redinger is fully aware of its
dangers: 'psychic phenomena', she writes, 'defy verbal description: if it is attempted, the results are usually misleading'.[19]
However, Redinger disproves her own indictment.

Focusing on the shaping events of George Eliot's imagination,
notably her childhood, adolescence and young womanhood,
Redinger stresses the idea of emergence. She repeatedly demonstrates the unity between early events and later actions. Concentrating on family conflicts (especially George Eliot's alienation
from her mother), as well as Eliot's self-doubts and the early
association between the imagination, day-dreaming and guilt,
Redinger explores the elements that alternately prevented George
Eliot from writing creatively until 1857 and yet provided her with
the materials for her fictions. This, the very substance of
Redinger's biography, is limitedly treated in Haight's account (cf.
pp. 205–7) of her life. Moreover, the elaboration of a comment
Eliot made to Sara Hennell in 1844 on childhood is the creative
source of Redinger's entire work: 'Childhood is only the beautiful
and happy time in contemplation and retrospect – to the child it is
full of deep sorrows, the meaning of which is unknown' (p. 50). To
define that meaning and clarify its significance is Redinger's goal.

Strikingly free from psychological jargon, Redinger nonetheless
is unafraid to psychologize about the progress of Eliot as a writer.

Summarizing her hesitancy to write yet possession of an intense imagination, Redinger explains that

> Had her imagination not held an autonomous position in her ego but functioned primarily as a defense against the various threats to her ego, it would have flourished during her unhappiest years and collapsed when she regained happiness and emotional security. Fortunately, her strongest defenses were against imagination itself, so that when they were broken down, it was at last free, and she was to be at her most creative during her happiest years. (p. 53)

Associating Eliot's Evangelicalism with her prose style, Redinger provides an original approach to understanding the novels. Her balanced and lengthy sentences, she suggests, were ways to conceal certain aggressive tendencies and protect 'the pith of their content' from hostile readers (pp. 78–9). Throughout the biography Redinger provides psychologically condensed explanations of Eliot's life (see pp. 286, 288–9) and in an effort to establish the identity of Eliot as a writer, she provides venturesome theories, imaginative interpretations and bold assertions.

Of course, Redinger is not without faults and they include an excess of speculation, a compressed criticism of the fiction, a desire for psychological certainty that leads, for example, to the suggestion that 20 September 1850, the death of Latimer in 'The Lifted Veil', is also the birthday of Eliot's 'life of creativity' (p. 401). The biography also has a truncated ending and an undue emphasis on the financial arrangements, publishing disputes and reaction of reviewers to Eliot's novels. Nonetheless, Redinger synthesizes ideas, clearly supports her opinions, unabashedly assesses previous lives, experiments with structure and seeks to understand, as immediately as possible, the importance of the subject's life. For Redinger, Eliot is an active not passive individual, one who 'occasionally has annoyed or disturbed me but has never bored me' (p. x).

One finishes *George Eliot: The Emergent Self* with a sense of knowing something of Eliot as a person. The conjecture, psychologizing and structure contribute to a dynamic narrative that involves the reader in the unfolding of the imaginative and psychological life of the subject. It satisfies our need to understand the pattern of creativity and thought beyond the record of events and allows the reader to participate in the unfolding events that become the substance of Eliot's fictions.

By concentrating on the major versions of the life of George Eliot I have by necessity had to avoid a series of other lives, notably dual biographies such as Anna T. Kitchel's *George Lewes and George Eliot: A Review of Records* (1933), Gordon Haight's previously mentioned *George Eliot and John Chapman* (1940), and K. A. MacKenzie's *Edith Simcox and George Eliot* (1961). There are also additional approaches such as Mary H. Deakin's *The Early Life of George Eliot* (1913), and Pierre Bourl'honne's intellectual biography (1933). The same year Haight's biography appeared, Rosemary Sprague published a popularized life that substituted explication of the novels for analysis of the life. F. W. Kenyon's *The Consuming Flame: The Story of George Eliot* appeared in 1970 as an example of a recent fictionalized account of her life, an imitation of Emilie and Georges Romieu's French fictionalization, *La Vie de George Eliot* (1930; trans. Brian W. Dons and published by Dutton in 1932).

From a survey of the major lives, however, one becomes more conscious of the problems of biographical expression, but like the frustrated biographer who adopts Flaubert's statement, 'we have too many things and not enough forms', one becomes more disheartened at the attempt at providing a single, workable conclusion incorporating the varied approaches displayed by the various biographies of George Eliot. Nonetheless, when a biographer recognizes that the life he writes is itself an aesthetic construct involving fictions, imagery, style and narration, parallel to the inner life of his subject, itself a fiction, the result may be a biography that is at the same time literary and truthful. It will also reflect the ambiguous, self-contradictory, illogical individual that is its subject. Redinger's life comes closest to this ideal through its sense of discovery and evaluation that involves the reader as well as the biographer. Every biography is of course incomplete, but Redinger comes nearest to coordinating the biographical form with the life-record to discern, in the words of Leon Edel, 'the complexities of being without pretending that life's riddles have been answered'.[20]

4 Writers as Biographers

Biographers are fixated on their heroes in a very peculiar manner. They frequently select the hero as the object of study because, for personal reasons of their own emotional life, they had a special affection for him from the very outset. They then devote themselves to a work of idealization, which strives to enroll the great man among their infantile models, and to revive through him, as it were, their infantile conception of the father. For the sake of this wish they wipe out the individual features in his physiognomy, they rub out the traces of his life's struggle with inner and outer resistances, and do not tolerate in him anything savouring of human weakness or imperfection; they then give us a cold, strange, ideal form instead of a man to whom we could feel distantly related. It is to be regretted that they do this, for they thereby sacrifice the truth to an illusion.[1]

More than any others, writers, especially novelists, are susceptible to the conditions Freud describes when they turn to biography. In their accounts of others, mostly of other writers, the author's choice, treatment and analysis of subject tends to follow a pattern of idealization, revision and rejection. The reason is simple. In most cases the writer's subject is a literary figure who directly or indirectly has had an influence on his work. The impact may be personal or artistic or both. Writing the biography, begun for such explicit and pragmatic reasons as defending a reputation, or clarifying facts, becomes an engagement and then rejection of a father figure whose influence must be shaken off. Writers as biographers challenge their forefathers through the reassessment of their lives. But only by engaging the facts, literary creations and careers of their predecessors can this unique group of biographers come to understand themselves and the origins of their own literary imagination. The subject of the biography has been and remains an influence on the writer but the writing of the biography becomes the act of confrontation, an effort to free oneself on the part of the biographer. Freud's cautious assessment of this dynamic between writer and subject outlines an important area of biography which further demonstrates its self-referential quality.

Examples of biographies by writers (I expressly mean creative writers and more precisely novelists; all biographies are of course by writers in the broad sense), include masterpieces like Mrs Gaskell's life of Charlotte Brontë or Sartre's account of Flaubert as well as other works such as Angus Wilson's *Kipling's Last Ride* or Evelyn Waugh's *Edmund Campion*. All of them, however, pose important questions about the relationship between the biographer and his subject, the presentation of material and the function of biography. This chapter will explore these matters through an examination of four examples: Mrs Gaskell's *Charlotte Brontë*, Henry James's *Hawthorne*, Trollope's life of Thackeray and Virginia Woolf's mock biography, *Orlando*. Each provides a different perspective on the same problem: what defines the unique association between the subject and the biographer and how does that association affect the writing of the biography? What, in fact, prompts the creative writer to write biography? And what can be learned about biography from the choices of Gaskell, James, Trollope and Woolf?

Dr Johnson argued that only when the biographer personally knows his subject is he able to write an adequate life. Nineteenth-century biographers followed this maxim, as seen in Lockhart's *Scott*, Carlyle's *Sterling*, Forster's *Dickens* and Froude's *Carlyle*. Within limits, this is also true of the writer as biographer. Mrs Gaskell knew Charlotte Brontë for nearly five years, while Trollope, of course, knew Thackeray. James did not meet Hawthorne, although he did know his son, while Virginia Woolf was intimate with her model–subject, Vita Sackville-West. A prerequisite for the writer inexperienced with biography appears to be some personal familiarization with the subject. For the most part, creative writers do not readily turn to historical figures for biographical projects, although exceptions to this generalization can easily be found such as Anthony Powell's account of John Aubrey or Graham Greene's life of Lord Rochester. When a writer composes a biography, however, the result is often critical not commemorative, reflecting a change in the conception of the subject. Initially conceived as a literary project growing out of sympathy or identity, the biography becomes a work of engagement or rejection of a literary inheritance in the search for

psychological independence. Linking the narrative of the personal life with the analysis of texts in the biography is the
re-evaluation of the figure in terms of the life of the author. This
refines Freud's description because it joins the life with the work
when they are both included, a union well understood by the
biographer when also a creative writer. Furthermore, conscious of
his own reputation, the writer realizes that he is creating a new
addition to his own *oeuvre* which should, in turn, embody his own
literary talent.[2] In short, biographies by writers have a distinct,
dual importance: on one hand the biography is a statement of
obligation and influence of one writer upon another and, on the
other hand, it is a distinct literary product demonstrating the
abilities of the writer. But biography is also a threat to the fiction
writer since the form imposes limitations and restrictions that in
some instances severely hamper the imagination of the author.
Virginia Woolf's problems in balancing fact with fiction in
writing *Roger Fry*, vividly recorded in her diary, illustrate the
difficulties.

Mrs Gaskell solved the problem of biographical form by relying
on her previously tested novelistic methods; Henry James
resorted to his practice of the critical essay and literary portrait
dealing with culture as much as with character. Trollope favoured
a more traditional approach, employing conservative biographical conventions in part because he was prevented from using
primary sources. Virginia Woolf, however, applied imaginative,
original ways to create fictional biography, uniting history with a
composite individual. 'The biographer's imagination', she confessed, 'is always being stimulated to use the novelist's art of
arrangement, suggestion, dramatic effect to expound the private
life.' These responses qualify Freud's analysis without invali-
dating it. Indeed, as we examine the biographies by these writers,
we will discover in Freud's remarks a principle that expands
rather than contracts in its usefulness.

Elizabeth Gaskell wrote the *Life of Charlotte Brontë* out of
friendship and caring that concealed a deeper desire to rectify the
impression promoted by reviewers of Charlotte Brontë's work and
life that she was a coarse and unwomanly individual. By stressing
her religion, self-sacrifice, familial responsibilities and commitment to literature, Gaskell aimed to correct the distorted and
maligned image. This desire coincided with her decision to write a
memoir of her friend to 'make the world (if I am but strong enough

in expression), honour the woman as much as they have admired the writer'. Two weeks *after* this note to George Smith, the publisher, a request arrived from Reverend Patrick Brontë to Mrs Gaskell to write the life of Charlotte.[3]

Reverend Patrick Brontë wrote to Mrs Gaskell only three months after his daughter died. Prompted in part by Ellen Nussey's suggestion that Mrs Gaskell could write a proper response to the unfair accounts of Charlotte's life, Patrick Brontë, against the wishes of his son-in-law, Reverend Arthur Nicholls, sought a thorough, truthful account. 'No quailing Mrs. Gaskell! No drawing back!' he told her in July 1855, when she came to visit Haworth.[4] Prophetically, the ensuing research, composition and publication of the two-volume life, which appeared in March 1857, created a *furor*.

The *Life of Charlotte Brontë* represents not only the accomplishments of literary biography but its dangers when unreliable sources, personal attacks and too personal an attachment to the subject exist. The issues converge on the matter of fact and its presentation in biography as the following retraction in the *Athenaeum* of 6 June 1857 makes clear:

> We are sorry to be called upon to return to Mrs. Gaskell's 'Life of Charlotte Bronte,' – but we must do so, since the book has gone forth with our recommendation. Praise, it is needless to point out, implied trust in the biographer as an accurate collector of facts. This, we regret to state, Mrs. Gaskell proves not to have been ... It is in the interest of Letters that biographers should be deterred from rushing into print with mere impressions in place of proofs, however eager and sincere those impressions may be.[5]

To understand the source of this reaction and the consequences for the biography is not only to review the major difficulties in biographical composition but to see more accurately the particular challenges faced by the writer as biographer. Foremost among those issues is that the novelist as biographer relies on fictional rather than biographical conventions to tell the story.

An analysis of Gaskell's *Brontë* must begin with an analysis of the relation of the author to the subject. Freud's comment that biographers choose their subjects 'for personal reasons of their own emotional life' remains an important guide. For Mrs Gaskell it was the need to reassert the importance of a woman novelist as a woman that was essential, presenting, through the life of Charlotte Brontë, a defence of her own identity as a woman and writer. A passage from *Aurora Leigh* which appears on the title page as an epigram to the biography vividly records this need:

> Oh my God,
> – Thou hast knowledge, only Thou,
> How dreary 'tis for women to sit still
> On winter nights by solitary fires
> And hear the nations praising them far off.

The solitude of an active mind prevented by circumstances from engagement with the world establishes a tragic prelude to the *Life*. But no longer will this passivity continue. Women must, despite their isolation, pursue their desires, especially to write. This theme organizes the biography in opposition to the provocative sentence Robert Southey wrote to Charlotte Brontë in March 1837: 'Literature cannot be the business of a woman's life, and it ought not to be.'[6] Implicitly, the struggle of Brontë to establish and survive as a writer parallels that of Mrs Gaskell and this identity draws the two writers together to unify the life.

The external impetus for the *Life* may have been to rescue Brontë from misinterpretations and distortions but the internal cause is the reexamination of Gaskell's own goals and achievements through recounting those of her friend. This is done not by surveying her work but by examining her life and her methods as a novelist. The biography is psychological in purpose, concentrating on the mind and character of Brontë which, in its telling, incorporates environment and setting. The biography remains, however, a psychological act of rescue expressed in Mrs Gaskell's letter to the by now well-known stationer, John Greenwood. Learning of Charlotte's death, Mrs Gaskell writes: 'I do fancy that if I had come [during her illness], I could have induced her, – even though they had all felt angry with me at first, – to do what was so absolutely necessary, for her very life. Poor poor creature!' Mrs Gaskell's biography fulfils her desire to save Charlotte Brontë and in the course of her act she protects, if not saves, herself. In her defence of Brontë's career, Gaskell supports her own. Written at the end of nearly a decade of literary creativity and success, and standing almost at the chronological centre of Gaskell's own *corpus*, the *Life* is both a reassessment of her own writing as well as her position as a woman and novelist, wife and writer, mother and author.[7]

Self-analysis, an important feature of the *Life of Charlotte Brontë*, takes the form of examining the dual nature of Charlotte Brontë. In a letter sent to George Smith on 4 June 1855, Gaskell clearly states the case. Anticipating objections from Patrick Brontë and Arthur Nicholls, she nonetheless writes 'the more she was known[,] the more people would honour her as a woman, separate from her character of authoress' (*Letters*, p. 347). In Chapter 16 of the *Life*, Gaskell reiterates this fundamental concern with the divided nature of women as writers and women. Commenting on the success of *Jane Eyre*, but conscious of the attendant *furor* over its authorship, Gaskell writes 'henceforward, Charlotte Brontë's existence becomes divided into two parallel currents – her life as Currer Bell, the author; her life as Charlotte Brontë, the woman' (p. 334). The paragraph continues to outline the different and often opposed duties of these two separate characters, duties that Mrs Gaskell herself frequently experienced. In this, perhaps the most feminist portion of the life, Mrs Gaskell expresses the dilemma of women writers in the nineteenth century, the tension and struggle experienced by Charlotte Brontë, which by implication Mrs Gaskell clearly understood. As early as February 1850, Gaskell complained to the artist Elizabeth Fox of the conflict between 'home duties and individual life'. 'The difficulty', she continues, is 'where and when to make one set of duties subserve and give place to the other' (*Letters*, p. 106). Virginia Woolf also responded strongly to this dimension of the biography, explaining to Madame Sue Ling in 1938 that the biography 'will perhaps give you a feeling for the lives of women writers in England in the 19th century – their difficulties and how she [Charlotte Brontë] overcame them'.

As an accomplished writer, Mrs Gaskell understood success but as a woman she also knew the conflict within the will of women, the difficult obligations of being a wife, mother, sister and friend. An example of this feeling in the biography is the tone of Mrs Gaskell's account of Charlotte's marriage. While happy and supportive of the event, Gaskell nonetheless understands its severe effect on Brontë's career as a writer. Arthur Nicholls would not tolerate a wife who wrote, regardless of her talent. There is, says Gaskell, one last letter that 'develops the intellectual side of her character, before we lose all thought of the authoress in the timid and conscientious woman about to become a wife' (p. 572). In describing the impending end to Brontë's writing career, Gaskell conveys her own sensitivity to the place of women in the home and their responsibilities as well as conflicts stemming from an interest in literature. William Gaskell, it should be added, never interfered with his wife's writing, aiding her in correcting, copying and proofing material, although he made it quite clear that only he would look after her business affairs, from contracts to payments.

The affinity between their lives as women and as writers overshadows the family, social and domestic differences between Brontë and Gaskell and results in a personal biography, the first successful biography of a woman by a woman. Although Mrs Gaskell did not experience the loneliness, deprivation and personal conflict of Charlotte Brontë, she nonetheless felt an identity through the effort to write, the life of duty and the moral courage Brontë continually displayed. 'The wonder to one is how she can have kept heart and power alive in her life of desolation', Gaskell wrote to her friend Tottie Fox.[8] However, the influence between the two writers is not directly literary – Mrs Gaskell was undecided about *Jane Eyre*, critical of *Shirley* and displeased with *Villette* – but moral. The common problems of being a woman writer in an age that gave little recognition and even less respect to such an occupation created a bond that resulted in the personal account. A sign of that affection was Mrs Gaskell's secret effort through Monckton Milnes to secure a pension or preferment for Arthur Nicholls in order to make him more acceptable as a son-in-law for Patrick Brontë and as a husband for Charlotte. Such sympathy and identity with Charlotte, however, created problems in the handling of biographical fact.

Detail not fact was Mrs Gaskell's principal concern. If she could concretely build the life of Charlotte, she could demonstrate her life as a moral woman. This took precedence over literary criticism of which there is little. Research for the *Life* was extensive and Gaskell travelled widely (including a visit to Brussels), interviewing friends, family members and associates of Charlotte, especially the Hegers, Ellen Nussey and Mary Taylor. G. H. Lewes, as well as Patrick Brontë and Arthur Nicholls, supplied letters, anecdotes and manuscripts. And in this work, especially in the reminiscences of Charlotte's schoolgirl friend Mary Taylor, then living in New Zealand, Gaskell found confirmation of her own view of Charlotte's life as one of duty and labour in a world that misunderstood and mistreated her. The importance of Mary Taylor is seen in Gaskell's use of her letter of January 1857 to conclude the life (p. 526).

Letters, of course, became the most useful documentary

evidence and, like Lockhart, Gaskell lets Brontë speak through them often and extensively, supplying a narrative only when necessary. But since her purpose was a defence of Brontë, certain facts had to be discarded. Specifically omitted was the attachment of Charlotte to M. Heger and recklessly handled was Branwell Brontë's dismissal from Mrs Robinson's employ. These major and other minor errors of fact and judgement (such as the controversial account of Cowan Bridge School or the exaggeration of Patrick Brontë's eccentricities) illustrate Freud's view that certain biographers 'devote themselves to a work of idealization', eliminating internal struggles or feelings that help to define but also disrupt the conventional life-portrait. In her effort to protect Charlotte Brontë from appearing immoral or provocative, and to defend Charlotte's own ideal view of Branwell and his role as the great hope of the Brontë family, Gaskell lacquers over episodes of personal emotion or involvement while uncharacteristically scandalizing others.

The controversy which resulted from Gaskell's semi-libellous statements led to a letter of apology in the press on 30 May 1857, approved by William Gaskell during Elizabeth Gaskell's absence. Ironically, she started a vacation in Italy six days after finishing the manuscript, on 13 February 1857. She returned to Manchester on 28 May, two days before the letter, dated 26 May, appeared in the papers. The required changes in the third edition of the life reflect the *furor* created by the shrill attack on Lady Scott (then Mrs Robinson) in the first edition, of which this selection is but a sample:

> The case presents the reverse of the usual features; the man becomes the victim; the man's life was blighted, and crushed out of him by suffering, and guilt entailed by guilt; the man's family were stung by the keenest shame. The woman . . . she goes flaunting about to this day in respectable society; a showy woman for her age; kept afloat by her reputed wealth.[9]

According to Gaskell, Mrs Robinson was also responsible for the premature death of Branwell and she did not hesitate to denounce this easily identifiable but unnamed woman in the text. Only a threatened libel action prompted her to revise the passage in a third edition published 22 August 1857. In a letter to Smith dated 29 December 1856, however, she admitted that it was 'a horrid story, and I should not have told it but to show the life of prolonged suffering those Brontë girls had to endure'. Nonetheless, Mrs Gaskell strongly believed she was telling the truth and upheld the duty of a biographer to be honest and candid. In a letter of 16 June 1857 to Charlotte's close friend Ellen Nussey, Gaskell defensively explained that she 'weighted every line with all my whole power & heart, so that every line should go to its great purpose of making *her* known & valued, as one who had gone through such a terrible life with a brave & faithful heart'.[10]

Underscoring the inclusion of the incident, however, is Gaskell's commitment to Charlotte's view of the event; she, in fact, was the original source of knowledge about the Mrs Robinson affair, later confirmed by Patrick Brontë to Mrs Gaskell. The episode is symptomatic of Gaskell's concentration on Charlotte's attitudes and self-image. But Gaskell's determination to show Charlotte as 'noble, true and tender . . . without mingling up with her life too much of the personal history of her nearest and most intimate friends' provided her greatest difficulty (p. 490). Her obligation to her image of Charlotte exceeded her commitment to the facts, as a conversation in *Mary Barton* between Job Legh and Mr Carson foretold. Carson's belief in the legitimacy of facts is matched by Legh's scepticism: 'You can never work facts as you would fixed quantities, and say, given two facts, and the product is so and so.'

The *Life of Charlotte Brontë* has been called 'the first and still one of the finest, psychological studies of the writer at work' despite its misuse of evidence and supression of material.[11] The statement, however, emphasizes one of the strengths of the biography. Through her analysis of environment, education and childhood, Gaskell focuses on the formative elements that both restricted and stimulated Charlotte's development as a writer. Her concern is with getting at the root of her dark imagination and, by analysing the nature of acute isolation and duty to a selfish father, she shows how the refugee of the imagination in a world of harshness manages to survive if not triumph.

But the biography succeeds in its own right as a literary work, in part the result of its narrative method which sustains an element of drama and discovery. Narratively in the biography the present is shared equally by the reader and Gaskell; we proceed as much in Gaskell's presence as that of the subject's. Phrases and sentences repeatedly bring the reader into an active present: 'I was once speaking to her about "Agnes Grey" ', 'A good neighbor of the Brontës . . . told me a characteristic little incident', are only two of many examples (pp. 186, 180). This device not only personalizes the biography but establishes a stronger sense of participation for the reader. One of the most important moments is when Gaskell explains that 'I have had a curious packet confided to me, containing an immense amount of manuscript, in an inconceivably small space; tales, dramas, poems, romances, written principally by Charlotte, in a hand which it is almost impossible to decipher . . .' (pp. 111–12). The reproduction of a manuscript page in the biography reinforces the participation of the reader as he unavoidably tries to unravel the minute hand, and discover new elements in Brontë's work. This involvement in the life intensifies the retrospective and anticipatory structure of the biography as one experiences the early signs of later themes. The presence of the narrator furthermore heightens the tension in this account of how 'a solitary life cherishes mere fancies until they become manias' (p. 67).

The sensitive awareness of the development of Charlotte's imagination leads to one of the most important dimensions of biographies by writers, their self-reflexiveness. Choosing a woman writer as the subject of her only biography, Mrs Gaskell decides to study the very social and artistic pressures she herself has undergone. In a writer she appreciates and a woman she loves, Gaskell seeks an explanation if not a confirmation of her own deeply felt aesthetic and personal convictions. These begin with her belief in the importance of art and value of the creative enterprise but they diverge with her sense that

> Miss Brontë . . . puts all her naughtiness into her books, and I put all my goodness. I am sure she works off a great deal that is morbid *into* her writing, and *out* of her life; and my books are so far better than I am that I often feel ashamed of having written them and as if I were a hypocrite. (*Letters*, p. 228)

But here again are two sides of the same coin. What Gaskell perceives as the negativism of Brontë's life (projected in her fiction), and the nobleness of her (Mrs Gaskell's) life leaves the two women in a similar condition: fulfilled by their art, satisfied by their ability to transform reality into imagination, they remain dissatisfied by their inability to overcome personal shortcomings.

Brontë's 'misbehaviour' and Gaskell's inadequacy are similar states of unhappiness that nonetheless create an identity between the two.

Gaskell concentrates most on what would appeal to a novelist, analysing the moods and actions of Charlotte and providing a highly realized environment. These presentations, based on what she believed to be accurate sources, persuade the reader of the truthfulness of her narrative. However, the biography is not entirely uncritical nor without self-censure. Two passages, one describing Emily Brontë's 'stern selfishness' in refusing aid from her sisters while gravely ill, the other explaining Charlotte's hostility to Christianity in terms of masking her attraction to it were suppressed by Gaskell before publication.[12] But Gaskell's attraction to the personal suffering, disadvantages and innate goodness of Charlotte, qualities she herself described in her writing, fashioned a sympathetic yet powerful life.

At various moments in the biography Gaskell declares herself above making judgements and in the penultimate paragraph to the work writes that she 'cannot measure or judge of such a character as hers. I cannot map out vices and virtues, and debatable land' (p. 526). However, in choosing to write of a friend and emphasizing desires and achievements which were similar to her own, Mrs Gaskell could hardly escape the responsibility. The detachment is false and sustained only by reliance on Charlotte's own voice through the many quoted letters. But always present, as we read the life, are not only the revelations about M. Heger or Branwell but Gaskell's remark that she resolved to withhold 'nothing, though some things, from their very nature, could not be spoken of so fully as others' (p. 490). This reticence is partly the result of the authorized nature of the biography and fear of offending Patrick Brontë or Arthur Nicholls, plus the presence and eagerness of many to criticize or complain during, as well as after, its writing. But displayed most prominently in the life is the influence of the subject upon the biographer, personalizing the narrative. Brontë has, in significant ways, stimulated, challenged and confirmed the commitment of the biographer to the career of literature. The work becomes a striking self-proclamation on the part of the author to a life devoted to art.

Written at the mid-point of Gaskell's career, culminating a decade of controversial but successful fiction, from *Mary Barton* (1847) to *North and South* (1855), the *Life of Charlotte Brontë* is a kind of summing up or review of Gaskell's development. It is also an apotheosis of her concern with current affairs. No other work of Gaskell's focuses so extensively on contemporary issues. In the *Life* she recognized features of herself and, through indirect self-engagement, was able to reassess her own work and direction. The consequence was a shift to less contemporary, less controversial novels. Historical fiction (*Sylvia's Lovers*) and rural life (*Wives and Daughters*) mark her later successes. And although she briefly contemplated a life of Sir George Saville and began research on a life of Madame de Sevigne, Gaskell never wrote a biography again (*Letters*, 463, 679, 925). In November 1856 she ended an anxious letter to George Smith over permissions and the use of letters by lamenting 'Oh! if once I have finished this biography, catch me writing another! I shall be heaved overboard at last, like the ass belonging to the old man in the fable' (*Letters*, 421). Yet, the *Life of Charlotte Brontë* remains one of the most fascinating biographies of the period as G. H. Lewes made clear in a letter written to Mrs Gaskell shortly after he and George Eliot read the first edition:

> The book will, I think, create a deep and permanent impression; for it not only presents a vivid picture of a life noble and sad, full of encouragement and healthy teaching, a lesson in duty and self-reliance; it also, thanks to its artistic power, makes us familiar intimates of an interior so strange, so original in its individual elements and so picturesque in its externals – it paints for us at once the psychological drama and the scenic accessories with so much vividness – that fiction has nothing more wild, touching and heart-strengthening to place above it.[13]

Strikingly, in the final sentence, Lewes cites the very qualities that unite the biography with the novel, while confirming the power of Gaskell as a writer, which her fiction and biography demonstrate: a psychological realism, descriptive power and sense of drama linked to history.

But Gaskell's confirmation of her worth as a writer and reaffirmation of her commitment to literature through the struggle of Charlotte Brontë were not experienced by later writers who became biographers. Indeed, later writer-biographers were similar in their drive for independence from, rather than acknowledgement of, the influence of their subjects. Two examples are

Henry James and Anthony Trollope who found, in the impulse to write lives, freedom from restraining influences. The result was biography as rejection. In James's *Hawthorne* and Trollope's *Thackeray* the authors confront and detach themselves from their mentors, establishing new identities. George Eliot's remark that a biography by a writer 'has a double interest, from the glimpses it gives of the writer as well as his hero' is especially pertinent to James and Trollope, for each uses biography as a means of self-discovery.

The opportunity to write a life of one's precursor is the opportunity to re-examine obligations and demonstrate new freedoms. Although the biography does not often state such relationships, the interpretation of the life and analysis of individual texts frequently reveals implicit criticism and rede-fined relationships between the subject and author. Literary lives by creative writers are always interpretative. Rewriting his subject's life, the author rewrites his own as he realizes that he must assert his own identity as a writer. Furthermore, the author is aware that what he writes will be judged both as an account of his subject and also as one of his literary efforts. Commenting on Carlyle's *Sterling*, Eliot again noted the dilemma: 'We care less about the subject than about its treatment.'[14]

Biographies by writers are often a confrontation between the subject and his dominating presence in the psyche of the author. The decision to write the life is as much psychological as it is professional and a necessary stage in the artistic development of the author. The biography becomes an acknowledgement of debts *and* a sign of independence. It is both an act of obedience that fulfils certain demands and a sign of rebellion satisfying certain needs which ultimately release the author from control by his subject. James and Trollope are no exceptions. Both begin with certain similarities to their subjects such as the difficulty for James and Hawthorne of surviving as an artist in America or the nature of realism in the novel for Thackeray and Trollope. But each author quickly divests himself of his subject. James declares his independence from America and Europe, Trollope his freedom from Thackeray.

Hawthorne and *Thackeray* both appeared in 1879 as part of the English Men of Letters series. The two works illustrate the biographer employing ideas and values inherited from his subject while asserting new, sometimes contradictory concepts and

ideals. Engagement with, and detachment from, the life of the
subject becomes the fundamental movement in the narrative of
the life, a movement that importantly alters the conception of
biographies by writers about writers. Trollope, publishing the life
at the end of a successful and popular career, renews his debt to
Thackeray while distancing himself from him. But while praising
Thackeray, Trollope also criticizes him, implying that he (Trollope) worked, but that Thackeray was often 'idle'. The biography
becomes reinterpretation, the result of his own freedom created by
the death of Thackeray which, in practical terms, permitted
Trollope to become the leading novelist on Smith & Elders' lists,
chairman of the prestigious house committees of the Garrick Club
and to ascend higher on the pole of popular Victorian novelists.[15]
Through the presentation of his own qualities, habits and
accomplishments, Trollope, not Thackeray, dominates the
biography.

Henry James similarly used biography to advance his own
situation as well as to clarify his fictional aesthetic. Like Trollope,
he is negative, criticizing the provincialism of Hawthorne and the
limitations of the symbolic romance in order to justify his own
recent decision to live in England, his new allegiance to the
realistic novel (represented by the publication of *French Poets and
Novelists* the preceding year) and his independence from a writer
in whom he no longer found sustenance. Identified as early as
1870 with Hawthorne, James, after writing the biography, turned
to a different model, more aligned with his new European life and
international themes: Turgenev.[16]

Revisionary biography, however, does not always enforce the
rejection of the precursor; it can also lead to a tenuous reconciliation. Trollope demonstrates this in his earlier admiration and
identity with Thackeray in his *Autobiography* (written in 1876)
while James revises his attitude towards Hawthorne in his 1897
essay and 1904 centenary letter. Such acts do not invalidate the
quality of revision in the biographies but demonstrate that
rejection may be a necessary stage in the growth of understanding
between the author and his subject. Following an initial and
perhaps prolonged phase of criticism, akin to the Freudian notion
of 'opposition between successive generations' which Freud
outlined in his essay 'Family Romances', there appears to be a
reunion or acceptance of the predecessor after the author has
clearly established his literary autonomy. The writing of a

biography by a writer of a precursor is the first stage in his – the author's – separation which leads to his literary independence. Later estimates, if they are written, confirm his independence by their reconciliation with the subject.

Neither Trollope nor James had much experience with biographical writing when they were asked by John Morley in 1878 to contribute to the popular English Men of Letters series. Trollope had only published a brief memoir of Thackeray in the *Cornhill* fourteen years earlier, and a short life of Caesar, while James had done no biographical writing, although a selection of his critical essays had been collected and published in book form. Morley approached Trollope because of his reputation and long public association with Thackeray; he wrote to James because of his emerging reputation, recent arrival in England and a decision to include several American writers in the series.

In spite of the family restrictions on what personal details could or could not be disclosed, Trollope was instructed to 'give as much as ever you can in the personal vein by way of background to the critical and descriptive' by Morley. To James, Morley confidently explained the situation with Hawthorne in this fashion: 'there is no reason why we should not for the purposes of literature consider Americans as English'.[17]Both Trollope and James accepted the offers and completed their volumes in short time – Trollope, working at his characteristically rapid pace, finished in just under two months; James took more time, spending nearly a year on the research and writing. Trollope's volume appeared in the early summer of 1879, James's in mid-winter of the same year. Throughout 1879, it should be noted, James worked hard to consolidate his literary presence, republishing a number of works that first appeared in America. These included *Daisy Miller* (February), a revised edition of *The American* (March), a revised *Roderick Hudson* (May) and *The Madonna of the Future and Other Tales* (October). *Hawthorne*, published in December, climaxed what Leon Edel has called 'the conquest of London'.

Despite Morley's editorial directions, the absence of any first-hand research into primary sources is noticeable in both *Thackeray* and *Hawthorne*. Writing sixteen years after the death of Thackeray, Trollope confronted the injunctions of Thackeray's daughters which prevented him from fully documenting the life of their father. Consequently, he presents only 'an account of his [Thackeray's] development ... [and] how he worked and struggled'.[18] Disappointed by the lack of material, Trollope relied mostly on reminiscences of Thackeray's friends, the letters of associates and his published works, although no uniform edition of the writings existed at the time. To some extent, Trollope possessed personal knowledge of his subject, but it was limited since he had known Thackeray for a period of only four years. Nonetheless, *An Autobiography* refers to the 'intimacy' between them and conveys the admiration Trollope had for Thackeray. However, this personal link remained undeveloped in the biography, a reflection of Trollope's reticence or insecurity in becoming too personal in his account.[19]

James relied solely on secondary materials, never having known his subject. Except for conversations with Hawthorne's son, Julian, his major sources were George Lathrop's 1876 biography, Hawthorne's recently published notebooks (which James found quite uninteresting) and his published books. So incomplete was James's research that he failed to read *Fanshawe*, Hawthorne's first novel, relying instead on Lathrop's account of the plot. The second sentence of the James biography notes the lack of 'data for a life' with the qualification that 'even if they were abundant they would serve but in a limited measure the purpose of the biographer'.[20] This confirms James's unconventional notion of what his biography ought to achieve: an interpretation of Hawthorne's work, the age and the man in that order.

The paucity of materials and research prevented both biographers from providing much new or corrected factual detail. In place of concrete information, they concentrated on judgemental and presumptive statements regarding lives they knew little about. Without reference or example, Trollope wrote of Thackeray 'though he so rarely talked, as good talkers do, and was averse to sit down to work, there were always falling from his mouth and pen those little pearls'. The substitution of the cliche for content indicates the absence of substantial or even anecdotal material. James similarly speculated: 'he [Hawthorne] must have proposed to himself to enjoy, simply because he proposed to be an artist, and because this enters inevitably into the artist's scheme.'[21] The opinion is James's, not Hawthorne's.

The inadequacy of research in both *Thackeray* and *Hawthorne* led to errors of fact. Trollope failed to identify the illustrations of 'The Great Hoggarty Diamond' as Thackeray's and mistook the main theme of the story as the exposure of the bubble companies, a point that Thackeray himself contradicted in Chapter 1 of 'Sketches and Travels in London'. Trollope also confused the role of Mr Honeyman in *The Newcomes* and made a serious transcription error in substituting 'his Maker!' for 'the Master' when recounting the death scene of Colonel Newcome. James erroneously gave 1818 as the date of Hawthorne's move to Maine instead of 1816 and failed to mention the friendship between Melville and Hawthorne that developed after Hawthorne moved to Lenox, Massachusetts in May 1850.[22] An explanation, though not an apology, for these errors, is the haste and impatience with the conventional methods of biography which both authors demonstrate. James's only other biography, a two-volume life of the American sculptor William Wetmore Story, is a more accurate and better researched work – a result in part of his having known the subject.

It is no surprise that as biographers Trollope and James show greatest interest in the literary development of their subjects and that both emphasize the artistic accomplishments rather than the personal lives of their subjects. However, neither writer explores the importance of personal experience upon the literary works. The biographical fallacy is curiously absent from both texts. Trollope preferred to survey the habits and idiosyncrasies of his subject, while James concentrated on the representative qualities of his subject, not his life as an individual.

An important topic in each biography is realism, perhaps the dominant literary characteristic of Trollope and James. Trollope consistently discusses it in the work of Thackeray, often to validate its presence in his own novels. James continually laments its absence in Hawthorne and, by its omission, infers its importance as an aspect of his own writing (cf. p. 73). His study of French novelists, published in 1878, intensified his understanding and support of the realistic novel. One detail that reflects the concentration of Trollope and James on the artistic rather than biographical elements in their work is their mutual use of the fine arts as the source of their critical vocabulary. Both *Thackeray* and *Hawthorne* discuss the aesthetics of literary form in terms of art and such artists as Titian, Rembrandt and Reubens.

To regard *Thackeray* and *Hawthorne* as unsuccessful biographies, however, is to stop short of understanding them for what they are – self-reflexive texts focusing on the intersections between the authors and their subjects. The thematic base of this reflexive condition is influence, supplemented by a concern over the means of maintaining a career as a writer, and the psychological dimension of sustaining one's literary identity. Industry, environment and technique are the three ingredients Trollope and James perceive as necessary elements in sustaining a successful career. Trollope, in particular, stresses the industry required to be a successful writer. Those who avoid the 'elbow-grease of the mind' and disregard the drudgery of the work will fail. Thackeray lacked these qualities, as Trollope is quick to point out: 'Unsteadfast, idle, changeable of purpose, aware of his own intellect but not trusting it, no man ever failed more generally than he to put his best foot foremost.'[23] James, just beginning the middle phase of his career, studies the craftsmanship of his subject less and the environment more. America, he argues, was, and is, not adequate, providing only a Puritan milieu which, to his credit, Hawthorne analysed in his fiction.

As part of his act of disengagement, Trollope emphasizes the virtues of his own practice – the early hours, productivity, stamina and diligence – which he understands as weaknesses in Thackeray. His literary shortcomings include the lack of a complete and harmonious story, the absence of a balanced satirical outlook, the failure to publish at regular intervals and the neglect of the social duty of a novelist to make others understand the nature of his craft. Such criticism was necessary for Trollope in order for him to assert his identity and free himself from an allegiance and dedication to Thackeray. He sustains an identity only in outward ways, citing such parallels as their mutual quest for Post Office positions and aborted search for political office (Thackeray failed at both). Trollope intimates, however, that these events are frivolous and do little to advance one's status as a writer; of course, his own successful career at the Post Office and equivalent attempt to become an MP in the 1868 election suffer from no similar judgement. Trollope never indulges in the strong feelings he holds for Thackeray, so evident in the 1864 *Cornhill* article. Only in the posthumously published *Autobiography*, written before the Thackeray biography, however, did he allow himself the free praise and personal admiration he repressed or hid in the 1879 volume.[24]

Less secure about his writing than Trollope, James focused on the theoretical issues of his subject's genre. He investigated problems of allegory, symbolism and imagination and the way they function to create the 'deeper psychology' of Hawthorne's novels which so appealed to him. But he rejected the symbolic emphasis found in Hawthorne and undid any association between himself and the writer. But in what James identified as the originality of the tales, he defined the form of writing he himself would soon display. Describing Hawthorne as 'a confirmed *habitué* of a region of mysteries and subtleties' who possessed a 'natural yet fanciful familiarity' with the psychological, James recognized, in the handling of conscience and state of mind, the catalyst to, and signal of, his own coming achievement. But this relationship between what he saw in Hawthorne and how he himself was writing was complex and not fully understood. For example, in a comment on Coverdale from *The Blithedale Romance*, James uses language which reflects himself and his characters. Coverdale, he wrote, was a man 'whose passions are slender, whose imagination is active, and whose happiness lies, not in doing, but in perceiving – half a poet, half a critic and all a spectator'.[25]

James's support of European culture and denigration of America in the biography clearly marks his renunciation of Hawthorne. But it also confirms a necessary stage in his own literary independence. Yet, in his letters written from Europe shortly before he published the biography, James complained bitterly about humanity in general and the English in particular. This ambiguity represents the failure by James to accept completely his new identity and new home. In June 1879, three years after he moved to England and while he was researching *Hawthorne*, James wrote to Grace Norton that the English have 'a certain number of great plump flourishing uglinesses and drearinesses which offer themselves irresistibly as *pin-cushions* to criticism and irony'. Such a discrepancy between his satiric view of the English and the celebration of English and European culture in the biography suggests a lingering uncertainty about his 1876 move not fully expressed in the biography. *The Europeans*, published a year before the Hawthorne biography, satirically conveys his critique of American society paralleled in the 1879 biography. In the ensuing debate, he defended his position by confidently telling William Dean Howells that an older civilization provided greater meaning and materials for a novelist.[26]

Both Trollope and James became disenchanted with their biographies, reflecting the dismay writers as biographers often experience when limited to historical narrative. To John Black-wood, Trollope confessed that he became quite bored with the project, telling him he found it a 'terrible job' because there was 'absolutely nothing to say – except washed out criticism'. However, he defensively added that 'it had to be done, and no one would do it so lovingly'.[27] James, too, became uncomfortable with his work, but the strong analytical quality of the book strength-ened his prose style and helped him to fashion a sustained if controversial argument on the conditions that encourage or defeat an American artist. Newly established in Europe and seeking confirmation of his decision to leave the familiar for the unknown, James wrote with a sense of urgency, knowing his artistic identity was at stake.

To the extent that both biographies diverged from the standard treatment and biographical practice of the late Victorian period, most fully represented at the time by G. O. Trevelyan's two-volume *The Life and Letters of Macaulay* (1876), both *Thackeray* and *Hawthorne* offended. Their readers were not bothered by factual error; perhaps they never detected it. However, they were disturbed by undocumented assessments and unconvincing con-clusions and became strongly agitated when those views departed from popular, accepted images. The cause of the harsh reception of Trollope's *Thackeray*, for example, was his emphasis on the personal inadequacies of Thackeray as a writer. The candour of Trollope's comments regarding Thackeray's indolence generated controversy and James Thomson's attack on the book, calling it mere 'scribbling' fit only for circulating libraries, is symptomatic of the reaction of the public.[28]

The diffident attitude towards American culture and under-valuation of Hawthorne's writing disturbed the readers of *Hawthorne*. Repetition of the word 'provincial', misunderstanding of the importance of Thoreau and an emphasis on the absence of realism in the fiction of Hawthorne were the substance of further criticisms. Most vexatious was James's opinion of the intellectual poverty of America that Howells and others opposed. But *Hawthorne* registers a significant stage in the evolution of James as a writer. The refined point of view, consistent narrative tone and ability to portray character psychologically are notable technical features. Thematically, it records his independence from a tradition through the reassessment of a primary influence which permits him to experiment with other forms and other subjects.[29] The biography also conveys the commitment of James to realism.

Nine years after the publication of *Hawthorne*, James extended his fascination with biography in 'The Aspern Papers' (1888). The story fulfilled a need to fictionalize the problems of biographical research, and allowed him to demonstrate dramatically the difficulties and frustrations of biography as a literary enterprise. Released from the problem of literary debt through the writing of an actual biography, James nonetheless continued his interest in biography with a fictionalized account of biographical writing. Curiously, the story is about an attempted biography of a writer by a writer; the subject is the displaced American poet Jeffrey Aspern, while the narrator/author is an American editor/writer. The plot, however, never allows the narrator to re-write the life of his subject although he speculates throughout on the possible interpretations of various moments in his subject's life. The parallel is striking in form and situation to the Hawthorne biography.

Both Trollope and James wrote biographies other than *Thackeray* and *Hawthorne*. Trollope published a two-volume *Life of Cicero* in 1880, originally essays in the *Fortnightly Review* of 1877, while James produced *William Wetmore Story and His Friends* in 1903. But without the challenge of writing a life that in direct or indirect ways affected the artistic life of the author, biography lost its vitality and creative energy for both. The result was conventional if not mediocre narratives of Cicero and Story. Writing to Henry Adams shortly after the Story biography appeared, James expressed his frustration with the 'art of a biographer'. It was, he said, a 'devilish art! – is somehow practically *thinning*. It simplifies even while seeking to enrich.'[30] What James failed to realize, however, is that when biography is revision, as it is when written by a creative writer whose subject is also a writer, biography remakes both the author and his subject.

In biographies by writers fictional techniques abound. Mrs Gaskell displays them in *Charlotte Brontë* in her treatment of landscape, setting and dramatic structure – as in the suspenseful progression from 'the deep valley of the Aire' to the tombstone of Charlotte Brontë in the opening chapter or in the dramatic rendering of Charlotte's plea to sleep aboard the Ostend packet bound in the morning for Brussels (ch. xxii). Trollope's fictional touches include his interruptive narrator who comments on the condition of his subject, noting that Thackeray lacked application or wrote haphazardly. James provides a careful character and cultural analysis focusing on the consciousness of his subject, as he will later concentrate on those of his fictional characters. The work is almost a testing ground of the Jamesian method of discrimination and evaluation, combining, as he says of Hawthorne, 'in singular degree the spontaneity of the imagination with a haunting care for moral problems' (p. 166).

Contemporary novelists have actually inverted these procedures, borrowing from biography so that their fictions take the form of biographies, echoing eighteenth-century models. *The Glass Bead Game* by Herman Hesse, *Doctor Faustus* by Thomas Mann, *The Real Life of Sebastian Knight* by Vladimir Nabokov or *Le Biographe* by Phillipe Beaussant are several examples. *Edwin Mullhouse, The Life and Death of an American Writer, 1943–1954* by Steven Millhauser is a further experiment in this style. But an earlier and, for biography, more influential work is *Orlando* by Virginia Woolf. Despite its praise and study by Woolf scholars, *Orlando* has been little discussed in terms of the evolution of biography, yet in its departure from conventional form and structure it points to new ways of writing lives.[31]

Through its satire of nineteenth-century biography, *Orlando* summarizes outmoded practices while indicating fresh directions. Importantly, the work not only contains a theory of biography but shows that theory at work. Among biographies by writers it holds a unique position, being at once criticism and fiction. Furthermore, *Orlando* shows how the limitations of biography can be overcome by the creative writer. The subjects of *Orlando* are the possibilities and potentials of biographical form. It is quintessentially biography as revolution, illustrating Thomas S. Kuhn's theory that a new method requires construction of prior techniques and 'a re-evaluation of prior fact'. *Orlando* also represents the engagement of the biographer with powerful, shaping forces but, in addition to asserting the narrator's personal freedom expressed in the time shifts, style and scope, the biography vitalizes the form of biography through its synchronic narrative, figurative language, shifting presentation of personality, scenic and historic variety and vibrant language. The work fulfils Woolf's remark on the concept of the work when she wrote 'it sprung upon me how I could revolutionise biography in a night'.[32]

Writing biography was always problematic for Virginia Woolf;
her greatest successes with the form were fictional, as in *Flush* and
Orlando. 'My God, how does one write a Biography?', she asked
Vita Sackville-West ten years after *Orlando* as she was beginning
to work on the papers of Roger Fry:

> How can one deal with facts – so many and so many and so
> many? Or ought one, as I incline, to be purely fictious. And
> what is a life? . . . And if one can't say, whats the good of trying?
> Yet its my favourite reading – short of shall we say Shakespeare
> and Sackville-West: biography.

This frustration in confronting the facts and welding them into
some unified aesthetic whole that also conveyed the personality of
the subject remained her greatest dilemma in attempting the
form. *Orlando*, however, provided her with a solution: the free play
with biography to test its limits and show its flexibility. Unlike
preceding writer-biographers, Woolf did not shy away from the
experiment but quickly and passionately wrote the work.

Parallel to the biographies by Gaskell, James and Trollope, a
literary figure is at the centre of *Orlando*: Vita Sackville-West. In a
letter written the day the idea of *Orlando* crystallized, Woolf
exclaimed to Vita 'its all about you and the lusts of your flesh and
the lure of your mind . . . I should like to untwine and twist again
some very odd incongruous strands in you'. Later letters inquire
about the facts, details, dates and history of Vita: 'Is it true you
grind your teeth at night? Is it true you love giving pain? What
and when was your moment of greatest disillusionment?'[33] *Knole
and the Sackvilles*, Vita's 1922 history of her family home, provided
additional details; *The Land*, her 1926 poem, provided certain
literary elements. Out of a dual effort to commemorate her
feelings for Vita, and as a stimulus to her creativity, Woolf burst
forth with *Orlando*, a work seen whole from its earliest conception.
It rapidly achieved large sales and established Virginia Woolf's
name in America as well as England; but our principal interest is
how the work revitalized biography.

Throughout the text, biography is both victim and victor.
Through the satire of nineteenth-century biography's reliance on
fact and documentation, the narrator engages the reader's
sensibility in reconsidering the difficulties of writing a life. *Orlando*
actually becomes a metabiography as two important passages

make clear. The first in Chapter 2 takes the reader into the confidence of the biographer:

> The biographer is now faced with a difficulty which it is better perhaps to confess than to gloss over. Up to this point in telling the story of Orlando's life, documents, both private and historical, have made it possible to fulfil the first duty of a biographer, which is to plod, without looking to right or left, in the indelible footprints of truth; unenticed by flowers; regardless of shade; on and on methodically till we fall plump into the grave and write *finis* on the tombstone above our heads. But now we come to an episode which lies right across our path, so that there is no ignoring it. Yet it is dark, mysterious, and undocumented; so that there is no explaining it. Volumes might be written in interpretation of it; whole religious systems founded upon the signification of it. Our simple duty is to state the facts as far as they are known, and so let the reader make of them what he may.[34]

The absence of facts befuddles the biographer who realizes that this 'dark, mysterious' incident is open to endless interpretation. Metaphor expresses the previously well-trodden path of the biographer but 'flowers' and 'shade' do not inveigle him. However, returning to the narrative, the biographer shows how Orlando's inexplicable seven-day trance leads to speculation, digression and question, which end in comic control:

> Had Orlando, worn out by the extremity of his suffering, died for a week, and then come to life again? And if so, of what nature is death and of what nature life? Having waited well over half an hour for an answer to these questions, and none coming, let us get on with the story. (pp. 64–5)

The change to solitary behaviour and fascination with death has no clear explanation for the biographer who is forced to continue his story. But he does indicate that it is the obligation of the reader to fashion meaning out of the strange behaviour. Excusing his failure to explain does not excuse the reader, who now must participate in the life through *his* active interpretation:

> For though these are not matters on which a biographer can

profitably enlarge[,] it is plain enough to those who have done a
reader's part in making up from bare hints dropped here and
there the whole boundary and circumference of a living person;
can hear in what we only whisper a living voice; can see, often
when we say nothing about it, exactly what he looked like;
know without a word to guide them precisely what he thought
– and it is for readers such as these that we write . . . (p. 69)

From impressions, insights and ideas about Orlando the reader
can formulate his character and his 'disease' which is literature.
The parody of biographical method here, the reliance on impression and interpretation because of the unreliability or
unavailability of facts, forces the reader as well as the biographer
to adopt new strategies of analysis and presentation.

Chapter 6 contains further parodies on biographical method
involving the reaction of the reader to a colourless narrative. The
recital of cold facts, in this case the months of the year, comically
leaves the biographer paralysed, as Orlando, merely sitting in a
chair and thinking, fails to act. The comic anger of the biographer
towards the subject here, generated by the impossibility of delving
into the mind of the subject or of narrating any action satirically,
exposes the shortcomings of traditional biography. When nothing
visibly happens, there is nothing to report: 'Still he looked, still he
paused. It is these pauses that are our undoing', remarks the
narrator (p. 75); 'If only subjects, we might complain (for our
patience is wearing thin), had more consideration for their
biographers!' (p. 241). Inaction is self-indulgence by the character, and an affront to the eager biographer: 'If . . . the subject of
one's biography will neither love nor kill, but will only think and
imagine, we may conclude that he or she is no better than a corpse
and so leave her', the narrator exclaims (p. 242). Such a charge to
the subject and such a digression deflates the stature of the
biographical hero while enhancing the position of the narrator.

Parodying the content of biography becomes a critique of the
nature of the genre *and* a challenge to find a new method. More
specifically, the biographer must learn how to convey the
thoughts of his subject. The satire, however, is double, since the
biographee has shown how difficult that task is while the narrator
espouses a belief that the psychology of the subject forms the very
substance of the life and the material of the biography. The year
before she wrote *Orlando*, Woolf complained that 'the Victorian

biographer was dominated by the idea of goodness. Noble, upright, chaste, severe; it is thus that the Victorian worthies are presented to us.'[35] *Orlando* is a reaction to that admiration, displaying a new equality between the biographer and his subject which, in turn, leads to a new honesty as well as criticism of the represented life. The focus of biography actually shifts from a given or fixed attitude to a search for value in the life. Biography no longer begins with a preconceived pattern.

Associated with the satire of conventional representation of character in biography is the more important and modern notion – symbolized by the sex and time changes in *Orlando* – that an individual can be a multiple number of selves. This concept reflects ideas of Freudian psychology and Bergsonian time and is one of the conclusions articulated in the last twenty pages of the work. This modern discovery, that we are a series of people of which a biography can provide only a limited number, emerges as a crucial idea which forces a re-evaluation of the nature of biographical expression: 'a biography is considered complete if it merely accounts for six or seven selves, whereas a person may well have as many thousand' (p. 278). But this realization frustrates the biographer's reliance on the record; calling for another self may not be an easy task since

> these selves of which we are built up, one on top of another, as plates are piled on a waiter's hand, have attachments else-where, sympathies, little constitutions and rights of their own, call them what you will (and for many of these things there is no name) so that one will only come if it is raining, another in a room with green curtains, another when Mrs. Jones is not there, another if you can promise it a glass of wine – and so on; for everybody can multiply from his own experience the different terms which his different selves have made with him – and some are too wildly ridiculous to be mentioned in print at all. (p. 277)

Such an interpretation of self necessitates a loosening of biography as the biographer realizes how little he knows and can convey of his subject in the work. Indirectly, it is a claim for psychological biographies, lives that can get to the interior of the life, penetrating the detail and record which, as *Orlando* demonstrates, can be erratic, inexplicable, inconsistent and untrustworthy.

Time is similarly confusing for the biographer and on this subject *Orlando* makes perhaps its greatest impact on biographical writing.

'The true length of a person's life, whatever the *Dictionary of National Biography* may say, is always a matter of dispute. For it is a difficult business – this time-keeping', declares the narrator of *Orlando* (p. 275). In conveying vividly and dramatically the nature of biological versus clock time, Woolf prepares the way for later biographical experiments such as Leon Edel's *Henry James* which consciously shifts back and forth in its attempt to convey time organically. Time in *Orlando* exists in the text as both a technique and experience, reflecting the varieties and experiments with time in the poetry and fiction of the 1920s as seen earlier in the work of Joyce and T. S. Eliot as well as in *Mrs Dalloway* or *To the Lighthouse*. Woolf alters biography to include the fragmented sense of experience and to introduce modernist biography which concentrates on the making rather than the content of the life. The continual awareness of the unreliability of the fixed *quanta* and the attempt to liberate biography from its literalness, substituting a new expressiveness through experimentation and fictionalization, underscore *Orlando*'s importance for subsequent biographers. The process of forming the life becomes the substance of the life. Pattern, coherence and myth become the new contingencies of history, as the consciousness of Orlando and the flow of thought replace dates, facts and exactness. An example of the telescoping of time is Orlando's sleep. In the manuscript of *Orlando* 1616 is cited as the date when Orlando awakes but, since he went to sleep in 1604 (implied narrative time), twelve years of historical time have passed during his seven days' sleep. The revision, however, discards the 1616 reference but shows a marked change in time and Orlando's personality from exuberant Elizabethan to melancholic Jacobean.[36]

Orlando provides non-fictional prose with a model of how to free itself from the limitations of chronological and historical time. The discrepancy between clock time and biological time establishes a new order and release for biography, allowing greater experimentation and development of a natural rather than imposed life. It also permits the biographer to encompass the modernist consciousness of disunity. Woolf, with Proust, demonstrates the freedom from time that permitted departures from diachronic to synchronic time in biography seen in such later works as A. J. A. Symons's *Quest for Corvo* or Andrew Field's *Nabokov: His Life in Part*.

Supplementing the innovations of character, time and structure, especially in narrative pause and digression in *Orlando*, is style. The adaptation of certain period styles as seen in the syntax, diction and vocabulary again demonstrates the versatility of the biographical form. Woolf displays the verbal energy that biography can encompass. More sustaining, however, is the use of metaphor. Through the development of Orlando's life, the parodies of biographical and historical details become metaphoric. Borrowed perhaps from Lytton Strachey, who frequently used metaphor as a short-handed means of expressing character, the prevalence of metaphor nonetheless advances the stylistic possibilities of biography. Unable to convey a complete or even definite account of Orlando via the record, the biographer turns to tropes; the most sustained is metaphor. This technique again both summarizes past practices while anticipating future developments in biography. It is not only grand metaphors such as 'damp' for the Victorian age or the 'disease' of literature that reappear but the minor metaphors such as sewing, with memory the seamstress, that provide the figurative and linguistic fabric of the text (cf. p. 74). And one result of this stylistic self-consciousness is the greater awareness of the organic development of time. Reliance on metaphor to interpret the subject undermines the naive faith in facts, dates and documents Woolf attempts to correct. *Orlando*, through its distinct styles, both identifies and separates different moments in time while maintaining their unity. This sensitivity to such contradiction accentuates the literary quality of the work as Woolf both exposes the problem of representation while also overcoming it.

In *Orlando* the use of fact indicates not only its elusiveness and instability but the new principle enunciated in 1927 by Woolf that life 'no longer consists in actions only or in works. It consists in personalities.' Woolf's ideas of biography parallel shifts in epistemology occurring at this time, beginning in physics with Einstein's relativity principle, Arthur Eddington's concepts of relativism and Werner Heisenberg's uncertainty principle. *The Nature of the Physical World* by Eddington appeared in the same year as *Orlando*. A biographer is not to disregard facts completely but to present them in a creative fashion: 'in order that the light of personality may shine through, facts must be manipulated',

Woolf explained.[37] This is the accomplishment of *Orlando* – the demonstration of moulding actual fact from English history and the background of the Sackvilles with the personality of Vita Sackville-West into a form that does not sacrifice its truth to fact, nor its fictional potential to historical limitation. *Orlando* enhances the continuity and unpredictability of personality in prose and shows biographers new ways to present life. With its exuberant narrative and organic sense of time (the hero ages only twenty years in the three hundred covered), *Orlando* shows how fact can become imaginative. As Orlando crosses barriers of time, sex and space with gracious ease encompassing disparate cultures, flux makes fact into order. Personality and action unite in a fluid, changeable but consistent figure. But this transformation of fact in biography did not occur in isolation.

The comic style, use of hyperbole and satire of biography in *Orlando* find their immediate inspiration in *Some People* by Harold Nicolson which Woolf reviewed on 30 October 1927. In particular, Nicolson's portraits of Lord Curzon and Lambert Orme illustrate the style Woolf extended:

> It would be impossible, I feel, to actually be as decadent as Lambert looked. I split the infinitive deliberately, being in the first place no non-split die-hard (oh, the admirable Mr. Fowler!), and desiring secondly to emphasise, what was in fact the dominant and immediate consideration which Lambert evoked. I have met many men with wobbly walks, but I have never met a walk more wobbly than that of Lambert Orme.

For Woolf, Nicolson was a clear example of the biographer as artist who renewed the Plutarchian love of anecdote because the 'pith and essence' of the subject 'shows itself to the observant eye in the tone of a voice, the turn of a head, some little phrase or anecdote picked up in passing'. Most crucially, he 'has shown that a little fiction mixed with fact can be made to transmit personality very effectively'.[38]

But another, important influence for Woolf was Lytton Strachey. Strachey's remark to Woolf that she 'should take something wilder & more fantastic, a frame work that admits of anything, like *Tristram Shandy*' has often been cited as the germ of *Orlando*. In the earliest reference to *Orlando*, Woolf echoes the remark and suggests the inclusion of Strachey in 'a grand historical picture, the outlines of all my friends' which might be 'a way of writing the memoirs of one's own times during peoples lifetimes . . . Vita should be Orlando, a young nobleman. There should be Lytton; & it should be truthful, but fantastic.' But there is little else of Strachey's external influence on *Orlando*. Of course, his extraordinary success with *Eminent Victorians* and *Queen Victoria*, the latter the most favoured of his works by Woolf, and his general ideas and exchanges on biography, plus easy way in talking about his books with Woolf, summarizes his overall impact on her ideas of biography. But more vital may have been his struggle with his last major biography, *Elizabeth and Essex*, which appeared one month after *Orlando*. In his two-and-a-half-year battle with the biography, it is likely that he and Woolf discussed matters of form and composition frequently.[39] A comparison of the two works illustrates numerous similarities. This is not so much a matter of influence as of exchange and the curious coalescence of biography with fiction at a particular time, 1928, and the attempt by writers like Nicolson, Woolf and Strachey to explore new ways of enlarging biographical writing with fictional techniques.

The year 1928 is a kind of *annus mirabilus* for biography. Not only do *Orlando* and *Elizabeth and Essex* appear but Andre Maurois delivers six lectures on biography at Cambridge, later published as *Aspects of Biography*. The journal *Life and Letters*, edited by Desmond McCarthy, is born and Edmund Gosse dies. Framing these publications are Harold Nicolson's *Development of English Biography* which appeared in late 1927 while early in 1929 F. A. Pottle published *Boswell's Literary Career*. As Woolf and Strachey illustrate and Maurois argues, fiction and biography strongly interact with one another. Several examples of biographical novels at this time include *O Rare Ben Jonson* (1928) by Francis Steegmuller and Rene Benjamin's *Balzac, La Prodigieuse Vie D'Honore de Balzac*, English translation 1929. In the arts, 1928 was a year of experiment and change witnessing the completion of *Remembrance of Things Past* with the publication of *Time Regained*, the premieres of Brecht and Weill's *The Three Penny Opera* and Schoenberg's *Variations for Orchestra*, the release of *Un Chien Andalou* and the publication of two works of extraordinary sexual license: *Lady Chatterley's Lover* and *The Well of Loneliness*. Language also found a new form that year with the appearance of the *Oxford English Dictionary* in twelve volumes. Biography participated in this climate of excitement and challenge, sharing in these developments.

An example of the critical response at this time to the merging of biography and fiction is A. J. A. Symons's 1929 lecture, 'Tradition in Biography'. Delivered in the 'Tradition and Experiment' series which included contributions by T. S. Eliot, Edith Sitwell and Rebecca West, Symons extends certain ideas Maurois outlines in the final chapter of *Aspects of Biography*. In particular, Symons emphasizes that 'Biography *is* the telling of a story – a *life* story.' It differs from fiction in that probability guides the novelist, fact the biographer. But the difference between the two is not vast: the novelist, like the biographer, is limited, although by *his* character and not that of his subject's. The biographer, Symons argues, also has 'a *certain* freedom of choice' allowing for creativity and imagination. Echoing Strachey, Symons adds that 'books like rose bushes, are improved by skilful pruning; to omit is as important as to mention'. The significance of the resemblance between fiction and biography at this time might be summarized by a remark of Geoffrey Scott's at the end of his successful 1925 biography, *Portrait of Zélide*. Of his subject, Isabella van Tuyll, he says 'I have sought to give her the reality of a fiction; but my material is fact.'[40] *Orlando* and *Elizabeth and Essex* reflect a similar effort.

The narrative voices of biographies by writers reinforce the freedom and self-reflexive nature of the genre. Gaskell's casual first-person voice, supplemented by a novelistic point of view, introduces a strongly personal note, establishing intimacy and subjectivity despite her focus on detail and stated objectivity. James contradicts this romantic style with his Victorian omniscience, criticism and evaluation of his subject's social and cultural context instead of private detail. This objectivity, however, contradicts Trollope's self-expression which almost distracts from presenting the life of Thackeray, although he avoids the intimacy Gaskell displays, and attends more carefully to the conventions of the genre. Woolf, in the most expressionistic of the biographies, highlights the possibilities and freedoms available for the biographer in his search for his subject, reflecting the *absence* of shared assumptions and values about a life.

Uniting these four lives is the quest for self-definition by the author in his search for aesthetic and moral values. Collectively, biographies by writers invite readers to perceive relationships between the author and his subject, as well as the biographer and his work. Like fiction or poetry at this time (ca. 1850–1930), biography undergoes a change from fixed ideas of structure and style to the more complex and self-conscious process of creation. Woolf's *Orlando* culminates the trialogue between the biographical form, the creative process, and the raw material of a life. But the shift from coherence to disunity in a life, the former the goal of *Charlotte Brontë*, the latter that of *Orlando*, marks a change that continues to unsettle contemporary biographers. The choices of biography pose new challenges to the telling of lives as life itself is no longer conceived as a prefigured pattern.

In the Preface to his award-winning biography *Edmund Campion* (1935), Evelyn Waugh wrote 'there is great need for a complete scholar's book on the subject. This is not it. All I have done is to select the incidents which strike a novelist as important and put them into a narrative which I hope may prove readable.'[41] This modest admission fails to convey the value of Waugh's biography but it candidly expresses a perpetual concern with biographies by writers. Do they provide reliable narratives and thoughtful interpretations, or are they merely works of admiration or attack based too closely on fictional methods? George Gissing could confidently assert that 'I believe a novelist would make the best biographer. I wish I had someone's life to try my hand upon' and there is evidence to support his view in the form of, say, Margaret Drabble's life of Arnold Bennett, Angus Wilson's account of Rudyard Kipling, or John Wain's narrative of Samuel Johnson.[42] But other writer-biographers have been less satisfying. Sybil Bedford, for example, ambiguously succeeds with her life of Aldous Huxley, confusing the reader by her own narrative insecurity although revealing new details and facts. But writers as biographers form a distinguished list – E. M. Forster, Robert Graves, Christopher Isherwood, Evelyn Waugh, Graham Greene, Edith Sitwell, Anthony Powell, to name a few. Their efforts reveal not only unique aspects of their own progress and identity as authors but important dimensions of biography as a form of literary expression. Studying the diversity of these lives and biographical approaches, however, raises the central issue of form and the fundamental question of whether or not any principles of biography exist to unify or organize the genre. Chapter 5 considers these matters in some detail.

5 Biography and Theory: Steps towards a Poetics

> A study of biographies by the dozen, though it often leaves one
> pretty much in the dark as to the people biographised, ought
> perhaps to give one some view as to the art of biography.
>
> Leslie Stephen, 'Biography'

Is there a theory of biography, a systematized set of principles
regarding the form and composition of the genre? Given the
multiplicity of lives and variety of styles of biographical
expression this seems an impossibility. However, a theory of
biography based on language, narration and myth provides a
possible model. More specifically, I believe that an analysis of the
function of tropes, the forms of narrative, and the nature of myth
in biography can establish a foundation for a theory that
emphasizes its generic properties. Shaping this approach is the
principle that the literary form of biography derives not from
observing a set of rules, nor from the documentation of a life but
from the literary act of composition and the dependence of the
biographer on language to express a life-story. What gives
biography its impact is not the point of view of the biographer, as
Strachey emphasized, nor the 'inner myth' of the subject, as Leon
Edel stresses, but the linguistic expression, narrative technique
and mythical elements employed by the author to tell his
story.

While we continually learn of the historical importance,
popularity or research difficulties of biography, we are rarely, if
ever, taught the principles of biography as a literary art.
Biography lacks both an Aristotle and a Northrop Frye. One
cause for this absence may be that biography exists in an
anomalous state. It is clearly based on fact but, as Frank Brady
has remarked, 'modern criticism hardly knows what to do with
the factual'. Ironically, the biographer himself often seems
'unaware that his work has either formal aspects or a general

151

strategy', a point confirmed by James L. Clifford in interviews with English and American biographers. As Michael Holroyd has noted, 'non-fiction is regarded by many critics as non-creative. They confuse invention with creation.'[1]

Another cause for the reluctance to theorize about biography may be the sustained antipathy towards that biographical criticism characterized in its excess by an extreme reliance on the life as the only source for understanding the work. Wellek and Warren in 1948 and, before them, the Russian critic Boris Tomasevskij in 1923 rejected the usefulness of such an approach.[2] The advent of structuralism following the New Criticism reinforced the resistance to biographical criticism, discouraging the possibilities of developing a theory of biography. Another reason for the failure to pursue a theory of biography is the anxiety of literary critics when the psychological approach, inevitably linked to biography, is applied. The lack of proper training, incomplete analyses and uninformed theorizing of biographers have frequently resulted in unsatisfactory psychological lives. But in general, critics have been reluctant to consider biography a creative task within the sphere of non-fictional prose. Emphasis on its historical, factual or documentary nature, often summarized by the term 'comprehensive', has restricted efforts to theorize about the genre. The limited number of theoretical essays on biography is not so much the failure of the form as the inability of readers to perceive biography as a fully defined aesthetic subject. The preponderance of literary studies of biography have clearly been historical.[3]

This situation, however, should not lead one to conclude that a modern theory of biography has never been attempted. In 1977, for example, Leon Edel published a work unabashedly titled 'The Poetics of Biography'. Written in a dialogue form modelled on Dryden's 'An Essay of Dramatic Poesy', Edel's 'Poetics' is an apology for the activities of the biographer and the value of his creation. Although his presentation is refreshing, his critique of the Boswellian model stimulating and his claim for the biographer's task inspiring – 'I would begin with the idea that a life – the recreation in words of a life – is one of the most beautiful and most difficult tasks a literary artist can set himself' – Edel's essay-dialogue falls back on unclear generalizations and platitudes when explaining how the biographer should shape his materials into a life without a well-defined guide. 'All that I can say', explains the character Plutarchus, 'is that a biographer must work by the illumination of his materials.'

The 'Poetics of Biography' is a defence of the genre rather than a systematic theory and repeatedly castigates those critics who have attacked biography while nonetheless using biographical materials in their own critical essays. It also criticizes those who write biography with no training as biographers. The most useful section is Edel's summary of the by now well-known characteristics of an ideal biographer. He is, Edel explains, one who

> writes a story of the progress of a life; he must allow himself to feel its failures, its obstacles overcome, its human ambiguities, its fallibilities, and the drama of personality and temperament. If he's a good biographer, he knows how to select and use significant detail. He can't allow himself to be too much the critic, lest his critiques of the work impede the march of the story. A critical biography is a contradiction in terms . . . The beauty of what a biographer does resides in his insights: we discern the complexities of being, without pretending that life's riddles have been answered.

In addition to these often cited qualities, Edel adds that the art of the biographer resides in making the reader feel that he is creating a mosaic of the subject's life along with the biographer. The process of discovery becomes a shared activity between reader and biographer through the text. 'A biography', he concludes 'is a kind of endless summary, in which the reader is made a party to a weighing of evidence.'[4] This idea of the reader participating in the biography is one of the newer aspects of current efforts to analyse biography, although no one has yet developed an approach akin to various reader-oriented theories of fiction or autobiography. But 'The Poetics of Biography' by Edel fails because it provides only dramatized generalizations instead of concrete and systematic specifics.

If a theory of biography is to emerge, it might begin where Edel ends. It should examine how the completed text deals with the subject in literary ways and show how the 'insights' of the biographer that Edel prizes are represented in the only tool shared by all biographers: language. We must begin by looking less at the historical development of the genre and more at the formal properties of individual texts. We must accept, as Ralph Rader has explained, that 'to the degree that any factual narrative is responded to as literature, its form may be analyzed as inherently the cause of an effect'. From the assumption that biography is a work of literature, we can, or should, elucidate a series of qualities that may unify disparate and varied examples. We must not forget, as Edmund Wilson reminded Arthur Mizener when he was writing his biography of F. Scott Fitzgerald, that the biographer 'has not only to choose and place every detail of his picture, but to calculate the tone of every sentence'.[5]

A biographer is above all a writer and how he presents the details of a life is perhaps even more important for responding to the life than the details themselves. Few critics of biography, however, have explored this aspect of the subject; it is still the accuracy of materials that takes precedence over the form of presentation. But the demands of readers upon biography, fashioned by developments in other genres, notably the novel, will not allow such concerns to continue to dominate the conceptualization of the subject.

A biographer, bounded by fact, still invents his form and, through language, directs his reader's impressions, images and interpretation of the subject. How he does this could become the focus of a theoretical approach initiated by the recognition of figurative language and its function in a biography. Furthermore, discourse in a biography is narrative and in that role assumes properties other than that of recording events. No biographer merely records a life; every biographer, no matter how objective he declares himself, interprets a life. In a 1978 manifesto on biography, Edel wrote that 'how a life has expressed itself is the real subject of the biographer'.[6] This statement is only partially true because it neglects the element of form and the way the reader/critic experiences the life of the subject. Perhaps Edel's statement could be rewritten more exactly to read 'how the biographer expresses the life becomes the real subject of the biography'.

When a biographer becomes conscious of language, conscious of how it alters what he describes from a factual representation to an independent verbal object, he transforms his craft into an art. His text moves 'toward a condition where . . . the words appear to become the object, so that they cannot be replaced by other words than the ones used to convey the same experience'. But in this process, the biographer also becomes conscious of the sense of contradiction at the heart of language, of the difference between word and meaning and, as a consequence, his awareness of alternate linguistic modes increases. The issue is how well can language incarnate reality; how faithful can a biography be to the complexities of human experience? However, in alternating various tropological strategies through such literary means as metaphor, metonymy, synecdoche and irony, the biographer can mediate the difficulty of ever achieving a definitive, objective life-account. 'The process of fusing events', we should remember, 'whether imaginary or real, into a comprehensible totality capable of serving as the *object* of a representation is a poetic process.'[7] Those who accept language as a transparent medium of representation and believe that if they only use the right word for describing an event the meaning will be clear, illustrate an inadequate sense of the creative nature of language and its role in biography. Such empiricists, who place their faith in language for conveying fact, write biographies of maximum detail and minimal interpretation, believing the latter to be the function of some other form of composition. But the principal interest in biography, the reason for its popularity with authors as well as readers, remains its ability to provide meaning for an individual's life, transmitting personality and character through prose. It furthermore nourishes the author's sense of identity and vitality through the act of recreating the subject's life. The challenge of biography as a genre is how, given the tool of language on one hand and the data of a person's life on the other, the biographer can create a work of truth and pleasure.

Elemental to biography is the sense of coherence, deriving from ideas of order – either a factual pattern arranged along a chronological axis or an interpretative pattern based upon a sense of the inner life of the subject. Froude's life of Carlyle illustrates the first, Freud's life of Leonardo the second. The former, however, identifies truth with fact; the latter questions that relationship or at least investigates it. For the analytical biographer, facts do not speak for themselves. Biographers nonetheless represent fragments of the past as a whole, an articulated composition of a life in language with its demands of organization, syntax and grammar which we identify as biography. Contiguity sometimes comes into conflict with fact and the result is 'creative fact', an amalgam of narrative and meaning or the 'rigid passage of events and actions' united with 'the slow opening up of single and solemn moments of concentrated emotion and meaning'.[8] But the act of fusing events into a totality is a poetic process.

In the chronicle of events or unprocessed historical record, Hayden White has written, 'the facts exist only as congeries of contiguously related fragments. These fragments have to be put together to make a whole of a particular, not a general kind.' The process is artistic in order 'to display an ordered world, a cosmos, where only disorder or chaos might appear'. The problem for biography is that readers accept facts literally, although their presentation is always figurative – that is, readers misinterpret the artistic ideal of coherence for the historical ideal of objectivity. By contrast, the configuration of the facts for the biographer is always imaginative. The excitement and interest in composing (and reading, I would argue) a biography derives not so much from the facts themselves but from the form of their presentation. For the biographer, the issue is not what are the facts but, as White explains, 'how are the facts to be described in order to sanction one mode of explaining them rather than another?' Readers, however, prefer the reverse, believing that what they read is the only way to present the facts. Nonetheless, different lives of the same person exist because there are alternate ways of ordering facts so that events 'in the same set are capable of functioning differently in order to figure forth different *meanings* – moral, cognitive or aesthetic – within different fictional matrices'.[9] The result of these compositional forces is what I call 'authorized fictions', the alteration of facts into new forms which, despite their original or inventive presentation, do not lose their authenticity. Such transformations, caused by the pressures of language and the act of composition, alter the shape but not the legitimacy of fact.

The obsession of empirical biographers with comprehending *all* the facts soon becomes subsumed by the nature of the genre and the limitations of its form. No biography can contain, nor would we want it to, all the facts. But neither do we want the biography which says 'just when we thought to elucidate a secret that has puzzled historians for a hundred years, there was a hole in the manuscript big enough to put your finger through'. Biographies should exhibit, however, an awareness of language and its limitations as well as its choices. The recognition, as Carlyle noted, that 'a well-written life is as rare as a well-spent one' is the responsibility of the biographer as much as it is that of the reader.[10] The goal of the biographer who conceives of biography as literature is the creation of life through art; by so doing, the biographer enlarges the life of his subject as well as that of the genre.

The representation of facts, once the biographer has determined them, necessarily involves figurative language or tropes. But the distrust of figurative language in non-fictional prose and the preference for seeing biography as a positivist, empirical genre have limited our ability to understand the function of tropes and how they organize the biography, shaping the composition of the life. The power of objectivism as a social and moral force in society has determined the way biography has been understood and written as a literal account of the subject. But a close examination of biographies reveals their tropological character, underscoring their imaginative energy and creative dimension. The presentation of tropes furthermore reveals how truth is relative to understanding. The tropes are actually guides or signs to the reader of the biographer's process of understanding or interpretation of the life of his subject which in turn creates new meaning for the life while establishing the biography as an independent text. Different biographies of the same individual offer not only different interpretations but disparate tropes. But it is primarily through these tropes that we become aware of the presence of the biographer, regardless of his narrative voice. In a biography the tropes actualize the experience of the life of the subject for the biographer.

In *A Grammar of Motives* Kenneth Burke identified 'Four Master Tropes': metaphor, metonymy, synecdoche and irony; each has a role in biography. Metaphor emphasizes the unity between reason and imagination through representation; metonymy links contiguous events or facts in the life through condensation; synecdoche conveys their integration; irony expresses their distance or separation. In this fashion the supposed objectivity of biography assumes the properties of rhetorical as well as fictional paradigms. How we comprehend a written life, then, becomes a function of how we understand its language. The operation of the linguistic modes within a biography not only determines the type of biography composed but the way we respond to it as a literary rather than a documentary text. A trope cannot substitute for a life but it can become the means for expressing that life. The very process of writing a biography, forging facts into a narrative, reorders the life in creative ways measured by the presence and function of tropes. Language rather than fact organizes and structures a biography while figurative language or tropes establish the verbal or literary life of the text. Individual biographies, however, indicate the predominance of one type of trope over another, most often metaphor or metonymy. This is not to deny the presence of synecdoche or irony in biography but the recognition of metaphor and metonymy as the most discernible and repeated 'Master Tropes'. I turn first to metaphor.

In a biography, referential and figurative language interact as the biographer locates a pattern or image that develops metaphorical qualities to shape the life of the subject. Indeed, for the biographer the attempt to unify the life becomes a quest for metaphor which has a dual meaning: metaphor simultaneously acts as the guiding or controlling trope of the subject's life while also embodying or projecting the biographer's conception of that life. The metaphor may either be self-generating, originating out of the life-materials, or imposed by the author from his own biases. Similarly, the language of a biography provides us with clues as to how the subject envisioned him- or herself. Metaphor is necessary for biography because it aids in expressing the structure of fictions promoted by the subject and allows the author to link his sense of the ideal or universal to the real and particular. Metaphor provides internal unity for the life of the subject and external unity for the author trying to fashion a text. The biographer locates coherence *in* the life and in the writing *of* the life through metaphor.

In his essay 'The Theory of Biography' Park Honan reaffirms the emphasis on the narrative or literary dimension of biography, which advances but does not damage the factuality of life.[11] Stressing the importance of understanding expressivist anthropology, which argues that written expression acts to clarify the author's self, Honan identifies a structure of time represented by a linear, diachronic plane in biography and a structure of feeling represented by a non-linear synchronic plane. He then cogently illuminates the qualities of those successful biographies that make them vital forms of literary writing. Most importantly, he stresses that narrative tactics on the part of the biographer do not compromise the accuracy or authority of the life of the subject.

Furthermore, Honan identifies the essential component of expressivist biography as language.

The responsibility of the biographer, in order to achieve what Honan calls the 'present-ness' or 'sense of experience-in-events', is to exploit the potentialities of style. This must be done to convey what is the essential function of any biographer: 'to keep the emotional, intellectual, and moral relationship with the biographee in focus' (p. 115). The synchronic narrative expressed through stylistic variety relieves the literalness of the life, providing interest and pleasure for the reader and the writer. The danger for the post-1700 biographer, however, is the massive weight of evidence, what Honan calls 'naming'. The biographer's and reader's escape from this burden is through the presence of a narrative persona and, more crucially, style. This is most pointedly registered through metaphor which enhances and enlarges the 'inner structure of feeling' in a biography. Metaphor prevents biography from being pushed into an account in the past tense of one person's life, thus removing it from the present-ness of the reader and biographer. The importance of metaphor is, then, as an element of style which permits the shifting of language in the biography from 'naming' with its emphasis on facts, documents and chronology, to the abstract idea of 'relationship' based on interpretation and analysis. Essential for understanding the biographer's perception of his subject is the recognition and analysis of his metaphor and its use or misuse in the life.

In his masterful study of metaphor, Paul Ricoeur provides further material for the understanding of the function of metaphor in biography. Summarizing the accepted view that metaphor is displacement, 'a trope of resemblance', Ricoeur goes on to argue that a metaphor is the rhetorical process by which 'discourse unleashes the power that certain fictions have to redescribe reality'.[12] Metaphor reorganizes the reader's and the writer's perception of things, transposing elements from diverse and often contrasting fields of experience and meaning (p. 236). Metaphor is both representative and descriptive and in a text acts to redefine or redescribe the world. The place of metaphor is the intersection between Honan's synchronic and diachronic axis of narrative; it combines the two, providing the moment when 'naming' becomes interpretation and the past becomes the present. Ricoeur supplies biography with a theoretical foundation and compliments the argument of Honan when he explains that '*expression* is the name of a metaphorical possession of the representational order' (p. 237).

From his earliest considerations of biography, Lytton Strachey understood the value of metaphor. This may have originated in his early interest in poetry, especially Shakespeare and Milton, as well as in the prose of Gibbon and Macaulay. The French provided other models, notably Fontenelle and Condorcet both of whom Strachey cites in the Preface to *Eminent Victorians*. Whatever the source, Strachey continuously sought the clearest and most direct metaphors for his subjects: 'let us have the pure essentials – a vivid image, on a page or two, without explanations, transitions, commentaries or padding', he declared in his essay on John Aubrey.[13] Metaphor became the major stylistic embodiment of 'the pure essentials', compressing opposite characteristics of his subjects into single figures of speech. With his emphasis on the relation rather than the accumulation of details, Strachey naturally found metaphor congenial because it permitted the vividness, richness of meaning and feeling discursive prose generally denied and facilitated the unity and harmony so necessary for the aesthetic telling of a life.

The opening paragraph of *Eminent Victorians* initiates the military metaphors that dominate the work. Describing the 'subtler strategy', Strachey outlines the action of the new biographer who will 'attack his subject in unexpected places . . . fall upon the flank, or the rear . . . [and] shoot a sudden, revealing searchlight into obscure recesses'. Following his own orders, Strachey then manoeuvres a series of battle metaphors to express the sense of attack, pursuit and combat that fittingly summarize the aggressive manner of his biography. The military metaphors in the text in fact shift from battle (Manning and Newman) to administration (Nightingale, Arnold), to, finally, defeat (Gordon). That Strachey chose a military metaphor as the essential one for the book establishes the work's quite essential Victorianism. For, as Michael Timko has argued, the central cultural symbol of the Victorian period was 'engagement, in both the sense of battle and quest'.[14]

Animal metaphors compose the second major group of metaphors in *Eminent Victorians* and they, too, support another aspect of the work that makes it more a condensation rather than exposé of Victorian ideas. Timko again explains: 'the consistent use of bestial imagery serves to emphasize the awareness of the

Victorians of the need to find irrefutable evidence to prove the humanity . . . of human beings' (p. 615). In response to Darwin's work, which seemed to jeopardize their fundamental humanity, the Victorians desperately sought to define their humanness in the face of 'a demonstrated participation in the bestial nature', an endeavour which was complicated by questions concerning man's ability to know things about himself and his world (p. 615). In his adoption of the various bestial images that appear in *Eminent Victorians*, Strachey displays the essentially Victorian character of his work in terms of its verbal texture and patterns of imagery.

Military metaphors, however, control the book, from the opening paragraph on Cardinal Manning to the final dramatic details of the death of General Gordon where the military metaphors collapse, only to be superseded by ironic images of imperialist success.

The cause of Strachey's fascination and involvement with military metaphors is complex. It is clearly an extension of the Victorian sense of engagement but it is also a reflection of the very war taking place at the time Strachey wrote *Eminent Victorians*. As early as 1908 Strachey began to find battle imagery attractive, especially to express the conflict between the educated and the philistines. France was a model to him of civilization; the correspondence of Voltaire and D'Alembert a catalyst. What Michael Holroyd calls the spirit of 'revolutionary ferment' grew until it culminated in the aggressive attitude and, I would add, language of *Eminent Victorians*. Social and financial freedom from his family coincided for Strachey with the war and confirmed his ability to sustain a radical spirit symbolized by his break with the *Spectator*.[15] His pacificism during the First World War did not prevent him from metaphorically employing the images of war to mark his, and the age's, independence from the preceding generation of Stracheys.

Supplementing the military metaphors in *Eminent Victorians* are those drawn from animals which mix the bestial with the natural. Birds are particularly favoured: Manning is an eagle, Newman a dove; Nightingale 'hatches' as a swan, becomes an eagle and is finally transformed into a tigress; Gordon is a hawk. Later, cranes and turkey-cocks embody aspects of Gordon's character and he is said to resemble an exotic bird as he peers northward through his telescope on the fortress roof at Khartoum. Ironically, he becomes the grim attraction for the very hawks he admired when the

Mahdi orders his head to be displayed between two tree branches on a public highway after his murder. Other animal metaphors in the biography include a bison (Lord Panmure), a stag (Sidney Herbert), a terrier (Dr Hall) and one particularly pathetic image, 'a thoroughbred harnessed to a four-wheeled cab' (Newman [p. 79]).

An additional, implied metaphor Strachey employs might be identified as 'Titanic'. The Fates, Chaos, Demi-Gods and Prophets are all found in the text as metaphors of the 'Titanic' forces Strachey promotes around his subjects to enhance their stature before he undermines them with irony. Manning's ambition struggles with and then defeats the Fates (pp. 3, 7, 57–8); Florence Nightingale brings a semi-Miltonic power to the disorder at Scutari. Possessed by a 'demon', she has a 'visionary plan' as she confronts the Hell at Scutari but gradually 'the reign of chaos and old night began to dwindle' (p. 144). Arnold reigns like an Old Testament prophet who 'involved in awful grandeur, ruled remotely . . . from an inaccessible heaven' (p. 204). General Gordon's life acquires classical references: it is a 'tragic history' governed by Fate and Fortune, although he possesses a certain divine aura: 'walking at the head of his troops, with nothing but a light cane in his hand, he seemed to pass through every danger with the scatheless equanimity of a demi-God' (pp. 234, 240–1).

Collectively, these metaphors, with their emphasis on grand and epical adventures, develop into a pattern that the subtext – the ironical tone and witty exposé of weaknesses, prejudices and inadequacies – undermines. This contrasting duality of meaning and metaphor in the work extends the formal operation of metaphor, which is to link the similar with the dissimilar, as well as join the referential with the expressive. By subtly dismantling the Titanic metaphors, Strachey displays the meaning of the lives he narrates and identifies the thematic nature of his work. *Eminent Victorians*, then, not only uses metaphor to express its possibilities but analyses metaphor to show its limitations.

There is also, however, a personal dimension to the use of metaphor in the book. While it operates stylistically to unite the public and private selves of his subjects, metaphor also joins the divisions of self within Strachey's own character. His personal conflicts over sexual issues ('what pity one can't now and then change sexes!', he once wrote to Clive Bell), and social behaviour (his outward shyness and diffidence was at odds with his growing self-confidence) found resolution through his use of metaphor. The military metaphors expressed his sense of independence and resistance, the animal, his determination to assert his own liberal humanism and the Titanic, his growing sense of self-assurance as both a writer and individual.[16]

Within *Eminent Victorians* there are other devices, of course, that sustain and contribute to the sense of unity such as shifts in narrative technique, the mixture of times and the conflation of sources. But metaphor, most clearly and consistently, infuses the language of the biography with the experience of unity in diversity. On the social scale, for example, the divisions in such Victorian institutions as the church, public health, education and the military that Strachey confronts are resolved most confidently and completely in the text through metaphor (see p. 201 for an example of these paradoxes). Furthermore, Strachey structurally extends such dualities through his use of foils for his major characters. Cardinal Manning has Newman; Florence Night-ingale, Lord Panmure; Thomas Arnold, W. G. Ward; General Gordon, Sir Evelyn Baring. Metaphor, however, links these opposite individuals in the book, providing a stylistic key to the thematic and social divisions of Victorian life.

In June 1918, one month after *Eminent Victorians* appeared, Strachey published a little-known essay on the war in Leonard Woolf's periodical, *War and Peace*. Entitled 'Traps and Peace Traps', the essay criticized the harsh interpretation given to the German peace proposals and contained a concise analysis of metaphor. Noting the danger implicit in metaphors, Strachey also admitted their attraction. Some are 'magical' and are the very substance of poetry, but others are pernicious traps used by journalists 'under a guise of brevity and vigor' to 'confuse'.[17] The critical reader must be alerted to the danger and deceit of these subversive metaphors. But Strachey did not diminish his use of metaphor in his later writing; he continued to use it whenever it would enhance, dramatically and imaginatively, his work, recog-nizing and exploiting its power to illuminate rather than to 'confuse'. In *Queen Victoria* a small crystal pebble functions as the metaphor for the Queen, while a serpent acts as the metaphor for Bacon in *Elizabeth and Essex*.

In metaphor Strachey found a way to combine copiousness of meaning with brevity of style. The effect of an arresting image replacing a tedious detail was not lost on his prose. In his biographical writing, metaphor functioned as a textual trope of compression and a personal trope of expression. Through its objectivity impartiality was present; through its originality imagination overshadowed history; through its stylistic variety fictions emerged from the restrictions of discourse. The result was the fashioning of biography into art. A prelude to that development and a postscript to this discussion is George Eliot's remark that 'all of us, grave or light, get our thoughts entangled in metaphors and act fatally on the strength of them'.[18]

Anticipating Strachey, however, James Boswell earlier relied on metaphor as a form of structuring and unifying biography. In his *Life of Johnson* (1791) metaphor organizes, represents and projects the life, although in ways less overt and less constant than later biographers. More inconsistent in their application, because of the greater variety of material, metaphors nonetheless perform a similar function of unifying and interpreting Johnson and Boswell in the text. Indeed, as Boswell dematerializes for long periods in the work, letting conversations, diary passages, historical documents or letters speak, metaphor, along with the narrator, remains the only consistent literary means of unifying the work. In the face of the discontinuity of the *Life*, metaphor remains a vital source of its harmony.

In the Introduction to the *Life* Boswell initiates the visual metaphor of painting (repeated in volume III) which justifies his presentation of Johnson's limitations. 'In every picture', he writes, 'there should be shade as well as light, and when I delineate him without reserve, I do what he himself recommended, both by his precept and his example.' Later references to the painting metaphor include a passage immediately following the concentrated summary of Johnson's idiosyncracies (where we are told that concluding a vociferous dispute he often 'used to blow out his breath like a Whale'! [June 1764]) and the use of Flemish painting to justify 'the minute particulars' he provides of his subject (22 September 1777).[19] But the major unifying metaphor of the *Life* which informs its contents is that of a monument.

Referring to the biography as 'My Great Biographical Monument', Boswell repeatedly identifies his work as 'an Egyptian Pyramid in which there will be a complete mummy of Johnson that Literary Monarch'. The metaphor for the biography is a monument; for Johnson, a monarch. In the advertisement to the first edition Boswell comments that the result of the zealous aid of many is '*an honourable monument to his* [Johnson's] *memory*'. The consistent use of the monarch metaphor indicates the supremacy of Johnson for Boswell and the famous interview between Johnson and George III displays the power of Johnson, not the King. Johnson is, in fact, in control and speaks to the ruler 'in his firm manly manner, with a sonorous voice, and never in that subdued tone which is commonly used at the levee and in the drawing room'. At the King's departure, it is Johnson who voices approval in the biography, not the King. The royal metaphor defines the nature of Boswell's admiration of Johnson, which is not based on the power of Johnson's mind for its own sake, but on its 'power to govern'.[20]

Boswell as a biographer is a kind of embalmer as he notes that his 'design in writing the Life of that Great and Good Man [is] to put as it were into a Mausoleum all of his precious remains that I can gather'. References to 'preservation' appear throughout the text, beginning with the introductory section where Boswell writes that 'had his other friends been as diligent and ardent as I was, he [Johnson] might have been almost entirely preserved. As it is, I will venture to say that he will be seen in this work more completely than any man who has ever yet lived.' Additional metaphors that figure importantly in the life include 'the spectator', one who looks on and observes. Even in writing about the life, Boswell could not prevent himself from describing it metaphorically. To a friend he wrote in 1786 that the *Life* 'of [his] revered Friend will be the richest piece of Biography that has ever appeared. The Bullion will be immense, whatever defects there may be in the workmanship.'[21]

'The greatest thing by far is to be a master of metaphor', wrote Aristotle and this seems to be especially true for biographers. Faced with the debilitating, sometimes overwhelming collection of data that record a person's life, the biographer must select, summarize and create the personality of his subject. This is most often and most effectively performed through the use of metaphor which, according to Ricoeur, functions 'to instruct by suddenly combining elements that have not been put together before'. Through metaphor, reality achieves fictional presence, prose becomes poetic. Metaphor suspends but also extends literal references and what it achieves for the biographer is expression – 'the name of a metaphorical possession of the representational order'.[22] The fictional and representational meet through metaphor. Consequently, biography becomes an enlarged trope of resemblance which provides a structure and method to identify the character of the subject while simultaneously projecting the assumptions of the biographer. Metaphor also synthesizes the facts of a life into an interpretative form and mediates artistically between the narrator and his subject to allow aesthetic distance. For readers, the appeal of biography is more than curiosity; it is, rather, the discovery and identity of metaphor which is the recognition of universal aspects of human behaviour through the particular actions of an individual life. Metaphor teaches us how the literal can provide us with some formerly undiscoverable insight about the figurative and how the synchronic can merge with the diachronic, for metaphor also breaks down divisions of time.

In biography, metaphor, an act of substitution and creation, functions to organize the text, releasing it from the literal and the 'naming' aspect, unifying the character of the subject while expressing the style of the biographer. Metaphor acts as a verbal and rhetorical intermediary between the life of the subject, its presentation in language and its understanding by the reader. Metaphor pleasurably contradicts what Bernard in *The Waves* calls 'the biographic style' which 'tack[s] together torn bits of stuff, stuff with raw edges'.[23] While expressing the disjunctive nature of the comprehensive or chronological biography, the metaphoric verb Bernard uses undermines the very objection he presents. Through its act of resemblance, metaphor evaluates a life in imaginative ways for reader, biographer and even subject. And through its articulation in the text, metaphor reassembles the life of the subject while synthesizing the art of the biographer.

But metaphor alone does not rule biography; it competes with metonymy, an agency of condensation which allows one entity to stand for another. Since a biography can never be a complete record, the biographer must rely on metonymic means to render the life of the subject. Or, to reverse the order, metonymy makes the tasks of the biographer, selectivity and synthesis, possible. Metonymy furthermore permits the substitution of signifiers between which there is a relation of contiguity rather than similarity. Displacement from one signifier to another is a primary feature of metonymy and closer to what Jacques Lacan calls 'the idea of that veering off of meaning that we see in metonymy'. This reduction, however, enhances rather than diminishes meaning. Another quality of metonymy is its promotion of realism, an idea first asserted by Roman Jakobson. 'Following the path of contiguous relationships', he explains, 'the realistic author metonymically digresses from the plot to the atmosphere and from the characters to the setting in space and time.'[24] Metonymy relies on the recognition of contiguity, a process repeatedly enacted in biography and expressed in the text through syntagmatic relations which metonymy unites.

Jakobson's suggestion of a link between realism and metonymy explains many of the attributes of biography which establish environment, place or period in the text. Through the application of metonymy, a biographer manages to create a sense of reality and understanding of character essential for the authenticity of the narrated life. Through their linking of discontinuous moments, facts or details, metonyms establish the realism of biography. A classic example of this procedure is Boswell's first meeting with Dr Johnson. In his *London Journal* of 16 May 1763, Boswell is laconic, reportorial and descriptive. He responds unfavourably to Johnson's appearance and behaviour: 'his dogmatical roughness of manners is disagreeable', he writes. But in the *Life of Johnson*, Boswell continually digresses from the figure of Johnson to suggest the setting, atmosphere and nature of their first meeting. He creates a scene rather than reports an event and, in Jakobson's words, follows 'the path of contiguous relationships' as in his allusion to Horatio when recounting the way Mr Davies announces Johnson's arrival or the lengthy account of Reynold's portrait of Johnson 'sitting in his easy chair in deep meditation' now happily owned by Boswell and the source of the engraving of Johnson accompanying the *Life*. By their convergence, these metonyms contribute to the overall presentation of Johnson analogous to the many perspectives Boswell hopes to present of his subject in the work. In the *Life*, metonymic devices dominate Boswell's narrative of 'every minute particular, which can throw light on the progress of his [Johnson's] mind'.[25]

Metonymy functions through the *Life of Johnson* organizing and structuring the reality of its subject. The conversations that comprise so much of the biography are themselves metonymic. From their exhibition of Johnson in his various attitudes and opinions, the reader pieces together the whole of his character and personality. That Boswell was conscious of this contiguity within the text is marked by his disappointment that Johnson's conversation could not be completely preserved 'as musick is written . . . transmitted to posterity *in score*' (II: 327). Boswell recognizes his own and Johnson's reliance on metonymy as he records Johnson's habit of shortening names and condensing them to nicknames for his friends. Beauclerk becomes 'Beau', Boswell, 'Bozzy', Sheridan, 'Sherry' (II: 258). In Boswell's *Life*, metonymy becomes the rhetorical equivalent of what William C. Dowling describes as the narrative absence of Johnson and comes closer, I think, to identifying the literary principle Boswell relied on most constantly.[26]

Metonymy does not remain, of course, the exclusive purview of Boswell. Among a variety of contemporary biographers it has a dominant role in their rhetorical strategies of recounting a life. A recent example is *E. M. Forster, A Life* by P. N. Furbank, a colleague and friend of the subject. A full and candid account of a writer who virtually renounced fiction after 1924, the life is nonetheless told in a non-dramatic, almost documentary style, conveying the troubled and at times confused life of a timid, semi-reclusive author who for nearly twenty-five years remained a resident of King's College, Cambridge. The longstanding homosexuality of Forster appears in Furbank's pages not as a scandalous or vulgar subject but as a genuine and deeply-felt element of Forster's character. But to render Forster and his circle – the biography is as much about English literary and university life as it is about Forster – Furbank relies not on highly charged metaphors but on metonymy. Describing Forster's Cambridge associate, for example, N. F. Barwell, Furbank turns to the metonymic expression of his attributes: 'Barwell, who just then was cutting a would-be Wildean figure about Cambridge, belonged to the "advanced" set, the Stracheyean set at Trinity. There was, at this time, a considerable difference between this set and the tea-drinking agnostics of King's . . .'[27]

Expanding his use of metonymy, Furbank titles volume II of the biography 'Polycrates' Ring' to evoke, by relation, the theme of the volume and the character of Forster. Essentially, this is the harm brought to Forster by his success (see II: 131–3, 279). Further metonyms include Forster as a father figure (II: 137 ff.) and as friend. This latter subject, in fact, becomes the controlling interpretative strand throughout the life, a metonymy for Forster's belief that 'the true history of the human race was the history of human affection' (II: 295). But, as Furbank emphasizes, Forster was not 'encased in Edwardian courtesy and could play the fool', relying again on metonymy (II: 295). In the final chapter of the biography, 'E. M. Forster Described', the innovative personal account by Furbank represents Forster almost entirely by metonyms. His mouth, gestures and speech are contiguously presented although unified through the trope of metonymy.

In this concluding chapter, Furbank summarizes, explaining that 'to a rather special degree, he [Forster] lived the imaginative life' and that on occasion Forster felt 'he could see through to "life": could hear its wing-beat, could grasp it not just as a generality but as a palpable presence' (II: 297). The reader, too, is able to do this in the biography through the operation of metonymy which allows him 'to conceptualize one thing by means of its relation to something else'.[28] Forster himself employs this device when he remarks to Furbank at the noise created by the accidental dropping of several coins on the floor of a hotel room they share. 'When they begin to sing', he comments, 'it's all over with them' (II: 297). Through his systematic reliance on metonymy, Furbank succeeds in conveying a reasoned, disciplined life of Forster, transmitting order and understanding while establishing a sympathetic and truthful sense of the man, rather than a sensational or sentimental portrait of a lost figure.

Tropes alone, however, cannot constitute a poetics of biography. A means for conveying them consistent with their function must exist which is found in narration, the prism through which the life is refracted. An early biographer of Edmund Burke recognized this when he wrote 'no one individual can know *all* the facts which may form the materials of an entertaining and useful life. *Variety of narratives*, if authentic, impartial and not trivial, will tend to the great ends of biography.'[29] Biography is, for Robert Bisset, not only fundamentally a narrative art but one of varying possibilities. Preeminently a narrative art, biography is part of a long tradition of narrative forms in prose writing originating in history and commemorative expression. Limited by fact, the biographer can still invent, shaping his reader's impressions, images and understanding of his subject through the narrative.

A helpful conceptual frame for the narrative distinctions that exist in biography is found in the division between narratives of contiguity and narratives of substitutions proposed by the French structuralist, Tzvetan Todorov. Narratives of contiguity emphasize the doing or performance of events, organized in chronological order. Sequence, temporality and causal logic shape the life which becomes the text. Narratives of substitutions accord meaning to events through repeated analysis of material presented at the beginning of the work or assumed to be understood by the reader – such as, George Eliot was a major novelist of the Victorian period whose private life involved conflict and disappointment as well as success and popularity. Narratives of substitutions structure themselves in cyclical ways with the narrative frequently turning back on itself. They concentrate on passage or transformation rather than on established states or conditions. The narrative of contiguity is linear and horizontal with history its major metaphor; the narrative of substitutions is vertical and circular with myth its major metaphor.[30]

The biographer's concern with design and presentation involves continuous narrative decisions, and often several narrative techniques appear in a single biography as in Harold Nicolson's *Byron: The Last Journey* or A. J. A. Symons's *The Quest for Corvo*. Narration also maintains point of view in biography which for the biographer is both a privilege and a responsibility. As the former, it provides freedom to create the story and shape the presentation of facts in an absorbing manner, establishing a pattern of significance. As the latter, the narration must be accurate, reliable and correct. The combination of the two should achieve the aim of a truthful portrait of the subject. Leon Edel summarized the problem in an essay entitled 'Biography and The Narrator' when he wrote 'the supreme fact [is] the modern biographer's constant struggle . . . against the irrelevant . . . The art of biography resides precisely in an arrangement of factual material so that truth is enhanced.'[31] Relationships or the 'arrangement' of such material define both the nature of the biography and the life of the subject.

Three types of biographical narrators appear to dominate the form, defined largely by their relation to the story and method of discourse. They have no historical order nor attachment and coexist at similar periods. They can be identified as the dramatic/ expressive, the objective/academic and the interpretative/analytic. The first emphasizes participation, the second detachment and the third analysis. Boswell represents the first, Lockhart the second and Strachey the third, or, among modern biographers,

A. J. A. Symonds, Leslie Marchand and Walter Jackson Bate. A presence in the narrative characterizes the dramatic narrator, either in terms of symbolic or actual presence through his role as a character (Gaskell) or commentator (Johnson in 'Life of Savage'). A specialized acquaintance with the subject also characterizes the dramatic narrative reflected in a unique relationship of the hero to the biographer which he frequently develops for dramatic effect.

In contrast, the objective narrator strives to eliminate himself from the presentation of the life, removing any sense of involvement because of historical distance or scholarly ideals. There is frequently, in such biographies, an announced absence of any thesis, as Leslie Marchand declares at the opening of his three-volume life of Byron, or Carlos Baker at the opening of *Hemingway*. The nineteenth-century 'Life and Letters' form initiated this approach with the narrator providing only discreet links between letters or records; the subject speaks best for himself, although some, like Mrs Gaskell, found commentary essential and provided interpretation of the material and life. A dual narrative often resulted, with the detached biographer placed against the autobiographical voice of the subject expressed through the documents. The scholarly biographies of the present century extended this method, allowing the amassed documents to replace the biographer in some cases, represented in the extreme by Edward H. Nehls's *D. H. Lawrence, A Documentary Life*. Such lives maintain an ideological faith in the primacy of fact and record, and a blindness to the shaping force of the biographer's presence through language, point of view and, of course, narration.

Interpretative narrators are not present in biography as characters but as commentators, playing the role of guide, establishing the meaning of the material for the reader. They are Virgils to the reader's Dante, doing, in a sense, the reader's job by analysing, judging or even rejecting data in comments which often present a well-defined thesis. They may also be advocates pressing for the prosecution or defence of their subjects, as Richard Aldington does in his life of D. H. Lawrence or T. S. Matthews in his defence of T. S. Eliot. The interpretative narrator is simultaneously the most difficult to sustain and the most absorbing to read. Walter Jackson Bate's life of Samuel Johnson, with his strong moral and psychological interpretation, or C. David Heymann's *Ezra Pound: The Last Rower* are examples.

Associated with narrative technique is the treatment of time, something shaped by the subject as well as the narrator. In biography one must always be conscious of how the content of a life may contribute to the nature of the narrative as much as the shaping power of biographer. No one biography is a pure example of a single narrative technique but individual biographies exhibit conscious narrative modes and emphases as the following will illustrate.

The dramatized or expressive narrator favours the first person, the objective narrator the omniscient voice and the interpretative narrator a limited voice. This immediately causes problems of reliability, involvement and understanding for each type. If the narrator is also a figure in the biography, how reliable is he in telling the truth? How does his participation shape the story? It is one thing to be present as Boswell is when he meets Dr Johnson in Thomas Davies's bookshop and quite another to read the account in his *Journal*. The dramatic narrator personalizes the biography and involves the reader, although sometimes at the expense of accuracy. His involvement creates a subjective element that sometimes affects the accuracy of presentation. Indeed, as William C. Dowling has shown, Boswell must turn to certain narrative solutions to maintain the 'illusion of accuracy', the most important the maintenance of a narrative naivete.[32] The majority of dramatized, participatory narrators are also naive and, in the course of their telling, progress from innocence to experience, from ignorance to knowledge of their subject. This traditional narrative paradigm links the biography with the picaresque archetype or the *bildungsroman* in fiction. The development of the narrator, in fact, becomes a secondary plot in the biography, equal in importance to what we are told about the subject. Ignorance, as Strachey noted in his Preface to *Eminent Victorians*, is not only 'the first requisite of the historian' but 'simplifies and clarifies . . . selects and omits, with a placid perfection unattainable by the highest art' (p. v).

The objective or detached narrator is omniscient and distances himself from the reader; fact, documentation and record separate the teller from the tale, depersonalizing the biography. This necessitates the omniscient form to sustain the illusion of a controlling order in an objective world. Research replaces experience and the result is usually a dull but accurate account, a reference book rather than a life-story. The interpretative narrator, however, respects the need for objectivity but also meaning, and intervenes at unexpected moments when he needs or senses that the reader requires an analysis of the life. Of crucial importance, however, is the recognition of a persistent narrative presence in biography, even when the narrative is discontinuous, broken up by excerpts from non-primary sources, or disrupted by digressions on historical or cultural events. Long scenes cast in dramatic dialogue, if the biographer chooses to reproduce or recreate conversation, or footnotes in the text further distract the reader. But the narrative stance determines the angle of vision through which the reader perceives the subject's life or, in different terms, maintains a narrative contract which exists throughout the work. This may be realistic if it is objective, ironic if interpretative or romantic if dramatic. Any narrative contract, however, goes beyond the referential and thematic to assist readers in composing a pattern meaning.[33]

But biographical narratives do not exist in self-enclosed worlds, excluding other approaches or forms of expression. There are frequently several narrative styles existing in one work as in Michael Holroyd's *Lytton Strachey* or Richard Ellmann's *James Joyce*. These critical biographies combine the detached, objective style with the interpretative, creating a biography that is both factual and critical. They often achieve this combination by separating the critical and the personal, avoiding the blend that Bate achieves. Both Holroyd and Ellmann deemphasize the continuous role of the interpretative narrator, preferring the clarity of alternating but clearly defined narrative voices. Ellmann's widely praised *Joyce* is particularly instructive.[34]

Following a defensive introduction which argues that we are still trying to understand Joyce, that we must see the events in his life as sources of his art, and that Joyce stands at the centre of modern life, Ellmann begins with a factual account of the Joyce family. Yet, it is the writings of Joyce that attract Ellmann to the life and shape the entire biography. The reliance on dates as chapter headings, interrupted only when literary criticism is announced, such as 'xxii. The Backgrounds of *Ulysses*', highlights Ellmann's primary attraction to Joyce's work. For all its basis in fact, the biography is written from the novels outward towards the life. Each chapter contains an epigram from a Joyce text and even the opening sentence of Chapter i begins with reference to Stephen Dedalus. Throughout the work, literary references are drawn into the narrative or, rather, the reverse seems to operate: literary works narrate life. Consequently, Ellmann restrains his interpretation of the life of Joyce, giving greater emphasis to a critical reading of his literary work (cf. pp. 48 and 55 or pp. 208–9 with 215–18, or p. 317). A good example of this pull to the literary rather than to the personal is the summing up of the first stage of Joyce's exile. It was, says Ellmann,

> the most bitter [and] had ended in Rome, when he succumbed to a mood of tenderness in planning 'the Dead.' It had been followed by three visits home. Now Ireland was visitable only in imagination. Joyce did not return, but he sent his characters back, and shared vicariously their presence in the Dublin scene as well as their partial estrangement from it. (p. 349)

The focus shifts back and forth from the personal to the literary, and quite naturally, it is the imaginary visitations of Joyce that will command the attention of the biographer for the remainder of the life. Nonetheless, Ellmann sustains a coexistent, although not balanced nor detached, interpretative narrative throughout the biography, creating a record, portrait and analysis of Joyce's work and life. He displays, in fact, the will-power of the biographer and a commitment to detachment in his resistance to dramatize or even enhance such events as the meeting of Joyce and Proust. The record, in its varying forms, is allowed to speak for itself. However, when he describes the descent of Joyce's coffin into the earth, Ellmann cannot resist retelling a pun at the expense of a deaf witness at the funeral who is told, in answer to the question who is it they are burying, 'Herr Joyce' (cf. pp. 523–4 with p. 755).

The narrative of a biography should no more be limited to a single style than a novelist to a single technique. As the subject changes, matures or alters, the biographer should be permitted the same freedom to shift his method. In the more experimental and adventurous biographies, shifting narrative voices coordinated with the changing focus of the story occur freely. In extreme situations, however, this can lead to confusion and misinterpretation as Sybille Bedford demonstrates. *Aldous Huxley* by Sybille Bedford is a two-volume life which begins with a disclaimer that the biographer undertook her task as a labour of love and in the 'spirit of detachment'. Yet, in the Preface she notes her forty-year friendship with Huxley, which has an unavoidable impact on the life, including her method of quotation: 'I have freely extracted, eliminated, juxtaposed, conflated as best suited my immediate purpose', she declares.[35] She has furthermore supplemented printed sources with conversations and private correspondence. The result is a documentary hodgepodge and narrative vortex. Chapters 1 to 3 of volume I employ a detached narrator but Chapter 4 unexpectedly veers to a dramatized, expressive voice who skips from the present to the past using an awkwardly identified 'we' (pp. 18–19). Clarifying parentheses interrupt the dramatic narrative, further undermining the new tone. In a section on Eton the narrator again becomes detached, although the tense shifts from a dramatic present to an expectant future. Soon, an interpretative voice appears, as in Chapter 4, part II with a comment on second marriages (p. 37) and, as the annoyingly short chapters from two to six pages in length proceed, the reader becomes increasingly disoriented.

The sudden appearance of the author as character in both the past and the present further confuses the narrative stability of the biography. She is an omniscient voice, first-person adolescent figure called 'Sybille' and a correspondent identified as 'S.B.'. The result is a discontinuous biographical narrative reflected in an erratic style that leaves the reader with no consistent means to construct or evaluate the life of the subject. A consequence is the lack of belief in, or identity of, the biographical narrator. As the narrative contract breaks, confusion overtakes the life. Time becomes a curious amalgam of past and present when the narrator interrupts, for example, to ask 'if for once I may be allowed to intrude what was then the future, the better to conjure up the past' (II: 250). The puzzling biography appears to advance the life of the narrator more than that of the subject.[36]

However, certain biographies turn these confusions into advantages. The very duty of a biographer, Bernard Crick has argued, is 'to show how he reaches his conclusions, not to pretend to omniscience; and he should share things that are moot, problematic and uncertain with the reader'. Crick and others also believe we need 'to present conflicts in evidence' and not falsely resolve them.[37] In this fashion, honesty towards the subject and the biography will be preserved and the artifice of a pattern or false coherence will be eliminated. Yet, the desire to establish a pattern and get inside the character is a powerful attraction for biography which leads to a third consideration in a proposed theory: myth.

Myth probably recurs with greater frequency than any other term in the discussion of biographical theory. For some critics, it identifies the primary job of the biographer as Leon Edel declares when he announces that the function of a biographer is no less than to discover the 'life-myth' of his subject. This process means being able to analyse psychological as well as historical evidence, the patterns that give life its shape. Phyllis Rose in her biography of Virginia Woolf echoes Edel, stating that the task of literary biography is to explore the personal mythology of the subject.

More than 100 years earlier, Arthur Stanley anticipated the concern with myth in his life of Thomas Arnold. In his Preface, Stanley wrote that there 'always exists in the case of any remarkable man' a conflict between

> the image of his inner life, as it was known to those nearest and dearest to him, and the outward image of a written biography, which can rarely be more than a faint shadow of what they cherish in their own recollections – the one representing what he was – the other only what he thought and did; the one formed in the atmosphere which he had himself created, – the other necessarily accommodating itself to the public opinion to which it is mainly addressed.

The division between public and private self separates myth and fact – but one always unites with the other. Yeats summarized the difficulty when he remarked that 'there is some one Myth for every man, which if we knew it, would make us understand all that he did and thought'.[38] Belief in this ideal, romantic as it might be, unites most twentieth-century biographers. However, the ambiguity of 'myth' is a handicap: on the one hand it suggests the essence of a person and on the other, the legend that person has created. For biography this is especially problematic because it finds itself with a dual activity, one assigned, the other assumed. The first is the desire to correct or revise the myth; the second is its own unconscious creation of new myths.

Biography is essentially a demythologizing form. Consistently, it functions to correct, restate or reinterpret false or distorted accounts of the subject. Boswell writes his *Life of Johnson* partly to correct the mistaken impression given by Hawkins and other biographers; Mrs Gaskell begins her life of Charlotte Brontë to counter the erroneous journalistic lives that maligned her subject; Carlyle writes his life of Sterling to counteract Archdeacon Hare's

biased view; Strachey revises the lives of his representative
Victorians to expose their shortcomings. As early as 1666 the
corrective impulse of biography was articulated. In his introduction to his life of Hooker, Izaak Walton explained

> I think it necessary to inform my Reader that Doctor Gauden
> (the late Bishop of Worcester) hath also lately wrote and
> publisht the life of Master Hooker; and though this be not writ
> by design to oppose what he hath truly written; yet, I am put
> upon a necessity to say, That in it there be many Material
> Mistakes, and more Omissions. I conceive some of his Mistakes
> did proceed from a Belief in Master Thomas Fuller, who had
> too hastily published what he hath since most ingenuously
> retracted. And for the Bishop's Omissions, I suppose his most
> weighty Business and Want of Time, made him pass over many
> things without that due Examination, which my better Leisure,
> my Diligence, and my accidental Advantages, have made
> known unto me.

Time is the culprit, for if Doctor Gauden had more of it, the polite
Walton surmizes, his life of Hooker would have been more
accurate and exact. Sensitive both to his own advantages and
possible errors, Walton, in the next paragraph, announces that he
would happily revise his life 'if there shall appear any Material
Omission'.[39] This attention to the corrective element of biography
shapes the genre into a form of revision more aggressive than
defensive but perhaps more conservative than radical in both its
structure and style.

Modern biographers are equally if not more determined to
correct distorted pictures of their subjects, as Leslie Marchand
notes in his *Byron* or Bernard Crick in his *George Orwell* (see pp. xxii
or xxvii). The desire and need to correct arise from the realization
on the part of the biographer that he is unable and unwilling to
provide a definitive life of his subject. Because of historical, social
and ultimately stylistic restrictions and interferences, no biography can duplicate the life of its subject. Despite all claims to
authenticity and objectivity, we read a personal view of the
subject, not a documentary history. Those modern writers who
objected to their biographies being written – Orwell, Auden,
Eliot, preceded by Thackeray, Hardy and Kipling – understood
the impossibility of 'getting it right' and the likelihood of

distortion, misunderstanding and confusion in the ensuing life-narrative. Implicitly they, and more recently various contemporary biographers, realized the truth of Freud's remark to an early prospective biographer: 'Anyone who writes a biography is committed to lies, concealments, hypocrisy, flattery and even to hiding his own lack of understanding, for biographical truth does not exist, and if it did we could not use it.'[40] Faced with this warning, all biography can hope to do is reanimate its subject through patterns of tropes, narrative technique or form. Through fact and revision, biography strives to demythologize the individual but inevitably, this becomes an ironic effort, since readers replace old myths with new if they read biography uncritically.

Northrop Frye summarizes the situation from a literary perspective. As a writer attempts to be more artistic, he cannot help but become more mythic: 'Symmetry in any narrative, always means that historical content is being subordinated to mythical demands of design and form . . .'[41] Myth emerges out of the author's need and the reader's desire for wholeness and order. Irony emerges out of the tension between the impulse to correct in the biography at the same time it generates new myths about the subject. In part this results from the effort to establish coherence in the text from the life and the tendency by readers to understand the life as representative. Biography necessarily universalizes the more it individualizes as it reveals the common experiences of such conditions as triumph, love or failure.

Biography translates individual effort into mythic experience. The representational aspect of the life, a picturing of the experiences of a single man, become elements of a universal type. It is a movement from metonymy to metaphor in biography, the transfer of an individual life-struggle into a general condition. And in universalizing the narrative, drawing on archetypes and conventions, biography moves from the realm of history to that of myth. Edel's assertion that when the biographer can discern a life-myth he has found his 'story' is only half the account because it does not consider what new myths, to be revised, are born. The 'story' of a life consists of the union between the facts, their imaginative pattern and the linguistic means to present them which the biographer generates in his text. 'Practically all biography has to begin with legend', Justin Kaplan has remarked, but the responsibility of the biographer is to correct, dispute or revise it.[42] This ironically generates new myths despite the research and factual authority of the biography.

A work which in its extremes displays the myth-breaking and myth-making aspects of biography is Brigid Brophy's unusual *Prancing Novelist, A Defence of Fiction in the Form of A Critical Biography in Praise of Ronald Firbank*. This remarkable book combines elements I have been outlining with extraordinary flair and drama, overworking metaphors, emphasizing narrative disjunctions, excessively displaying the drive to correct. The peculiarities of presentation, with the narrator acting as observer and analyst, provide a continual process of intra-action as this paragraph illustrates:

> Harold Nicolson was in Spain (where his father was British Ambassador) in 1905. That was the year in which Firbank turned 19 (in January), went (in February) to stay in Madrid in order to learn Spanish, and became (in June) a precociously published (at his own expense) novelist (or at least novella-ist).[43]

Parentheses act as factual repositories of detail that dislodge the narrative continuity and tone, a habit developed to extreme in the biography. Belief in the narrator as a reliable voice becomes suspect as the erratic tone continues. For example, the narrator momentarily dramatizes herself to explain that 'Firbank's passion for fruit reads to me (even when I deliberately put aside the partisanship of my own vegetarianism) as a symptom of his being crypto-vegetarian' (p. 158). On the same point we are then told that Firbank's love for caviare and champagne does not invalidate his vegetarian instincts (p. 158).

But the issue of myth overrides almost all other concerns in the life. Firbank is himself the object of his own self-promotion, of a cult he fabricated as well as fashioned about himself. Brophy's task is to separate the myths from reality, a job she performs with avidity. Firbank's penchant for eating little – 'a single grape (for tea) and a single pea (for dinner)' – are contrasted to his prodigious appetite for fruit (p. 157). The *contre-temps* over the dedication to *Prince Zoubaroff* leads to the fact that in 1920 no Firbank cult had yet emerged. The belief of Evan Morgan that there had been such a cult in the 1920s is, writes Brophy, 'probably just an extra flight of the Firbank as cult-writer myth'. She then adds

It is, perhaps, a myth that seeks to justify the world's unjust neglect of Firbank by pretending that Firbank and some unnamed admirers of his work constitute a conspiracy to promote him by somehow unfair means. But the myth adds that the conspirators, though villainous in intention, were not clever enough to succeed; for a cult is not recognition. (p. 163)

It is indeed the myth of her hero that Brophy must contend with in the biography. Did Firbank actually invent Haiti for his fiction as he invented New York? Is he the originator of modern camp? Did he usually write in purple ink? Did he truly keep his books in closed cupboards at Oxford because the coloured bindings did not fit his decor? To answer these questions Brophy uses imaginative, energetic, unorthodox and unexpected means, clarifying how much Firbank actually originated myths like his own cult in advance of the fact and possibility (p. 372). Ironically, however, new myths such as his elegance and homosexuality originate (p. 184). The very appearance of the biography stimulated a new interest in Firbank and his work, creating new legends and tales. *Prancing Novelist*, with its multiple aims, defence of the novel, unusual presentation (at times parodying the biography, especially in its citations and use of sources) provides a remarkable example of the struggle of biography at the crossroads of form, at the threshold of new directions, pulled by the myth of its subject in one direction, and fact in another.

What unites and synthesizes biography, however, what equates its performance with the desires of its readers, is the belief that biography 'can deliver the essential person and that there is a core personality, the "real Me", which we will find if only we dig deep and long enough'.[44] Biographers and readers believe in this myth, the former often forcing their materials into artificial patterns to locate this coherence while the latter base their evaluations of biography on their ability to identify with the supposedly 'real Me' in the text. But what if the subject resists such a categorization? Does it invalidate the biography as a work of literature? Clearly not. In fact, there has recently been a call for a new, open form of biography precisely to record the multiplicity of selves we all possess. The idea of a single, coherent personality in a biography denies the many selves that we are, as Virginia Woolf dramatized in *Orlando*.

The desire of biography to deliver an enclosed self is actually a myth about biography that must be dispelled. Biography, as James Clifford has suggested, is 'probably less often true to the way life is than to the way we might like it to be'.[45] The illusion of unity is always experienced by the reader and biographer but not the subject. One way to express this openness is to encourage biographers to be more aware of the rhythm and energy of narrative which they can then apply to the rhythms of a person's life. Just as events in a life have different values, so should the narratives of that life reflect these different strengths. All events should not be treated equally. The interpretative narrator is aware of this as he selects and evaluates key moments but the detached or expressive narrator, paradoxically, is not. Just as we read in rhythmic units, so too, perhaps, biography should be structured and written in rhythmic units. Rhythm is 'man's triumph over chronology' Robert Scholes has said; let biographers apply this concept to the writing of lives as Woolf early in *Orlando* had hoped.[46] Furthermore, biographers might rely on synecdoche more readily than chronology, letting the part stand for the whole, writing biography of *praxis* rather than *historia*, replacing a dependency on comprehensive lives with more analytical, selective lives. The problem for biography, however, remains the ability to translate the growth of a person, his inner as well as outer development, through language and symbolic structures. It is a matter of transforming fact into literary reality.

In its process of demythologizing and creating myth, biography parallels the central archetype of death and rebirth. Reading lives both destroys and creates our image of the subject which is one of the great attractions to biography: even though the historical figure dies, the biography continues his presence – in itself a mythic, phoenix-like activity re-creating and perpetuating the self. Biography, in its gratification of wish-fulfilment, embodies a dream; in its stress on moral example, it becomes an allegory. In this way biography sustains its duality in mythic as well as generic ways. But the tension between dream and allegory remains within the text, as Otto Rank noted when he described 'the real problem of biography':

> Biography is as little an object science as history is, even when it endeavors to be so, and would never fulfill its purpose if it were. The formative process of the biography begins long before the actual attempt to picture the life of the artist; after all, the main

purpose is the picture of the creative personality and not merely of the man of actuality, and the two portraits can naturally never be wholly identical. The effort to make them so is, however, the avowed tendency not only of the biographer but of the artist himself and of his public, present and future.[47]

In the conflict that results from the effort to merge the actual and imagined individual resides the double bind of biography. Its task of reconstructing while deconstructing intensifies the difficulty of its factual and literary nature. Language, however, mediates the problem, especially metaphor, which unites the verbal and the mythic. Metaphor, in fact, becomes the access of literature to myth. Biography is the genre that has as its assignment the reanimation of life which, in Thomas Mann's words, is the creation of 'life as myth'.[48] But when biography reveals a life at odds with its accomplishments a dilemma results for both the biographer and the reader. There is a harshness in the chronicle of reality which often undermines the image, literary or otherwise, of the subject. But in adapting the two in some mythic form, we reconcile the fact with the image until we either persuade ourselves of its unreality or reinforce its illusions.

6 Experiment in Biography

Why should a man spend days in authenticating dates and deciphering obscure records when he can evolve all that he wants so much more easily from his own imagination?

Edinburgh Review (1857)

Why must a biography so rigorously enslave itself to chronology? Why can't it operate like other works of art and find its own kind of order for the job at hand?

Paul Fussell, 'Boswell and His Memorable Scenes' (1967)

At the close of *The Development of English Biography*, Harold Nicolson predicted an unhappy future for biography because it would be unable to unite the scientific with the literary. Science, along with objectivity and detail, would isolate biography from art. Fifty-three years later, however, Leon Edel perceived a new future for biography precisely because of the way it has adapted the new social sciences, especially anthropology and psychology, to writing lives. The result, he states, is 'a new province for biographical adventure and knowledge'.[1] But has biography conquered the antagonism Nicolson forecasted by discovering original ways to unite literary and scientific methods of understanding character with new means of recording human life? A survey of current approaches to life-writing provides an affirmative answer. Responding to shifting epistemological, literary and cultural changes, biography has replaced its attachment to chronology with themes, its linear development of a life with a spiralling narrative and proleptic use of motifs. To read contemporary biography is to discover new ways of structuring a life by pattern or spatial form rather than by time or history.

It would be foolish to think, however, that the inventions of modern biography are completely original. A study of the history of biography reveals the continuous adaptation of classical and post-Renaissance models to innovative modern accounts. Plutarch's set of contrasting, dual lives which makes up his *Lives of*

183

the Greek and Roman Emperors is an early example of group biography as *Bernard Shaw and the Actresses* by Margot Peters is a late example. Xenophon's departure from static eulogy and untidy chronology in his *Agesilaus* (ca. 360) in preference for a factual history of his subject and a non-chronological, systematic analysis of character anticipates such modern studies as Richard Ellmann's *Joyce*. In such a fashion, Xenophon, who went on to write an influential life of Cyrus combining fact and fiction, solved the problem of how to define a character without eliminating the variety of events that comprise an individual life. Plutarch, however, was the most widely imitated classical model, and Edward Jessup's *The Lives of Picus and Pascal* (1723) and Joseph Spence's *Parallel: in the Manner of Plutarch* (1757) are two representative examples.

The eighteenth century was the great age of pre-modern biographical experiment, with nearly every decade providing examples of biographical novelty. This was in part the result of the interaction of biography with the emergence of the novel. Among the most remarkable forms of biography at this time were John Hill's epistolary biography of *Dr. J.H., Inspector General of Great Britain* (1752) told in letters from a gentleman in town to a friend in the country, and Thomas Francklin's life of Lucian (1780) in the form of a dialogue between Lucian and Lord Lyttleton in heaven. Pseudo-fictional biography was also highly popular as in William Hayley's 1787 biography of the Earl of Chesterfield and Samuel Johnson in dialogue form. John Dunton's *Life and Error* (1705), however, went further: it constructed a life in alternate chapters – in one, how the life was lived, in the other, how it should have been lived! A consequence of this experimental biography was William Bingley's three-volume work, *Animal Biography* (1802), subtitled 'authentic anecdotes of the lives, manners and economy of the animal creation', a work anticipating Virginia Woolf's *Flush*.[2]

Of course, the eighteenth century did not monopolize experimental biography, which had such inventive precursors as Sir Thomas Storer who published a metrical *Life and Death of Thomas Wolsey* in 1599. *The Mirror for Magistrates* (1559) in the 1610 edition contained a poetic account of Cromwell by Michael Drayton. Satirical biography appeared in 1680 in the anonymous *Life of Mr. Stephen Marshal*, a parody of popular ecclesiastical lives. Other examples include Izaak Walton's *Life of Sanderson*, with its conversations between the biographer and the Bishop, or the *Eikon Basilike*, a biography of Charles I by John Gauden in the form of an autobiography, reversing the later practice of Thomas Hardy whose biography, identified as being written by his wife, was in fact authored by himself. Additional experimental lives of the sixteenth and seventeenth centuries are John Capgrave's *Liber de Illustribus Henricis* (1446–53), a collection of lives of famous individuals whose Christian names were all Henry, and George Sikes's *Life of Sir Henry Vane* (1662) which attempts to present only the inner life of its subject, neglecting most historical or factual detail.

But in the age of evidence, the nineteenth century, biography appeared less adaptable to experimental forms. An exception, however, was *Imaginative Biography* by Sir Egerton Brydges. Anticipating Landor and Pater, but following Walton in his *Sanderson*, Brydges created fictitious conversations between various individuals, believing that placing 'an Imaginary Superstructure on the known facts of the Biography of eminent characters' was a valid activity.[3] However, the importance of history in the period, highlighted by Gibbon, Carlyle, Macaulay, Lecky and others, emphasized documentation, industriousness, fact-gathering and objectivity. The result was serious, comprehensive lives rooted in the record. Letters, documents, diaries – all took precedence over interpretation or narrative method. Controversy occurred only with the revelation of new material resulting in estimates of the subject that contradicted previous interpretations, as in Froude's *Carlyle*. Aesthetically, there were few risk-takers; change or innovation seemed to occur only through institutional or economic means as in the rise of the popular series biographies or dictionary lives. Experiment existed in fiction with such pseudo-biographical works as Lamb's 'Conversations with Elia', Landor's *Imaginary Conversations* or Pater's *Imaginary Portraits*.

In the twentieth century, biography has reasserted experimentation, linking itself to fiction rather than history. This is partly the consequence of Strachey's psychologizing, candour and stylistic energy and partly a reaction by biography to new forms of fictional expression. Joyce, Woolf and Lawrence have affected biography as well as the novel. With the general move to self-conscious fictions and narrators, biography has become more aware of how it tells its story. Biography furthermore recognizes the impossibility of ever achieving the unity or completeness of self former biographies presented or the cohesiveness represented by history. A seventeenth-century belief in the 'circle of life' – the phrase is Izaak Walton's – altered in the nineteenth century because of the volume of records and reliance on fact. The quantity of information gave a fuller but less architectural shape to the subject, resulting in informative but unstructured lives. Our own age, reacting against the belief that the collection of data and empirical record could convey the life of a subject and sceptical of the chronological pattern of a life, has become more self-consciously aware of method. Although the technical convention of omniscience survives in biography, the concept of a shared value system – of there being a single self for the subject – does not.

Today, how a life is written is as important as how that life was lived. The result of literary modernism, psychology and an awareness of the power of fictions, as well as the problematic nature of language, this view of biography has led to biographies whose boldness and scope significantly differ from their predecessors. 'It is not', as Frank Kermode has written, 'that we are connoisseurs of chaos, but that we are surrounded by it, and equipped for co-existence with it only by our fictive powers.'[4] For biography, this means locating new ways of reconciling disorder and illogic through the use of fictions. Finding Strachey too acerbic but his methods appealing, wanting to psychoanalyse the subject but unskilled in psychoanalysis, eager to incorporate fictional methods but not practised in such forms, biographers have been challenged to fashion new ways of telling a life. Three important responses to this challenge are psychobiography, group biography and contextual biography.

Psychobiography – or psychohistory, as some term it – is currently the most captivating experimental and yet controversial approach to biographical writing. Originating in Freud's life of Leonardo, psychobiography has its modern exponent in Erik Erikson and such followers as Bruce Mazlish and Cynthia Griffin Wolff. The emphasis in this approach is not on the facts but 'trends' in a subject's life, not the record, but interpretative moments that define the psychological truth of the subject. *Praxis*, characteristic conduct, summarizes the approach as the biographical process becomes one of association rather than accumulation. Motivation and inner strength, as contributors to achievement, become the psychobiographer's concern. In reaction to the narrowly Freudian interpretation of subjects and in response to uncritical and oversized lives, psychobiography has turned to examine inner conflict but placed within a historical context, enlarging the Freudian method of analysis by adding social and cultural detail. It seeks exemplary moments (instead of exemplary lives) through significant detail organized in an original form. But until recently, psychobiography has been associated more with historians than with literary critics or literary biographers.

The aim of psychobiography is to match the retrospective, external view of a life with an internal, contemporaneous perspective of the individual. Erik Erikson has applied and advanced this method in *Young Man Luther* (1958) and *Gandhi's Truth* (1969), demonstrating the ways psychoanalysis can illuminate a life by focusing on a crucial event or moment of crisis. Erikson established a pattern of developmental sequence for the individual, his well-known eight-stage human life-cycle. Adding to Freud's three stages of psychosexual development (oral, anal and phallic), Erikson describes interpersonal patterns of action such as getting and taking which are typical of our growth. He also provides for psychobiography a psychosocial vocabulary for the unfolding pattern of development and makes one aware of the need to examine the interaction between the individual and his age. Sequence and moment become the coordinated, not contrasting, elements of psychobiography, viewing 'each present moment as the outcome of his subject's life history'.[5] Correspondence between individual life and the community's moment and sequence also occurs and concerns the psychobiographer whose job is to link the two together. *Young Man Luther*, subtitled *A Study in Psychoanalysis and History*, announces this combination. For Erikson, in general, ideals and identity replace drive and sexuality and in his stress on social as well as biological and familial impulses, he extends Freudianism from the notion of repetition to growth for an individual. In Erikson individual and collective history intersect.

Psychobiography makes it possible to write a more open form of biography and meet Edward Mendelson's charge that the tendency of modern biography 'has been a progressive narrowing of focus, an ever increasing concern with the interior organization of its subject and a lessening of attention to its subject's relations with the world outside'. Mendelson fails to recognize the coordination between moment and sequence, the individual life and the general culture that Erikson and others such as Jerrold Seigel and Bruce Mazlish have declared to be the primary quality of psychobiography. Mendelson's announcement that we must write 'biographies that focus on the *effect* of literary works on the author and the world around him, not the internal *affects* that may or may not have shaped those works' has already been anticipated by psychobiography.[6] The new model is Max Weber not Freud. Mendelson's call for attention to the external and social matters shaping an author is precisely what distinguishes the best of these new biographies.

Norman Holland has perhaps most cogently stated the purpose of the new biography in his discussion of psychoanalysis and literature. Reversing Freud's use of art as a clue to a writer's past and his childhood neuroses, Holland suggests that we look forward and see the life in its totality, recognizing 'the human being as playing infinite variations upon a continuing, central identity theme . . .'[7] This parallels Leon Edel's wish to delve behind the mask of his subject with the similar goal of finding 'the organic unity that links all the aspects of his [the subject's] life together, by focusing on the underlying themes whose developments and variations constitute the determining elements of his history'. These words are not those of Holland or Edel but of Jerrold Seigel in his biography of Karl Marx, a recent and successful example of psychobiography. Seigel considers the inner consistency and pattern of meaning in the life of Marx, and his narrative and point of view are determined by his approach: 'I have sought the coherence of his life history in terms of symbols and patterns suggested by his own thinking or by that of people close to him.' The importance of self-analysis for the biographer – one element in the task of the biographer to which Robert Gittings alludes and Edel prizes in his 'Poetics' – is made clear by Seigel when he says in the Preface to his book, 'my relationship to Marx is frankly ambivalent . . . Writing this book has been an attempt to understand and come to terms with my own position.' But accompanying this approach is the awareness that 'the inner determinants of Marx's life history' cannot be understood independently of the historical and social forces that 'shaped the life of his time'.[8] Family, culture and history all enter significantly into the narrative. The result is a vivid, original and revealing portrait.

Criticism of psychobiography, however, has been almost as vocal as its praise.[9] Summarized, objectors find it reductionist in its stress on psychological pattern in the determination of personality. Models assume the status of facts as intellectual circularity dominates logic. Social, economic or even historical factors are excluded while facts are misused or invented. There is, furthermore, a tendency to universalize rather than individualize figures, in addition to focusing only on the psychopathological. Psychobiography believes in a certain timelessness of behaviour and discounts historical differences in methods of thinking and behaviour. Most crucially, say its critics, it distorts facts by imposing a theory that is often mechanically applied and which tends to disparage its subjects. Combined with repeated charges of incompetence among its practitioners, who are trained neither as psychiatrists nor biographers, psychobiography has suffered frequent attacks while attaining a high degree of recognition and popularity. This reflects a modern fascination with matters psychological, a puzzlement if not absorption with psychoanalysis, and the needs of readers to discover the reaction of the self to crises. There is, today, a deep desire for interpreting rather than reporting a life. For readers of biographies it is not the facts alone that are of interest but their application, meaning and use in presenting a life. But formulating an approach on the establishment and then analysis of the interior life of a subject is a practice as dangerous as it is appealing. The largest criticism of psychobiography may be the question of what constitutes its evidence? Do the facts justify the interpretation? The severest criticism of psychobiography appears to be its attachment to internal consistency within the text, rather than correspondence to a set of facts outside the work.

Curiously, psychobiography has so far had a greater appeal to fields other than literature, notably history, music, economics and even science. Siegel's biography of Marx, Fawn Brodie's of Thomas Jefferson, Maynard Solomon's *Beethoven*, Arthur Mitzman's *The Iron Cage, An Historical Interpretation of Max Weber* or Frank Manuel's *A Portrait of Isaac Newton* are examples. Literary studies have been less adventurous, preferring, still, the security of the conservative, fact-gathering life such as Park Honan's new account of Matthew Arnold or Matthew J. Bruccoli's narrative of F. Scott Fitzgerald. Helene Moglen's *Charlotte Brontë: The Self Conceived* or Cynthia Griffin Wolff's life of Edith Wharton, however, are two exceptions in literary biography. A striking example of psychobiography that incorporates historical, literary and cultural interests is Bruce Mazlish's 1975 study, *James and John Stuart Mill, Father and Son in the 19th Century.*

In seeking to maintain a balance between 'the claims of restricted historical context and sweeping universal concept' and aware of the complexities of social and intellectual matters which proceed 'in subtle accord with personal development and transformation', Mazlish suggests a new direction for biography.[10] Through his symbiotic, dichotomous manner, the linear quality of the book, with its sequential chapters and divisions into separate sections, assumes an original structure for biography. He repeatedly moves from social reality to psychological reality as new ideas become part of John Stuart Mill's psychological growth, revising and redefining the private and social past. In the later half of the book, Mazlish turns away from the formative years and the mental crisis of John Stuart Mill to discuss his involvement with the age in the form of Carlyle, Bentham, Comte, Harriet Taylor and others. The aim is to identify a recurrent pattern in each of Mill's personal relationships.

Through the continual exchange of macro and micro elements, presented as the tension between nineteenth-century social change and Mill's personal mental crisis and growth, a curious dialectical rhythm operates in the life that is one moment sweeping and broad, the next, specific and precise (cf. p. 8). In joining ideas to their social and personal contexts, the foundation of the dual biography and its emphasis on generational conflict remains clear. Progress or advance comes from reaction and Mazlish demonstrates this in Mill's life through the themes of rebellion and adaptation, rejection and exemplification (cf. p. 427). The image Mazlish creates is that known in mathematics as a strange loop: 'to understand one generation, we must accordingly ascend to the generation before it, and then descend to the generation after' (p. 434; on the paradigm of the strange loop see Douglas M. Hofstader, *Gödel Escher Bach* [New York: Basic Books, 1979]).

This last comment has, by extension, an interesting application to the appeal of psychobiography. Nineteenth-century biography was impersonal, displaying an allegiance to documents and facts. It reflected identity and comfort with the reigning public culture. But the loss of faith in the impersonal, the recognition of the power of instability and the gradual prominence of personality made the previous biographical forms inadequate. In the quest for the personality of the subject, biography welcomed psychology and in the effort to establish intimacy for the biographer and reader with the subject, it turned to psychobiography as a form of psychohistory. Since intimacy has become a moral good, any legitimate means to establish closeness between reader and subject is continually promoted. Erasing the impersonality of the historical or documented life leads not only to a greater effort at knowing the inner life of the subject, but also to the development of the 'creative fact'. In the effort to promote intimacy via the text, the imagination rather than the record takes precedence in an attempt to bond the life of the subject with that of the reader. It only remains for psychobiography to apply more clearly and consistently the principles it has enunciated in the area of history to that of literature. As long as we value what Richard Sennett has labelled the intimate society, the attractions of psychobiography will remain for would-be biographers as well as readers.[11]

A consequence of the intimate society, where personality rather than objects dominate, where motives rather than acts are important, is the emphasis on community, which is the formation of a collective identity. This is a kind of reassurance through the act of general self-definition. These factors are at work in the resurgence of a second major experimental form of biographical writing today, group biography, where the sense of community establishes a shared personality. In 1921 Freud published *Group Psychology and the Analysis of the Ego*, in which he tried to describe the characteristics of group psychology in terms of the collective mental life. Furthermore, the stress on human interaction rather than individualism challenges and parallels the changing emphases in the presentation of character in the modern novel. Group biography may be, as Margot Peters has suggested, 'the belated development in biography that parallels the early twentieth century development of the novel', or an extension of the nineteenth-century novel's concern with social forces and social identity altered to reflect the group instead of the class.[12] Regardless of the exact cause, the reemergence of group biography in the last twenty-five years is the reassertion of a need to understand communal experience.

Characterized by a series of themes or actions that link various individuals, group biography has existed since the mid-nineteenth century. *Heroes and Hero Worship* or *Representative Men* or even *Eminent Victorians* stressed thematic associations extending and tightening the associations Plutarch suggested and Johnson's *Lives of the Poets* confirmed. But gradually, a common identity began to unite the figures in a group life as in *Bernard Shaw and the Actresses* by Margot Peters or Stanley Weintraub's *London Yankees*. Other recent group lives include John Pearson's *Facades: Edith, Osbert and Sacheverell Sitwell* (1978) and Michael Korda's *Charmed Lives*, subtitled *A Family Romance* (1979). Additional examples are *Lorenzo, D. H. Lawrence and The Women Who Loved Him* by Emily Hahn (1975) and the recent *Group Portrait: Joseph Conrad, Stephen Crane, Ford Madox Ford, Henry James and H. G. Wells* by Nicholas Delbanco (1982). One sees again the interaction with fiction. In 1971, Henrich Böll published *Group Portrait with A Woman*; in 1963, Mary McCarthy wrote *The Group*.

In group biography, one becomes defined by the many. The group biography in fact becomes a protest against the erosion of a viable communal life and marks the socialization of biography as it incorporates several lives, not a single life. A danger, however, is that we may falsely believe that interchanges in society are the only disclosures of personality. In its effort to reassert community, the group biography also establishes place or milieu, the context for a movement. This effort of placing individual lives within a larger environment creates a multidimensional quality for biography and enlarges its scope as well as its appeal. This, too, may be a form of psychobiography as the moment and sequence of a single life becomes multiplied by several or many connected lives. Such an identity, in turn, corresponds to the moment and sequence in the community at large. The group biography then establishes various shared themes that reinforce and integrate the lives of its individuals. The person and his age, the focus of the psychobiography, extends itself in the group biography to include people and their time. For the individual, identity is ego-structure; for the group, it is ideology and the successful group biography measures both the impact of society upon our lives and the desire to expand the self. Three works in particular illustrate the resources of the group biography: the first deals with Paris in the 1920s, the second with the Fabians, the third with Bloomsbury. All three enlarge the idea of a pattern or theme in a single life to include the coherence that might occur in society. This necessary fiction is both historical and literary.

Charmed Circle, Gertrude Stein and Company by James R. Mellow, published in 1974, is a skilful blend of a group and its history. The cast of characters is as multitudinous as its subjects but the work also includes analyses of modern art, twentieth-century literature, family relations and the literary career of Gertrude Stein. It begins with an effective description of 27 Rue de Fleurus and its profusion of art. We learn, for example, that the studio was so overcrowded that 'Picasso and Matisse drawings were tacked to the double-doors that led to the cramped dining room'.[13] In the biography, detail is colourful but brief as Mellow narrates the early life of Stein in only thirty-one pages but dwells extensively on her life in Paris. Balancing environment with character, Mellow compliments action with atmosphere. Encounters are the key events in the biography and the Steins' first meeting with Matisse, their early involvement with Picasso, Gertrude's affair with Alice B. Toklas are all highlighted. His method of integrating the lives unites event, meaning and character as Mellow explores how Gertrude Stein's life-style informed her writing.

The colourful participants in *Charmed Circle* dramatically contribute to the events that surround the three principal characters and provide a natural locus for the drama of the group. Norman and Jeanne MacKenzie, however, deal with less flamboyant and less well-known personalities in their group biography, *The Fabians* (1977). Beginning with a meeting in October 1883, at the apartment of Edward Pease, the MacKenzies provide brief sketches of their players, enlarging the range of protagonists as the political movement develops. George Bernard Shaw enters and quickly dominates Chapter 2, while Annie Besant takes over Chapter 3. Interspersed with intellectual history and political thought is a loose, anecdotal narrative of the shaping of the Fabian Society. The personalities of the figures and their interaction, however, seem to take precedence over their platforms and organization. History mixes with private incident as the Fabians form themselves in a political unity marked by the dramatic, unexpected impact of the *Fabian Essays*, published in December 1899.

What emerges from this group biography is a cultural and political history of England between 1885 and 1914 with a shifting cast of central characters. Beatrice and Sidney Webb dominate three of the four chapters of Part Two. Shaw is omnipresent and dominates or, at the very least, manipulates the balance of the narrative until he comes into conflict with the late entrant, H. G. Wells. Ideology and life-style interact in this work which is organized around anecdote and intellectual history. The sketch of an age that emerges, however, overshadows the less interesting aspects of the Fabian programme and plans for social action, although the MacKenzies summarize the Fabians as a group that 'sought to reconstruct society on new moral principles'.[14]

Another group that had reconstruction as its unstated aim, although it was aesthetic and not social in intent, was Bloomsbury. Leon Edel's *Bloomsbury, A House of Lions* (1979) is the latest study of what detractors have identified as 'the engine-room of modernism'. Edel's work, however, demands our attention because it illustrates the use of the group biography matched with a psychological approach by one of our most articulate practitioners of the art. Edel's biography, however, is incomplete, stopping short in its narrative at 1920 with the suggestion that as 'elderly lions' the lives of Bloomsbury took on different shapes.

Edel refers to his work as 'a mosaic of facts and interpretations' to suggest the independent yet connected nature of his narrative and materials.[15] He deals with nine characters in one volume but, in contrast to Mellow, his range is smaller and less expansive; in contrast to the MacKenzies, he focuses less on the age and more on society. Edel explains that the biography began as a set of individual biographical essays that required 'brevity, lucidity, selective detail and above all, a light ironic touch' but the weight of material caused a shift in purpose to a more homogeneous form in an attempt to answer the question 'what *was* Bloomsbury?' (p. 11). Edel's answer is found in his 'episodic structure and . . . psychological interpretation of Bloomsbury's past' (p. 13). These comments on the evolution and shape of the book, especially the emphasis on the 'light ironic touch' for the style and content, help us to understand the work and its goals.

Dealing with the fashionable subject of Bloomsbury, however, poses dangers to any biographer, not the least being the overshadowing of one figure by another, a worry in any group biography. Edel avoids this through the first half of his work by maintaining the separate strands of his story and by following the separate lives of his characters. Leonard Woolf, Clive Bell, Lytton Strachey, Maynard Keynes and others are individually treated with entire chapters or portions of chapters devoted to each separate life. An understated and unsatisfactory sense of their interaction, however, emerges in the opening sections of the book. Although there are hints of future coalescence, the strategy of Edel is to treat individual lives equally, even if their contributions to Bloomsbury were unequal. There is a continual process of assembling and disassembling the characters in the story.

A welcome but diminished scepticism, however, is present in this generally romantic biography of Bloomsbury. Discussing the parties of Bloomsbury, Edel admits that the celebrated gatherings 'sound like intellectual parties anywhere. We must take it on trust that they were remarkable' (p. 150). A casual, almost neglectful approach to the literary accomplishments of Bloomsbury suprises the reader. But in spite of overwriting that verges on the melodramatic, the book maintains a narrative pace generated and sustained by the personalities found in contact with one another. The biography is constantly progressive, in part the result of Edel's decision to tell it 'in biographical form, as if it were a novel, and be loyal to all my materials . . .' (p. 13). Except for the opening section on the early death of Leonard Woolf's father and the Carrington–Strachey affair, the psychologizing in the work is surprisingly limited. But one moment where it is unusually heavy-handed is in Edel's estimate of Strachey's conversion of the negative aspects of his youth into the positive achievements of his maturity. 'The answer', writes Edel, is in 'the synthesis of his life myth. He was able to metamorphose his ambivalence toward his mother . . . into historical metaphors . . . Writing [his] books offered him the gratification of his double role in life, his androgynous quest for a place in the sun.' In an unpardonable pun, however, Edel adds that 'in his books Lytton Strachey identifies only partially with the males; he is on the side of the queens' (pp. 229–30).

The brief chapters of the book, divided into briefer subsections, represent the atomistic form of Edel's biography and stylistically reflect his overall theme concerning Bloomsbury expressed in this sentence: 'while they were aware of their individual strengths, they had no sense of their collective power' (pp. 253–4). The comment is also a critique of Edel's biography, for the division of subjects and individuals has taken place at the expense of a unified whole. The answer to the question what is a successful group biography is found in the biographical portrait that can only be completed when all the lives in the group are joined. The central formal problems in group biography, however, remain focus and proportion.

Psychobiography and group biography are not the only new forms of biographical writing. Dual biographies such as Nigel Hamilton's *The Brothers Mann* (1979) or biographies of minor figures such as Geoffrey Wolff's *Black Sun* (1976), a well-written account of Harry Crosby, social rebel, eccentric and 1920s publisher, also flourish. Metabiography, the biography about biography, also continues in the mould of *The Quest for Corvo*. *The English Climate, An Excursion into a Biography of John Galsworthy* (1979) by James Gindin is a lyrical example, while the misadventures of Mark Harris in trying to write of Saul Bellow are a comic variation of Symons's quest. The segment biography has also appeared, the work that analyses only a portion of the subject's life. A good example is Paul Delany's *D. H. Lawrence's Nightmare, The Writer and His Circle in the Years of the Great War* (1978). This work combines group biography with the detailed survey of a selected period; the individual life and cultural period overlap and illuminate each other.

But what appears largest on the canvas of biography is contextual biography, a contrast to its predecessor, circumstantial biography. (By contextual I do not mean the form of literary criticism Murray Kreiger and others outlined in the 1960s involving irony, ambiguity and paradox in the self-contained literary text. See Kreiger, 'The Existential Basis of Contextual Criticism', *Criticism*, VII: 4 (Fall 1966) 305–17.) Circumstantial biography is the large biography of undigested fact which concentrates on what sociologists label the 'instrumental tasks', those daily activities that act as means, not ends, in our lives. Biographers have tended to treat such data as significant reality for the subject, assuming the data will establish themes and patterns of meaning in and of themselves (i.e. without narrative interpretation). But as the life swells with detail, it shrinks in interpretative analysis. There is an indiscriminate equalization of circumstances in both meaning and importance; any 'peaks' disappear in the level horizon. In contrast to this form, contextual biography integrates the subject with his time while emphasizing only critical moments or events. The foreground does not deal with details of the subject alone but with the union of the individual and his art, society or age. It recasts the group biography, giving prominence to the hero against a stream of events rather than other figures. The engagement of the hero with his world and how the two interact form the basis of contextual biography, which tries to see and understand the complete environment and figure, his period and his work. Social relations control the significance of circumstantial detail. Surprisingly, these lives do not result in voluminous sociological tracts but carefully focused books that link biography to sociology, anthropology, history or politics. Three examples are *Dostoevsky* by Joseph Frank, *The Unknown Orwell* and *Orwell: The Transformation* by Peter Stansky and William Abrahams and *Conrad in the Nineteenth Century* by Ian Watt. The Orwell biography represents the major features of this method.

In *The Unknown Orwell* (1972) and *Orwell: The Transformation* (1979), Peter Stansky and William Abrahams, a historian and literary critic, combined to write an unusual biography that in nine parts (five in volume one and four in volume two) analyses the shift in George Orwell's identity against the sociocultural changes that occurred throughout his life. Originally to have been a group biography, 'a study of a number of young English writers of the 1930's . . . who had fought on the side of the Republic in the Spanish Civil War', the two-volume biography led to a different focus: 'a study of Eric Blair becoming the writer George Orwell'.[16] This change, they demonstrate, 'allowed Eric Blair to come to terms with his world' (p. xiv). From Eton, and the Indian Imperial Police in Burma to London, Paris, Southwold, Wigan, Spain and, finally, London, the story of George Orwell is coordinated with those events in England and Europe between 1903 and 1950 that strongly influenced his thought. Combining with the man and his time, as well as his work, are the themes of class and socialism – as well as a set of tensions variously labelled as 'the patriot and the radical, the idealist and the sceptic, the sahib and the victim' (p. xv).

Representing the contextual approach to the life are the opening pages of the biography which confront the matter of class. And the complexities of class identity introduce the problem of personal identity for the Blair family which Orwell inherits. The history of his family is explained, then, as a peculiar continuum downwards, ironically ending with 'Blair' and starting upward again as Orwell. As the biography proceeds, accounts of Anglo-Indian life in the late Victorian and Edwardian period contrast with life in Henley-on-Thames, and then life in the 'public schools', first at St Cyprians and then Eton (cf. I: 85). Further oppositions include the conditions at home while England was at war, the effects of post-war disillusionment (I: 104) and later British influence in Burma. Interspersed with these broad passages that convincingly establish the context for understanding Orwell are interpretative sections dealing with the paradox of his real versus fantasy life (the actual and the mythic) and sense of imposture (I: 112–15). His increasing unease as a Burmese policeman and growing identity as a writer (I: 164–9; 170–6), his shaping political views (I: 196–7) and his descent into an abyss are additional contrasts the biographers explore.

Throughout the biography, criticism of Orwell's writing is restrained and included only when it signifies a certain social or cultural dimension of his life. Overriding the biography are the themes, linked to cultural or social elements, that shape the transformation of Eric Blair into George Orwell (cf. I: 187). The moral and political theme, more articulated than the struggle to become a writer theme, begins to emerge as the shaping factor in his work. The issues that gradually overtake Stansky and Abrahams are generic and provide depth as well as breadth for the biography. How does he become a writer? How does he choose an appropriate style? How does he translate experience into the stuff of his writing? What are the major influences on his work? These generic concerns are part of the biography's interest in the stages of growth, and the organic development of the hero, another aspect of contextual life-narratives. Hence, the shift from becoming a writer to becoming Orwell with the focus on movement and process. This concern also permits variations in time and the fluctuation in presentation suggested by Virginia Woolf, Hayden White and Robert Scholes.

However, such 'freedom' and interest in the context of their subject does not seduce Stansky and Abrahams into writing without discipline. As they state when summing up the events in the winter of 1933, when, among other things, Hitler became Chancellor of Germany – 'We are not writing "history" using Orwell as an exemplary or typical figure (he was neither)' (II: 25). This awareness of the ease with which they could make Orwell symbolic heightens the contextual basis of their presentation which they do not limit nor deny.

Beginnings and endings clearly linked to social and political changes in Orwell's life organize the biography. There is no sense of finality but continuity. Even his death seems not to have occurred and its place is not in the traditional location as the culminating event in the biography. References to his epitaph, date of death, burial, and form of death, occur as early as pp. xv–vi of the Prologue to volume one, while intermittent references exist throughout the two volumes. The final section of the biography deals with one of the 'peaks' that interpretative, contextual biography emphasizes: Orwell's 1937 visit to Spain. Orwell's enthusiasm and then disappointment with the war and, finally, his dramatic escape with his wife and two associates is particularly well handled. The stress on the political milieu of Orwell's activities, the infighting among republican forces, the danger that surrounded him, as well as the importance of these events for Orwell's writing, are made clear. The final pages of the biography provide, in the context of Spain, not his death but his birth, and explain that his commitment to democratic socialism, solidified in Wigan Pier and Barcelona, made it possible for him to find his way as an artist while making peace with himself – 'and it was for this that he became George Orwell' (II: 226).[17] The final section also dispels the legends of Orwell, notably the one that presented him as 'abstracted . . . into a kind of saintliness . . . [Spain] cost him his innocence, but not as might have seemed inevitable, his idealism', the authors conclude (II: 225). Stansky and Abrahams have written a biography that understands its subject and its time, which grows out of their earlier, parallel biography, *Journey to the Frontier* (1966) a study of Julian Bell and John Cornford. Through their contextual approach, they link Orwell to his society, whether it is Burma, France or England and, while creating a striking picture, indicate a new direction for biographical writing.

Edward Mendelson has written that modern biography has become progressively narrower in focus, displaying 'an ever-increasing concern with the interior organization of its subject, and a lessening of attention to its subject's relations with the world outside'.[18] Stressing only the internal, psychological relations of the subject has limited the perspective of biographers to 'the inner workings of the self' (p. 20), parallel to the concern of criticism with literature as 'a complex of internal and self-referential relations' involved with irony, self-contradiction or deconstruction (p. 20). Mendelson calls for biographies that integrate the author with society, as well as the writer with his audience. This means 'external and social matters ranging from the economics of publication to the larger question of a modern writer's social role' (p. 24). Not Freud but Max Weber is the model in the effort to understand, through biography, the changing role of the author and his work. Contextual biography achieves this. In examining the life with the work in its social/historical context, the biography provides a broader vision and greater breadth to the subject while expanding the nature of the genre. Contextual biography incorporates the concern of group biography with the social aspects of psychobiography creating a form that enlarges the foundations of biographical writing. To the extent that biography attempts to shape a life rather than 'portray a life experience', contextual biography redresses the emphasis on chronology to one of totality.

But biography will no doubt take directions other than the contextual and perhaps the most tempting is that represented by fiction. How can a biographer disregard the technique, style and influence of such contemporaries as Nabokov, Borges or Hawkes? Novelists, one notes, cannot overcome their attraction to biography as seen in such fictional renderings of biographers as Sartre's *Nausea* or Bernard Malamud's *Dubin's Lives*. As biographers become more self-conscious about their means of presentation, authorial presence will become more problematic. Turning less to what will happen in the biography and more to how that happening will occur will result in new means of narrative presentation, as Andrew Field has shown in his unusual biography of Vladimir Nabokov.

The uniqueness of *Nabokov: His Life in Part* is the participation of the subject as a character/commentator in the text.[19] The biography begins with the subject conversing with his biographer but, as the text proceeds, Nabokov enters at odd and unexpected moments to correct, criticize or converse with the biographer. This engaging style establishes an unusual intimacy but also undermines the apparent objectivity of the primary narrative. The secondary narrative of Nabokov's commentary to Field creates play within the text that questions the accuracy, although not the truthfulness, of the primary narrative. The result is a trialogue between the subject, the biographer and the record. What the work emphasizes is, again, the ambiguity of fact, the slipperiness of relying on the subject as a source but, as well, the possibilities of biographical form.

Supplementing the drama of Nabokov's response to the record, noted by bold face insertions in the narrative, is the autobiographical account of the author who describes his various meetings with the subject from 1968 to 1971. Using a tape recorder gives Field an advantage Boswell might have envied and the result, we believe, is a verbatim account of his conversations with Nabokov. But more intriguing is the interplay between Nabokov, his own sense of the past and the biographer's perception of it. A continual problem with this method, however, is curbing Nabokov's desire to write his own biography and the impossibility of the two figures actually understanding each other and their motives. Nonetheless, the biography is an unusual and intuitive attempt to convey the record and experience of writing a biography with the cooperation of the subject, including his asides, interruptions and contradictions in the text. And what emerges is a dramatic illustration of the relativity of fact.

Increasingly, biographers will become more conscious that their methods of presentation inescapably involve alterations to the 'facts', that the process of re-presenting material becomes a reality as important as the subject described. Renouncing nineteenth-century history and fiction as models, with their compendious detail, stable narratives and positivist beliefs, biographers will probably explore the flexibility and possibilities of the form. This has already occurred in one distinguished biography, *Marcel Proust* by George D. Painter. Rejecting criticism of his use of detail because it is necessary for a complete biography and fundamental for an understanding of Proust's fiction, Painter also acknowledges his potentially disruptive structure. Four long digressions interrupt the narrative, he explains, because of the necessity to understand all aspects of Proust's life and work. They are on the topography of Illiers, Proust's hosts and acquaintances in society, the Dreyfus Affair and Proust's study of Ruskin. In themselves the digressions provide fascinating units within the overall structure and suggest how the purely historical or analytical can exist within the biographical. None of the digressions disrupt the life but, rather, contribute to it, confirming a statement Painter makes about Proust that applies equally well to himself: 'though he invented nothing, he altered everything'.[20] Experiments with narration are also beginning to appear, as in the new and radical *Edie, An American Biography* by Jean Stein. This life of the pop star Edie Sedgwick is told in a documentary manner by a chorus of witnesses who speak with, and against, each other through quoted transcripts. The comments are edited but the narrator has, in the manner of Joyce, removed herself completely from the text.

Experiments in biography will probably reflect a shift to greater dramatic presentation with the scene becoming the basic compositional unit of biography replacing linear narrative. Units of space rather than time may unite the work which will possess a metonymic scheme. Instead of the bare recitation of the facts or historical summaries, there will be more interesting and meaningful interpretative moments, fashioning the life in the psychological present of the subject and reader. The novel may again point the way for this new phase as seen in the work of Beckett, Calvino or Barth. The concentration of theme, plot and character of a biography in a single, telling scene or event suggests new possibilities for biographical form. Indeed, a succession of moments rather than a causal sequence may alter the way we structure lives in biography as synchronicity becomes a useful method of establishing simultaneous connections or contrasts in biography. An intrinsic pattern narratively presented may be established by juxtaposition as well as by continuity.

A basic challenge associated with narrative time in biography may be how to make biography more lifelike, dispelling the false sense of the essential self or single shape to an individual's life. The novel faced this crisis at the beginning of the present century. Life, it recognized, is disordered and fragmentary and 'does not say to you: In 1914 my next door neighbour, Mr. Stock erected a greenhouse . . .'[21] Biography must find ways of uniting the retrospective and anticipatory in the manner suggested perhaps by Mazlish, reaching back to a previous generation and then leaping forward to one that defines the present. A recent example of this formulation of the present is Patricia Craddock's life of Gibbon which uses Gibbon's *Memoir* as the principal text. Beginning with events from the *Memoir*, Craddock compares them to the record, refining, analysing and redefining situations. At the same time, she projects attitudes and ideas that will formulate later writings and situations for Gibbon. In *Young Edward Gibbon*, a literary present encompasses a past while predicting a future.[22] Freedom from strict chronological sequence, as Woolf exhibited in *Orlando*, as Edel demonstrated in his life of Henry James and as Stansky and Abrahams do in their life of Orwell, should be accepted by more biographers as they compose a life.

A work that illustrates some of the innovations I have been describing is *Lewis Carroll, Fragments of a Looking-Glass* by the French critic–biographer, Jean Gattégno. In this biography, published in French in 1974 and two years later in English, Gattégno substitutes *bricolage*, the building up of an image or object in parts, for the traditional linear development and historical narrative of a life. The division of the book into an Overture, Variations and Coda initiates the departure in form. The first section contains a short statement of purpose plus a chronology of Carroll's life. The second, the body of the work, develops a series of topics of varying length in alphabetical order like entries in a dictionary. They begin with 'Alice' and end with 'Zeno's Paradox'. After nearly 300 pages, the Coda, actually a brief summary of the tracings of the life that have preceded it, concludes the book.

Gattégno's recognition of the impossibility of ever producing 'any "unity" that will totally encompass Lewis Carroll' results in his decision to use a collage technique. As he explains, the only way to get near the dual figure of Charles Dodgson/Lewis Carroll is 'by bringing together these various worlds, though in no kind of hierarchy of importance'. And there is no suggestion, he emphasizes, that 'fitting the last piece of the puzzle into place is the end of the story'.[23] This open-ended biography, conscious of its own incompleteness, nonetheless relies on letters, diaries and works by Carroll to shape its composite picture. It also extensively relies on the reader to organize the life since there are few if any restrictions on how he reads it; he is free to enter it at any place and in any order. The assembly and reassembly of the life becomes a literal experience as the reader pieces the life together in the order he chooses. And as a consequence, Carroll emerges in an appropriately playful and enigmatic manner. Reading the life constructs the life with its truth that of the narrative rather than of history.

Not surprisingly, however, it is in the novel and the drama that some of the most extreme experiments with biographical form are occurring, especially among European writers. Max Frisch, the Swiss–German playwright, in his drama *Biography, A Game* (1967) considers what would occur if we could rewrite our biography and live it over differently. Philippe Beaussant, a French novelist, in *Le Biographe* (the Biographer) (1978), writes a novel subtitled *A Narrative*. It recounts a historian's study of the Congress of Vienna who discovers that memoirs have more truth than archives and becomes a biographer interested in individuals rather than events. Every biography, Beaussant has argued, tends to the imaginary as every fiction, in its exploration of time and individual psychology in action, tends towards biography. Eves Navarre in his novel *Biographie* (1981) considers similar changes as the novelist writes his own life in a biographical form, ending on the day *Biographie* is published. The subtitle of the work is 'un roman'.

Behind these and other attempts at new forms of biographical writing is Sartre whose faithlessness to calendar time in his search for single, organizing truths in biography has influenced, or at least challenged, conventional biographical form. Rejecting experimental detail in order to locate an ideal order 'intentionally false to the ambiguity of actual experience', Sartre establishes a new direction in his biographies of Genet, Baudelaire and Flaubert summarized by the problematic question, 'What can one know about a man today?' Roland Barthes has also presented several new directions in his life of Fourier, an assemblage of bits of information, knowledge and images. Of the Flaubert biography, Sartre remarked that 'I would like my study to be read as a novel' to break down further distinctions between the forms.[24] Practitioners appear willing to press towards new and original methods but critics seem less generous in responding to these new attempts and less cognizant of their potential.

Fictional biography again seems the most advanced in its exploration of new forms and it is fictional narrators from *Orlando* to Jeffrey Cartwright of *Edwin Mullhouse* who recognize that

> Memory and chronology simply do not make good bedfellows. Indeed, it sometimes seems to me that I should abandon the madness of chronology altogether and simply follow my whims . . . A curse on chronology! And again, a curse on chronology!

The frustration of the fictitious biographer Cartwright comes not from the hypocrisy of clock time that suggests a man, melancholic on Friday, must hang himself on Saturday, nor from the vulgar itch to get to the good part' but 'simply to the difficulty of the thing, the impossibility of fitting everything into its proper niche'.[25] The admittance of such problems by biographers would result in not only more imaginative but more honest and, hence, authentic biographies, works that were truer to the nature of life-writing and the subject rather than to the biographer's conception of him.

The solution to the dilemma of mimesis versus invention in biography may yet be through 'creative fact'. Virginia Woolf's term is not the impurity of fact but a near oxymoron recognizing the confusion, complexity and disorder of our lives and the determination not to make a biographical life a falsely ordered world. It is the response of biography to the kinds of perceptions modern literature has been grappling with since the late nineteenth century and a way of transforming biography into art via the imagination of the biographer. The result, often at the sacrifice of historical fact, is the establishment of an 'authorized fiction', an imaginative presentation of detail based on the understanding of the biographer of how his subject lived, psychologically and physically. Such a biography may sacrifice detail and, possibly, accuracy but not truth.

The nineteenth-century fear of objectifying impulses has been replaced by a twentieth-century belief that the disclosure of the self is a moral good. Biography has responded to this social and moral change by becoming, itself, more intimate, both in revealing more personal details and in presenting those details more creatively. The employment of facts, their representation as certain forms of plot structures in a biography, transforms them from chronicle to 'story' and involves theories of language and narrative form. Together, language, narration and myth establish configurations in biography recognized if not experienced by readers. Language constitutes the subject as it describes it, becoming both the content and the form. Narration gives it a voice, while myth orders the details into identifiable units. This does not falsify fact but enhances it. Fact expands from a record to the revelation of a human being. Biographers and readers must remember that 'there are *no* facts which *everyone* needs to know' at the same time they realize that no fact is without its fictions.[26]

7 Conclusion

[The writer] can describe a scene by describing one after another the innumerable objects which at a given moment were present at a particular place, but truth will be attained by him only when he takes two different objects, states the connexion between them – a connexion analogous in the world of art to the unique connexion which in the world of science is provided by the law of causality – and encloses them in the necessary links of a well-wrought style; truth – and life too – can be attained by us only when, by comparing a quality common to two sensations, we succeed in extracting their common essence and in reuniting them to each other, liberated from the contingencies of time, within a metaphor.

In this passage from *Time Regained*, the final volume of *Remembrance of Things Past*, Marcel Proust explains that meaning in literature comes only from the interpretation or analysis of the object, not from its mere presence. Relations not facts establish significance. Biography also recognizes the importance of this quality as it becomes more aware of the value of narrative design, structure and style, as well as the position of the reader and the subject in the text. Elizabeth Gaskell as a character observing Charlotte Brontë holding her brother's group painting while also narrating the scene graphically illustrates the complexity of the situation. The unmediated, comprehensive life, avoiding or unconscious of its own method, no longer satisfies; in its effort at completeness it only creates a greater awareness of its incompleteness. Replacing the positivist hope that the record of a life can be captured is the stronger awareness of how fictions regulate and articulate our past. History, as Hegel reminds us, 'combines in our language the objective as well as the subjective side. It means both the *historiam rerum gestarum* and the *res gestas* themselves, both the events and the narration of the events.'[1]

As biography acknowledges its duality of record and narration, it becomes a more vigorous and self-conscious literary form. But part of this consciousness is its understanding the fundamental paradox of biography, that it can gain completeness only by selectivity. Consequently, biography has displayed an increased awareness of narrative strategies and plot structures that enhance the meaning of the life to the reader. In part this is a consequence of the mid-nineteenth-century attraction to brief lives which stimulated the need for interpretative biography, as well as a response by biography to the influence of fiction and the more creative fashioning of a life. Biographers realize that the inclusion of fictional elements is unavoidable through the process of language, narration and myth but that such lives are also more truthful to the individual because they express the less orderly, sometimes unstructured details of human experience. Paradoxically, language in biography does not record as much as it reinvents a life. Tautologically, what creates this self-awareness is the pressure of language and the power of literary convention.

Experiment with structure, time and point of view in biography signals a new biographical consciousness responsive to changes in the novel and non-fiction writing. Increasingly, biographies appear more aware of this perplexing question: 'is it not an astonishing proposition and a fearful paradox to say that someone writes someone else's life? . . . can a life be written?'[2] The critical issue today has become, in fact, what is meant when a biographer refers to 'my' life of Dickens or Somerset Maugham or Isak Dinesen? Implicit in the conception and explicit in the text is the appropriation of data by the biographer to his vision of the subject and method of composing the life. The act of writing overtly, through stylistic and rhetorical means, and covertly, through theme, structure and interpretation, remakes the life. Those biographers who recognize the limitations of the comprehensive life concentrate on the nature of their subjects in an attempt to articulate the inner life of the individual even at the sacrifice of fact. Emphasis on causality rather than chronology, configuration instead of detail, significance instead of information, characterizes their work.

Correspondingly, the effort to examine and present the inner life satisfies and clarifies the psychological needs of both the biographer and reader. The biographer obtains a certain power over his subject in understanding the psychological and moral forces that shape his subject's life. This knowledge gives him a certain verbal and moral authority as he recharts the life of the subject under his direction. The challenge, however, is to represent the emotions and ideas of the subject through adequate language of which metaphor and metonymy become the major vehicles. For the reader this allows a similarly powerful sense of completeness and sense of psychic wholeness as the life of this subject becomes a unified story possessing a recognizable literary, psychological and mythic pattern. This in turn suggests to the attentive reader that within his own fragmented existence, there is a teleological unity. Ernest Kris in fact has argued that biographical models influence human lives by shaping our super egos, a process he labels 'enacted biography'.[3]

This process of identification, however, involves the act of mutual discovery on the part of the biographer and reader. Both must contribute to the understanding of the subject, a task performed by the author when he fails to answer all the questions posed by his subject or his subject's life. Laurence Sterne recognized this situation in the eighteenth century when he wrote in *Tristram Shandy* that 'no author, who understands the just boundaries of decorum and good-breeding, would presume to think all: The truest respect which you can pay to the reader's understanding, is to . . . leave him something to imagine, in his turn, as well as yourself.' Virginia Woolf realized the importance of this unique relationship when she wrote that biographer and reader 'both together must *puzzle out* what actually did take place on a given occasion . . .' Leon Edel restated the condition which recognizes the ultimately incomplete nature of every biography when he wrote that a successful biography discerns 'the complexities of being without pretending that life's riddles have been answered'.[4]

Conceived as an heuristic activity, biography fulfils its analytic purpose through incompleteness, engaging the reader's imagination in the task of evaluating the subject. The phenomenology of reading biography is the activity of perceiving the function of language in the work simultaneous with understanding the history of the subject. The narrative as the shaping factor of the events becomes pre-eminent. The aim of biography is not so much to convey the 'facts', which it linguistically cannot do objectively, but to present an attitude, perspective or point of view regarding those 'facts'. It accomplishes this through its rhetorical and linguistic properties, most noticeably in its use of literary tropes.

Consistently, however, the drive to understand the inner life, the Plutarchian desire to perceive and express character through telling personal detail is at odds with an Aristotelian focus on mimesis, on external event. The stress on the record, noted by Roger North in 1740 when he remarked that biographers sought 'to rectify want of art by *copia* of matter', has long been in conflict with the issue of selectivity, and biographical criticism has often been trapped by this dilemma.[5] But recognizing biography as a narrative exemplifying the art of telling resolves this contradiction. Here, the theories of fiction presented by Frank Kermode and the ideas of history articulated by Hayden White are helpful. Accepting the notion of 'regulative fictions' – for biography I have called them 'authorized fictions' – assists us in understanding how transformed fact assumes imaginative yet legitimate value. The respect of biographical narratives for the facts does not mean they cannot be altered to improve their understanding which the literary act of composing or writing a biography performs. 'Too strict distinction between meaning and truth', Kermode suggests, 'would leave few historical narratives capable of interesting us.' These remarks apply equally well to biography. Furthermore, we must remember that 'narrative is not opposed to analysis and problem-solving' and the boundary between an event and the telling of that event, fact and story, continually shifts and occasionally merges with itself. The current debate between historians over quantifying versus narrative history is instructive for understanding the nature of biography and its future.[6] Can the collection and ordering of data in a person's life ever give us complete knowledge of the truth, or must one recognize the fundamental inability of ever knowing the past exactly and therefore accept its fictions? Such questions are basic to understanding the future of biography.

Samuel Johnson declared that the principal value of biography is in 'giving us what comes near to ourselves, what we can turn to use'. For modern readers and writers of literary biography this means a more sympathetic as well as more psychologically and more literarily informed 'use' of biography – avoiding an emphasis on the mass of data at the expense of conveying the vital struggles that confront the subject and the biographer. Lytton Strachey once remarked that a biographer's equipment should consist of three things – a capacity for absorbing facts, a capacity for stating them and a point of view.[7] I have stressed all three in an effort to show how in biography language alters fact and draws on fiction to clarify its form.

Notes and References

INTRODUCTION

1. Elizabeth Gaskell, *The Life of Charlotte Brontë*, ed. Alan Shelston (Harmondsworth: Penguin Books, 1977) ch. VII, p. 155. This is a reprint of the 1857 first edition.
2. Frank Kermode, *The Genesis of Secrecy. On the Interpretation of Narrative* (Harvard University Press, 1979) p. 117.
3. David Novarr, *The Making of Walton's Lives* (Ithaca: Cornell University Press, 1958) p. 495. Nearly thirty years ago Novarr modestly noted the disregard of form in the study of biography. More aggressively, Leon Edel presses the case for the formal analysis of biography in 'Biography: The Question of Form', *Friendship's Garland, Essays Presented to Mario Praz*, ed. Vittorio Gabrieli (Rome: Edizioni de Storia e Letteratura, 1966) pp. 343–60, and more recently in 'Biography: A Manifesto', *biography*, 1:1 (1978) 1–3.
4. Edward Gibbon, *An Essay on the Study of Literature* (1761, French; New York: Garland Publishing, 1970) pp. 99–100. Gibbon adds that the rarest quality is meeting 'a genius who knows how to distinguish them [the types of facts] amidst the vast chaos of events, wherein they are jumbled and deduce them, pure and unmixed, from the rest' (p. 100).
5. On Donne, see Novarr, *The Making of Walton's Lives*, p. 56; on Boswell, Robert Gittings, *The Nature of Biography* (Seattle: University of Washington Press, 1978) p. 32; Thomas Carlyle, *History of Frederick II of Prussia Called Frederick the Great*, ed. John Clive (University of Chicago Press, 1969) pp. 5–6; Lytton Strachey, *Eminent Victorians* (1918; New York: Capricorn Books, 1963) pp. 6, 184; Virginia Woolf, *A Writer's Diary*, ed. Leonard Woolf (New York: Harcourt Brace Jovanovich, 1973) p. 281; Gore Vidal, 'French Letters: Theories of the New Novel', *Matters of Fact and Fiction* (New York: Vintage Books, 1978) p. 75.
6. Thomas Carlyle, *Sartor Resartus*, ed. C. F. Harrold (New York: Odyssey Press, 1937) p. 203; Friedrich Nietzsche, *The Will to Power*, tr. Walter Kaufmann and R. J. Hollindale, ed. Walter J. Kaufmann (New York: Random House, 1967) p. 301. In the same work Nietzsche also declares there are no facts, 'only interpretations' (p. 267).
7. Hugh Kenner, *The Counterfeiters, An Historical Comedy* (Bloomington: Indiana University Press, 1968) p. 61.
8. In answer to the question what was new in his biography of F. Scott Fitzgerald, the third since 1954 in English, Matthew J. Bruccoli replied 'more facts'. This rallying cry summarizes Bruccoli's sense of the responsi-

210

bility of a biographer shared by many: 'he should assemble a great many details in a usable way, relying heavily on the subject's own words', 'Preface', *Some Sort of Epic Grandeur, The Life of F. Scott Fitzgerald* (New York: Harcourt Brace Jovanovich, 1981) p. xx. Froude, the biographer of Carlyle, made the same point when he wrote 'the facts must be delineated first . . . We must have the real thing before we can have a sense of a thing', quoted in 'Preface', *Studies in Biography*, ed. Daniel Aaron (Harvard University Press, 1978) p. vi. Ovid, however, was aware of certain dangers: 'I will sing of facts, but some will say that I invented them', *Fasti*, Book vi, 1:3.

9. On Lockhart's departure from fact in his biography of Scott see Francis R. Hart, *Lockhart as Romantic Biographer* (Edinburgh University Press, 1971) pp. 41–3 and *passim*. Virginia Woolf, 'The Art of Biography', *Collected Essays* (London: Hogarth Press, 1967) IV: 228. Phyllis Rose, *Woman of Letters: A Life of Virginia Woolf* (New York: Oxford University Press, 1978) p. viii. Helene Moglen in *Charlotte Brontë: The Self Conceived* (New York: W. W. Norton, 1976) calls for a new biography that 'places chronology at the service of causality, that risks partiality in the interest of emphasis' (p. 14).

10. Hayden White, 'The Historical Text as Literary Artifact', *Tropics of Discourse, Essays in Cultural Criticism* (Baltimore: Johns Hopkins Press, 1978) pp. 84, 91–2. All further references are to this edition. White outlines his notion of emplotment in the 'Introduction' to *Metahistory, The Historical Imagination in 19th Century Europe* (Baltimore: Johns Hopkins Press, 1973) pp. 5–13. On narrative, fact and story also see Cushing Strout, 'The Fortunes of Telling', *The Veracious Imagination* (Middleton, Conn.: Wesleyan University Press, 1981) pp. 3–28. On basic plot structures see Northrop Frye, *Anatomy of Criticism* (Princeton University Press, 1957) pp. 158–238.

11. See Ina Schabert, 'Fictional Biography, Factual Biography and Their Contaminations', *biography*, 5:1 (Winter 1982) 1–16, for an important discussion of fact, fiction and biography related to aesthetic integrity.

12. Pirandello in Lester G. Crocker, *Jean-Jacques Rousseau, The Quest* (New York: Macmillan, 1968) I:x.

13. Karl Popper, *Conjectures and Refutations, The Growth of Scientific Knowledge*, 2nd edn (New York: Basic Books, 1965) p. 46. See also David Fischer, *Historians' Fallacies* (New York: Harper & Row, 1970) and Ralph Rader, 'Fact, Theory and Literary Explanations', *Critical Inquiry*, I (December 1974) 254–72. Lytton Strachey, *Eminent Victorians*, p. vii. My italics.

14. Emil Ludwig, 'Introduction: On the Writing of History', *Genius and Character*, tr. Kenneth Burke (1927; New York: Harcourt Brace, 1928) p. 5. James L. Clifford, *From Puzzles to Portraits, Problems of a Literary Biographer* (Chapel Hill: University of North Carolina Press, 1970) p. 111. Robert Bernard Martin author of *Tennyson* (1980), echoes Johnson in a 1982 interview: 'S.C.: "What proportion of the biography would be educated guess or extrapolation?" R.B.M.: "Very, very little that is unsupported by fact. No, what I think you have to do is to guess and then verify it."' Stephen Cahan, 'Interview–Review: Robert B. Martin', *biography*, 5:1 (Winter 1982) 78. Martin added that perhaps the greatest danger 'to the academic in writing biography is that he's too often the victim of fact' (p. 85). For a similar view expressed by a literary historian, see David Novarr, *The Making of Walton's Lives*, p. 486: 'every biographer has in his mind, if not a

character-image, a sense of character images, a pattern, a sense of a certain
unity, a sort of musical tone which explains or clarifies his subject'.

15. Harold Nicolson, *The Development of English Biography* (London: Hogarth
    Press, 1927) pp. 154–5.
16. Leon Edel, *Henry James, the Master* (Philadelphia: J. B. Lippincott, 1972)
    p. 20. Edgar Johnson modifies this view when he states that the role of the
    imagination in biography is 'not so much in inventing as in perceiving
    relationships between different areas of fact and relationships between
    different degrees of relationship'. Edgar Johnson, 'The Art of Biography',
    Dickens Studies Annual, 8 (New York: AMS Press, 1980) p. 3.
17. Robert Louis Stevenson, *The Letters of Robert Louis Stevenson*, ed. Sidney
    Colvin (New York: Charles Scribner's Sons, 1899) II: 350–1. Dated 18 June
    1893 from Samoa.

CHAPTER 1: BIOGRAPHY AS AN INSTITUTION

1. [George Eliot,] 'Sterling', *Westminster Review*, lxii (Jan 1852) 247–9.
2. John Sterling in Thomas Carlyle, *The Life of John Sterling, Centenary Edition,
   The Works of Thomas Carlyle* (London: Chapman & Hall, 1897) XI, 138. In
   1882 Leslie Stephen was also to refer to the great eighty-five-volume
   Biographie Universelle, Ancienne et Moderne (1811–1862), founded by J. F.
   Michaud and his brother L. G. Michaud (Paris: Michaud frères, 1811–62)
   as a model for the *Dictionary of National Biography*. The subtitle indicated the
   scope of the dictionary: *Histoire, par ordre alphabétique, de la view publique et privée
   de tous les hommes qui sont fait remarquer par leurs écrits, leurs actions, leurs talents,
   leurs vertus, or leurs crimes.*
3. John Watkins, 'Preface', *Universal Biographical Dictionary* (London: n.p.,
   1800) in Waldo H. Dunn, *English Biography* (London: J. M. Dent and Sons,
   1916) p. 157. On being paid not to write lives see Carlyle, 'Sir Walter Scott',
   Critical and Miscellaneous Essays, Centenary Edition, The Works of Thomas Carlyle
   (London: Chapman & Hall, 1899) XXIX, 26–7.
4. Anon., 'Contemporary Literature', *Westminster and Foreign Quarterly Review*,
   68 (Oct 1857) 581. The comment follows a review of Robert Carruthers, *Life
   of Alexander Pope including extracts from his Correspondence*, 2nd edn enl. (London:
   H. G. Bohn, 1857) pp. 580–1.
5. There is surprisingly little on Plutarch's influence on English writing after
   Shakespeare. See Rudolph Hirzel, *Plutarch* (Leipzig: T. Weicher, 1912)
   pp. 139–50, 192–200. Gilbert Highet, *The Classical Tradition* (New York:
   Oxford University Press, 1949) pp. 394–6; Edmund G. Berry, *Emerson's
   Plutarch* (Harvard University Press, 1961), ch. 1. For a brief but important
   assessment by a late-Victorian biographer see Sidney Lee, 'Principles of
   Biography', *Elizabethan and Other Essays*, ed. Frederick Boas (1929; Freeport,
   NY: Books for Libraries Press, 1968) pp. 46–50. Charles Dickens, *Our
   Mutual Friend* (1865; London: Oxford University Press, 1963), New Oxford
   Illustrated Dickens, Book III, ch. 6, p. 476.
6. Edward Fitzgerald to John Allen, *Letters of Edward Fitzgerald*, ed. Alfred and
   Annabelle Terhune (Princeton University Press, 1980) I, 192. Fitzgerald

referred to the *Parallel Lives* as 'one of the most delightful books I ever read' (ibid.). John Aldington Symonds, *Letters of John Aldington Symonds*, ed. Herbert M. Scheuller and Robert L. Peters (Detroit: Wayne State University Press, 1968) II, 289, 400.

7. George Bernard Shaw to Archibald Henderson, *GBS Collected Letters, 1898–1910*, ed. Dan H. Laurence (London: Max Reinhardt, 1972) p. 510; R. C. Trench, *Plutarch, His Life, His Lives and His Morals* (London: Macmillan, 1873) p. 43. Other admirers of Plutarch included Bacon, Goethe, Wordsworth and Emerson.

8. Plutarch, 'Alexander', *Plutarch's Lives*, tr. Bernadotte Perrin (London: Heinemann, 1928) Loeb Classical Library, vol. VII, I, 225. Plutarch, 'Pericles', *Lives of the Noble Grecians and Romans*, tr. Dryden, rev. Arthur Hugh Clough (1859–60; New York: Modern Library, 1932) p. 183. This translation vividly conveys the meaning of the original.

9. Samuel Smiles, *Self Help with Illustrations of Conduct and Perseverance*, intro. Asa Briggs (1859; London: John Murray, 1958) pp. 39–40. All further references are to this edition. [Francis Jeffrey], 'Memoirs of Sir James Mackintosh', *Edinburgh Review*, LXII (1835) 209.

10. Plutarch, 'Lucullus', in R. H. Barrow, *Plutarch and His Times* (London: Chatto & Windus, 1967) p. 56. I have chosen Barrow's translation for its contemporary quality.

11. On collective biography see Phyllis M. Riches, *An Analytical Bibliography of Universal Collective Biography*, intro. Sir Frederick Kenyon (London Library Association, 1934), and Robert B. Slocum, *Biographical Dictionaries and Related Works* (Detroit: Gale Research, 1967). Also see Waldo H. Dunn, *English Biography*, pp. 195–7 and Pat Rogers, 'Johnson's *Lives of the Poets* and the Biographical Dictionary', *Review of English Studies*, XXXI: 122 (May 1980) 149–71.

12. Thomas Carlyle, *The French Revolution* in Edmund G. Berry, *Emerson's Plutarch* (Harvard University Press, 1961) p. 28. A curious example of this shift back and forth from brief to enlarged lives is Robert Southey whose short life of Nelson appeared in 1813. His own life, however, became the subject of a six-volume biography by his son, C. C. Southey published in 1850.

13. Plutarch, 'Timoleon', *Plutarch's Lives*, tr. Dryden, rev. Clough, p. 293. Sigmund Freud, *Leonardo da Vinci, A Study in Psychosexuality*, tr. A. A. Brill (New York: Vintage, 1947) p. 109. Leon Edel has developed this idea in ch. 1 of *Literary Biography* (1957; New York: Anchor Books, 1959).

14. Smiles, *Self Help*, p. 348. Smiles added that 'the chief use of biography consists in the novel models of character in which it abounds' (p. 350).

15. Waldo H. Dunn, *English Biography*, p. 189. Most recently, A. O. J. Cockshut has treated Smiles as a biographer although he focuses only on hidden, thematic tensions rather than the literary quality of his lives. See *Truth to Life, The Art of Biography in the Nineteenth Century* (New York: Harcourt Brace Jovanovich, 1974) ch. 7. Richard Altick in *Lives and Letters* (1965; New York: Alfred A. Knopf, 1969) devotes two paragraphs to Smiles with a lengthy quotation substituting for a solid analysis, see pp. 88–9.

16. Thomas Carlyle, *Past and Present, Centenary Edition, The Works of Thomas Carlyle* (1843; London: Chapman & Hall, 1847) X, 298.

17. Craik in Charles Knight, *Passages of a Working Life During Half a Century* (London: Bradbury and Evans, 1864) II, 134. For details of the society see vol. II, ch. vi.
18. *Self Help*, p. 55; 7500 copies of *Stephenson* were published in 1857; 25 500 were in print to 1863, 60 000 to the end of the 1880s. See Richard D. Altick, *The English Common Reader* (University of Chicago Press, 1957) p. 388. By comparison, Croker's 1831 edn of Boswell's *Johnson* sold only 50 000 copies up to 1891. An American edition of *Stephenson* appeared in 1858. As recently as 1975 the Folio Society of London reprinted the book. One example of the influence of the biography is *Adam Bede*. See David Moldstad, 'George Eliot's *Adam Bede* and Smiles', *Life of George Stephenson*', *ELN*, 14 (1977) 189–92.
19. [A. K. H. Boyd,] 'George Stephenson and the Railway', *Fraser's Magazine*, 56 (Aug 1857) 192; 'The Life of George Stephenson', *Westminster and Foreign Quarterly*, 68 (July 1857) 214–34; 'George Stephenson and Railway Locomotion', *Quarterly Review*, 102 (Oct 1857) 496. On the art of the biography see *Fraser's*, 56: 193; *Quarterly Review*, 102: 503, 507.
20. Samuel Smiles, *The Lives of George and Robert Stephenson* (1863; London: Folio Society, 1975) ch. XI. This combined life is the most accessible edition. All further references are to this version.
21. George Eliot, Journal, 26? July 1857 in *The George Eliot Letters*, ed. Gordon S. Haight (Yale University Press, 1954) II, 369.
22. 'The Life of George Stephenson', *Westminster Quarterly*, 68 (July 1857) 214.
23. W. E. Gladstone in Smiles, *Autobiography of Samuel Smiles*, ed. Thomas Mackay (London: John Murray, 1905) p. 256.
24. Samuel Smiles, *Selections from the Lives of the Engineers*, ed. Thomas Park Hughes (Cambridge: MIT Press, 1966) pp. 80–2, 302. I have used this edition for its accessibility, useful introduction and bibliography. All further references are to this edition.
25. See Palgrave, *History of Normandy and of England* (London: J. Parker & Son, 1857) II: 65; Harold Nicolson, *The Development of English Biography* (London: Hogarth Press, 1927) pp. 126–7.
26. Little has been written on Morley as a critic or biographer although the following are helpful: Lytton Strachey, 'A Statesman: Lord Morley', *Characters and Commentaries* (London: Chatto & Windus, 1933) pp. 222–31; Edward Alexander, *John Morley* (New York: Twayne, 1972); A. O. J. Cockshut, 'Morley's Gladstone', *Truth to Life*, pp. 175–92; and William Hayley, 'John Morley', *American Scholar* (Summer 1982) 403–9.
27. Alexander Macmillan to Malcolm Macmillan 2 October 1877 in C. L. Graves, *The Life and Letters of Alexander Macmillan* (London: Macmillan, 1910) p. 342. Gladstone, in fact, did a primer on Homer for Macmillan, while Grove contributed one on geography.
28. Morley in Charles Morgan, *The House of Macmillan* (London: Macmillan, 1943) p. 115.
29. John Morley, *Recollections* (New York: Macmillan, 1917) I, 92; Morley to Macmillan, Macmillan Archives, British Library, London.
30. Macmillan to Morley, Macmillan Archives, British Library, London.
31. Macmillan to Morley, 9 November 1877 in Graves, *Alexander Macmillan*, p. 343; George Eliot to Macmillan, ibid., pp. 343–4.

32. All references and materials from the Macmillan Archives, British Library, London.

33. John Morley, *Diderot and the Encyclopedists* (London: Chapman & Hall, 1878) I, 18.

34. Morley, 'Byron', *Critical Miscellanies* (London: Chapman & Hall, 1871) pp. 255–6. In his essay 'The Man of Letters as Hero', Morley asks whether a biography can 'effectually and truly reveal the inward history, which is, after all, the real tissue of the man's being'. *Nineteenth Century Essays*, ed. Peter Stansky (University of Chicago Press, 1970) p. 61.

35. See John Gross, *The Rise and Fall of the Man of Letters* (1969; Harmondsworth: Penguin Books, 1973) pp. 121–4; Myron Tuman, 'The First English Men of Letters Series', *Contemporary Review*, 235: 1363 (Aug 1979) 70–5.

36. Mark Pattison, *Milton* (1879; New York: Harper and Brothers, 1894) p. 28.

37. Morley, 'Mr. Mill's Autobiography' (1874), *Nineteenth Century Essays*, p. 152; 'Condorcet', *Critical Miscellanies* (London: Chapman & Hall, 1871) p. 110.

38. Morley, 'Mr. Mill's Doctrine of Liberty', *Nineteenth Century Essays*, p. 135.

39. Morley, *Voltaire* (1872; London: Macmillan) pp. 301–2; 'A New Calendar of Great Men', *Nineteenth Century*, no. 180 (Feb 1892) p. 390. Morley explained, for example, that 'Little books are often laughed at as a sort of tinned intellectual meats; but many have no doubt found how extremely difficult it is to write them well. To tell the story of even a great man's life in some two hundred pages or so might seem to those who have never tried an easy matter enough; but it will not seem so to any who have tried it' (ibid.).

40. Morley, 'Byron', *Critical Miscellanies* (London: Chapman & Hall, 1871) pp. 256, 257; 'Mr. Pater's Essays', *Nineteenth Century Essays*, p. 233.

41. Morley, 'Harriet Martineau', *Nineteenth Century Essays*, pp. 256–7. All further references are to this edition.

42. Anon., 'English Men of Letters, ed. J. Morley, *Johnson*, by Leslie Stephen', *Athenaeum*, 2645 (6 July 1878) p. 11; 'Shelley', *Athenaeum*, 2662 (2 Nov 1878) p. 553; 'Hutton's Scott', *Athenaeum*, 2646 (13 July 1878) p. 46; 'English Men of Letters', *Athenaeum*, 2645 (6 July 1878) p. 13. E. F. Benson wrote one of the most negative assessments of the series declaring they were 'a shelf of disillusionment'. His attack on the unsuitability of writers' lives for biography appeared in the *Contemporary Review*, LXVIII (1895) 131–2.

43. Stephen to Morley on the first anniversary of *Johnson*, 16 Feb 1879, in F. W. Maitland, *Life and Letters of Leslie Stephen* (London: Duckworth, 1906) p. 335; Morley to Macmillan, 5 Feb 1878, Macmillan Archives, British Library; 'So be it', Morley to Macmillan, Macmillan Archives, British Library; Maitland, p. 302; Stephen to C. E. Norton, 23 Dec 1877, Maitland, pp. 304–5; Morley to Craik, 8 March 1878, Macmillan Archives, British Library.

44. Maitland, *Leslie Stephen*, p. 286.

45. Maitland, ibid., p. 306; Leslie Stephen, *Johnson* (London: Macmillan, 1878) p. 2. All further references are to this edition.

46. Stephen to Gosse in Maitland, *Leslie Stephen*, p. 346; on Browning and Froude, Maitland, ibid., p. 465; Morley to Stephen, in Maitland, ibid., p. 465.

47. Gosse, 'Biography', *Encyclopaedia Britannica*, 11th edn (Cambridge University Press, 1910) III, 953. All further references are to this edition.

48. Matthew Arnold, 'The Literary Influence of Academies', *Lectures and Essays in Criticism*, ed. R. H. Super (Ann Arbor: University of Michigan Press, 1962) pp. 241–2. For details on European biographical dictionaries see Sidney Lee, 'A Statistical Account' (1900), *Dictionary of National Biography*, ed. Leslie Stephen and Sidney Lee (London: Oxford University Press, 1938) pp. lxii–lxiii. All further references are to this edition. The Oxford edition of the *Dictionary of National Biography* first appeared in 1917, reprinting twenty-two volumes of the main dictionary (original in sixty-three volumes) with the twenty-second the *Supplement*. Vols 1–21 were originally issued between 1885 and 1890, ed. by Leslie Stephen; vols 22–26, 1890–1, ed. by Stephen and Sidney Lee; vols 27–66, 1891–1901, ed. by Lee alone. 'A Statistical Account' was first published in June 1900 as the Preface to vol. 63, the last volume of the first series. The 'Postscript to the Statistical Account' was published in 1908. They both appear in vol. I of the Oxford reprint.

49. The clearest history of the shaping of the *Dictionary of National Biography* is Alan Bell's article 'Leslie Stephen and the *DNB*', *Times Literary Supplement*, 3951 (16 Dec 1977) p. 1478. A fuller account can be found in the 'Memoir of George Smith' written by Sidney Lee in vol. I of the *DNB*.

50. 'Literary Gossip', *Athenaeum*, 2872 (11 Nov 1882) p. 629.

51. Leslie Stephen, 'A New Biographia Britannica', *Athenaeum*, 2878 (23 Dec 1882) p. 850. All further references are to this version Sir Egerton Brydges, *Autobiography* (London: Cochrane and McCrone, 1834) I, 94. Brydges was the author of the inventive work *Imaginative Biography* (London: Saunders and Otley, 1834), which he defined as 'an Imaginary Superstructure on the Known facts of the Biography of eminent characters', ibid., p. i.

52. Stephen, 'Addison', *Dictionary of National Biography* (1885; London: Oxford University Press, 1938) I, 130A. All further references are to this edition.

53. [R. C. Christie], 'Biographical Dictionaries', *Quarterly Review*, 157: 313 (Jan 1884) 229. All further references are to this version. The essay also includes an estimate of the popularity of biography among readers. Cf. 'Contemporary Literature', *Blackwood's*, CXXV: DCCLXII (April 1879) 482–96, which also astutely surveys the status of nineteenth-century biography.

54. Stephen to Lee, 1 Aug. 1893, Ms. Eng. miscd. 180/271, Bodleian Library, Oxford.

55. Stephen to Gosse in Bell, 'Leslie Stephen and the *DNB*', *TLS*, 3951 (16 Dec 1977) 1478.

56. Maitland, *Leslie Stephen*, pp. 385, 378–9, 383; Leslie Stephen, *Some Early Impressions* (London: Hogarth Press, 1924) p. 162. Passages from *Some Early Impressions* first appeared in the *National Review*, XLII (1903). See the review by Gosse in *Silhouettes* (London: Heinemann, 1925) which begins by lamenting the neglect of Stephen's writing; Maitland, ibid., p. 368.

57. Sidney Lee, 'Principles of Biography' (1911), *Elizabethan and Other Essays*, ed. Frederick J. Boas (1929; Freeport, NY: Books for Libraries Press, 1968) p. 55. Leslie Stephen, *The Science of Ethics* (1882; New York: G. P. Putnam's Sons, 1882) pp. 35, 74, 30.

58. Lee, 'A Statistical Account', *Dictionary of National Biography*, p. lxxviii.

59. Stephen, *Some Early Impressions*, pp. 163–4; Maitland, *Leslie Stephen*, p. 383.

60. Sidney Lee, 'Postscript to the Statistical Account' (1908), *DNB*, p. lxxx;

Maitland, *Leslie Stephen*, p. 371; Sidney Lee, 'Principles of Biography', *Elizabethan and Other Essays*, pp. 50, 51; Maitland, ibid., p. 372.

61. Sidney Lee, 'The Perspective of Biography', *Elizabethan and Other Essays*, p. 63.

62. Samuel Schoenbaum, *Shakespeare's Lives* (Oxford: Clarendon Press, 1970) p. 572; Sidney Lee, 'Shakespeare', *DNB*, vol. 51 (Rpt. vol. 17): 1292A; Schoenbaum, ibid., pp. 512–14. In the one-volume biography, the *Life of William Shakespeare*, Lee consciously avoids aesthetic commentary preferring 'an exhaustive and well-arranged statement of the facts of Shakespeare's career, achievement, and reputation that shall reduce conjecture to the smallest dimensions consistent with coherence, and shall give verifiable references to all the original sources of information'. Lee, 'Preface', *A Life of William Shakespeare* (London: Smith, Elder and Co., 1898) p. vi. By 1899 – one year after publication – the biography was in its 4th edn.

63. Stephen to Moore in Maitland, *Leslie Stephen*, p. 381; *Some Early Impressions*, p. 158; Lee, 'A Statistical Account', *DNB*, p. lxiii; Maitland, ibid., p. 397; Tout in Maitland, p. 370.

64. 'Dictionary of National Biography, Vol. I', *Athenaeum*, 2985 (10 Jan 1885) p. 43: 'Dictionary of National Biography, Vol. IV', *Athenaeum*, 3025 (17 Oct 1885) p. 502.

65. 'The Old Saloon', *Blackwood's*, CXLI (Feb 1887) 310, 311, 313.

66. [R. C. Christie,] 'Dictionary of National Biography, Vols. I–X', *Quarterly Review*, 164: 328 (Jan–April 1887) 352, 364, 380. Of the E. A. Freeman affair, Christie remarks that 'surely a Dictionary of *National* Biography ought to consult the wants of a nation, and not the whims of a few scholars' (p. 358). Some readers were never satisfied, however. Reverend John Washbourn, Rector of Rudford, Gloucester, sent regular criticisms to Stephen, from vol. 1 to 35 until the rector's death in 1893. Another clergyman, W. C. Boulter, contributed papers of correction to *Notes and Queries* throughout the entire eighteen-and-a-half-year project.

67. Leslie Stephen, 'Biography' (1893), *Men, Books and Mountains*, ed. S. O. A. Ullmann (London: Hogarth Press, 1956) pp. 131, 128.

68. Max Beerbohm in S. N. Behrman, *Portrait of Max* (New York: Random House, 1960) pp. 104–6.

69. Claude Levi-Strauss, *The Savage Mind* (1962; University of Chicago Press, 1970) p. 23; Sidney Lee, 'Principles of Biography', *Elizabethan and Other Essays*, p. 44; Levi-Strauss, pp. 24, 23.

70. Edmund Gosse, 'Preface', *Critical Kit-Kats* (London: Heinemann, 1896) pp. ix–x; *Portraits and Sketches* (London: Heinemann, 1912) p. viii.

71. See Sidney Lee, 'The Perspective of Biography', *Elizabethan and Other Essays*, pp. 64–5; on the parallels between Scott's life and *Zélide* see Meryle Secrest, *Being Bernard Berenson* (New York: Holt, Rinehart & Winston, 1979) p. 304; Geoffrey Scott, *The Portrait of Zélide* (1925; New York: Charles Scribner's Sons, 1926) pp. 215–16.

72. Edmund Gosse, *Tallemant des Réaux or the Art of Miniature in Biography* (Oxford: Clarendon Press, 1925) pp. 8–9, 14, 21, 23.

73. Stevenson to Gosse in Evan Charteris, *Life and Letters of Edmund Gosse*, p. 105.

74. Charles Whibley, 'The Limits of Biography' (1897), *Biography as an Art*, ed.

James L. Clifford (New York: Oxford University Press, 1962) pp. 110, 109; 'The Indiscretions of Biography', *English Review*, xxxix (Dec 1924) 772.

75. T. S. Eliot, 'Charles Whibley' (1931), *Selected Essays*, new edn (New York: Harcourt Brace World, 1964) p. 444. Eliot's praise of Whibley's writing reflects his important role in Eliot's life and career: Whibley was patron to the *Criterion* and recommended Eliot to Geoffrey Faber as a talented young man eager to enter publishing. Edmund Gosse dedicated his 1925 collection of essays, *Silhouettes*, to Whibley.

76. On the original title of *Eminent Victorians* see Michael Holroyd, *Lytton Strachey* (New York: Holt, Rinehart & Winston, 1968) ii, 66; Max Beerbohm, 'The Spirit of Caricature' (1901), *A Variety of Things* (London: Heinemann, 1928) pp. 148–9.

77. Lytton Strachey, *Portraits in Miniature* (London: Chatto & Windus, 1931) title page. All further references are to this edition. The quotation, from Horace, *Satire*, Book 1 Satire 10 reads, in a modern verse translation, 'You need / terseness, to let the thought run freely on without / becoming entangled in a mass of verbiage that will hang heavy / on the ear', *The Satires of Horace and Persius*, tr. Niall Rudd (Harmondsworth: Penguin Books, 1973) p. 67. Strachey, *Eminent Victorians* (1918; New York: Capricorn, 1963) p. vi; Michael Holroyd, *Lytton Strachey, A Critical Biography* (New York: Holt, Rinehart & Winston, 1968) ii, 33–4, 658, 665. Strachey's literary executors emphasize Strachey's talent as a miniaturist in the introduction to a recent collection entitled *The Shorter Strachey*: 'Close observation of detail and exquisite care in its selection and presentation' summarize his virtues. 'The limitations of the smaller canvas brought out his strengths – concision and precision', they add. Michael Holroyd and Paul Levy, 'Preface', *The Shorter Strachey* (Oxford University Press, 1980) p. vii.

CHAPTER 2: BIOGRAPHY AS A PROFESSION

1. Samuel Johnson, 'Rambler No. 60', *Essays from the Rambler, Adventurer and Idler*, ed. W. J. Bate (Yale University Press, 1968) pp. 112–13.

2. Surprisingly little has been written on literature and even less on biography as a profession. See A. S. Collins, *The Profession of Letters 1780–1832* (New York: E. P. Dutton, 1929) and C. H. Sisson, 'The Profession of Letters or Down with Culture', *Art and Action* (London: Methuen, 1965) pp. 1–9, as well as John Gross, *The Rise and Fall of the Man of Letters* (London: Macmillan, 1969). John Garraty in *The Nature of Biography* (New York: Alfred A. Knopf, 1957) devotes a single paragraph to biography as a profession on p. 102. He cites Sainte Beuve in France, John Forster in England, James Parton in America as examples. Richard Altick in *Lives and Letters* (New York: Alfred A. Knopf, 1965) provides two pages on the topic (pp. 189–90). James C. Johnston in *Biography: The Literature of Personality* (New York: Century, 1927), introduced by the biographer Gamaliel Bradford, has twenty-one unfocused pages on the topic 'Life Writing as a Deliberate Professional Undertaking'. He suggests Izaak Walton as the first professional biographer; however, only pp. 65–6 deal directly with the topic. Harold Nicolson

refines Johnston's view calling Walton 'Our first *deliberate* biographer' and the 'first Englishman consciously to write artistic biography'. He, rather than David Masson 'revived Eademer's admirable practice of introducing original letters into the text' and included 'imaginary conversations'. *Development of English Biography* (London: Hogarth Press, 1927) pp. 66, 69. In a single sentence Nicolson also refers to the professional biographer and his emergence in the nineteenth century. See p. 127 and, later, p. 156.

3. G. H. Lewes, *Ranthorpe*, ed. Barbara Smalley (1847; Ohio University Press, 1974) pp. 32–3. On Forster and Lamb see John Forster, 'Biographical Memoir of Charles Lamb' in Thomas Noon Talford, *Memoirs of Charles Lamb*, ed. Percy Fitzgerald (London: W. W. Gibbings, 1892) pp. 276–85. Talford wrote of Forster that he was, for Lamb, 'a friend of comparatively recent date, but one with whom Lamb found himself as much at home as if he had known him for years' (pp. 216–17). On Forster and Hunt see Edmund Blunden, *Leigh Hunt* (London: Cobden-Sanderson, 1930) passim; for a description of the Forster–Landor relationship see R. H. Super, *Walter Savage Landor* (New York University Press, 1954) pp. 470, 455–6.

4. John Forster, *Walter Savage Landor, A Biography* (London: Chapman & Hall, 1844) I: 1, 2. Criticizing the opening sentence of Forster's *Dickens*, Wilkie Collins pencilled in the words 'after Walter Scott' following the opening, appositive clause, 'the most popular novelist of the century', in his copy of the *Life*. Collins in Kenneth Robinson, *Wilkie Collins* (London: Bodley Head, 1951) p. 258.

5. Whitwell Elwin, 'John Forster', *Forster Collection: A Catalogue of Printed Books* (London: South Kensington Museum, 1888) p. xiv. No biography of Forster exists, although Jane Hennings's dissertation covers the years up to 1856 in detail and Malcolm Elwin surveys the general facts in his now outdated *Victorian Wallflowers* (London: Jonathan Cape, 1934). See Hennings, 'John Forster: A Literary Biography to 1856', *DAI*, 40: 5874A (1956, Yale). Established in 1845 by the Lunatics Act, the eleven Lunacy Commissioners were charged with detailed inspection of all types of asylums in England. Composed of medical men and laymen, the commissioners were continually embroiled in maintaining and improving the standards of mental health in England. From January 1856 until 1861, Forster was Secretary; from 1861 until 1872, when poor health forced his retirement, Forster was a commissioner and travelled widely about the country. Two medical members became close friends of his and were named in his will. Did his awareness of mental illness influence his conception of character and understanding of the self in his biographies? Only more detailed research into Forster's own life can convincingly answer the question. On the Lunacy Commission see Andrew T. Scull, *Museums of Madness, The Social Organization of Insanity in 19th Century England* (New York: St Martin's Press, 1979) and their Annual Reports, 1842–1912.

6. Forster's contributions were as follows: vol. II, 'Sir John Eliot' and 'Thomas Wentworth, Earl of Strafford' (1836); vol. III, 'John Pym' and 'John Hampden' (1837); vol. IV, 'Sir Henry Vane' and 'Henry Marten' (1838); vols VI & VII, 'Oliver Cromwell' (1839). Forster is identified as 'John Forster, Esq. of the Inner Temple'. His contributions were reprinted in five volumes in 1840 as *Statesmen of the Commonwealth*.

7. John Forster, 'John Dryden and Jacob Tonson', *The Pic Nic Papers*, ed. Charles Dickens (Philadelphia: Lea and Blanchard, 1841) p. 46.

8. Memorandum of Agreement, 17 February 1835 in Deed Box of John Forster, Esq. Box FD 5, Forster Collection, Victoria and Albert Museum, London. The Deed Box is the source of all subsequent agreements cited in the text.

9. Chapman to Forster, 21 November 1872, Deed Box of John Forster, Box FD5, Forster Collection, Victoria and Albert Museum. Comparison of Forster's pass books from Drummond's Bank between 1838 and 1877 records his increasing wealth. In January 1839 his monthly balance was £122.25. By November 1843 it had grown to £1359 but thirty years later in November 1873 it had mushroomed to £6773. Forster's pass books are in his Deed Box at the Victoria and Albert Museum.

10. See Richard Renton, *John Forster and His Friendships* (London: Chapman & Hall, 1912); R. C. Lehmann, *Memoirs of Half A Century, A Record of Friendship*, ed. R. C. Lehmann (London: Smith Elder, 1908) and Malcolm Elwin, *Victorian Wallflowers* (London: Jonathan Cape, 1934).

11. William Macready, *The Diaries of William Charles Macready, 1833–51*, ed. William Toynbee (London: Chapman & Hall, 1912) II: 395, 396, 397.

12. R. C. Lehmann, *Memoirs of Half A Century*, p. 126. Cf. Bulwer's laudatory statement written on a packet of letters from John Forster printed in Elwin, *Victorian Wallflowers*, pp. 178–9.

13. William Ainsworth in Elwin, *Victorian Wallflowers*, p. 191. Forster, however, praised those who helped him. The day after Hunt died Forster wrote, on 29 August 1859, that 'he influenced all my modes of literary thought at the outset of my life – very probably he led me, at least, confirmed me in Literature as a profession – and but for him I might have been a popular leader on a circuit, with all its present and prospective rewards – It is better as it is – At least, I am content as it is –' Diary extract copied in Mrs Forster's Private Diary, 1882; extract sent to Whitwell Elwin. Of his uncle who financed his education, Forster wrote on 10 August 1853 on hearing of his death, 'my best friend all through life. I hope I have not ill repaid his kindness to me.' Forster Collection, Huntington Library, San Marino, California.

14. Malcolm Elwin, *Victorian Wallflowers*, p. 194; Thorton Hunt on Forster, ibid., p. 195. On Forster as a professional biographer see Waldo H. Dunn, *English Biography*, p. 183. Dunn links Forster's love of biography to his appreciation of history which biography crystallized. He is hostile, however, to Forster's narrative abilities and refers to his lives of Goldsmith, Landor, Dickens and Swift as 'good works of craft' lacking 'the dramatic instinct', although the Landor and Dickens 'must remain authoritative'. The biographies are works to be consulted, not read, he concludes (p. 184). The effusive Albert Britt in *The Great Biographers* (New York: Whittlesy House, 1936) praises Forster as 'the first professional biographer in that he was the first man to make in any sense a profession of the study of other men's lives' (p. 128). He does, however, criticize Forster for monopolizing Dickens; a new life is needed, he adds, 'to save Dickens from the smothering clutch of overrighteous affection' (p. 133). John A. Garraty in *The Nature of Biography* (New York: Alfred A. Knopf, 1957) links Forster to Sainte Beuve in France and James Parton in America as three writers who treat biography as a

professional occupation (p. 102). But summarizing Forster's current reputation is Elwin's criticism: Forster, 'the most Johnsonian figure of the
nineteenth century [is] remembered only as a Boswell' (*Victorian Wallflowers*,
p. 202).

15. A characteristic attack on Forster's failings, criticizing his lack of artistic
    sense, style, prejudice and inability to systematize is found in 'The Letters of
    Charles Dickens', *Athenaeum*, 2718 (29 Nov 1879) 687.

16. Francis R. Hart, *Lockhart as Romantic Biographer* (Edinburgh University Press,
    1971) pp. 41–3. Anticipating his own argument is Hart's earlier article,
    'Boswell and the Romantics: A Chapter in the History of Biographical
    Theory', *English Literary History*, 27 (1960) 44–65. See especially 56–8. J. W.
    Croker, 'Memoirs de Louis XVIII', *Quarterly Review*, XLVIII (1832) 456.

17. William Hazlitt, 'Boswell Redivivus', *Conversations of James Northcote, Complete
    Works of William Hazlitt*, ed. P. P. Howe (London: J. M. Dent, 1930–4) XI:
    350. John Forster, *Life of Dickens* (London: J. M. Dent, 1966) II: 376. Froude
    was also criticized for altering texts. C. E. Norton wrote that 'almost every
    letter in the life [of Carlyle] which I have collated with the original is
    incorrectly printed, some of them grossly so'. *Early Letters of Thomas Carlyle*,
    ed. Charles Eliot Norton (London: Macmillan, 1866) ii: 376. Froude
    defended himself in *Carlyle: History of His Life in London, 1834–1881* (London:
    Longmans & Co., 1884) I, i–7; II, 408–12 and in *My Relations with Carlyle*, ed.
    Ashley A. Froude and Margaret Froude (London: Longmans & Co., 1903).

18. John Forster, 'John Hampden', *Eminent British Statesmen, The Cabinet
    Cyclopedia*, ed. Dionysious Lardner (London: Longman, Rees *et al.*, 1837)
    II: 306. All further references are to this edition.

19. Forster writes 'it seems to me that what Clarendon says (in one of his
    passages of covert and falsely coloured meaning) of Hampden's character so
    far bears out Lord Nugent, and that they both conspire in this instance to
    reflect no additional honour on the patriot'. *Eminent British Statesman*, III: 335.

20. John Forster, 'Oliver Cromwell', *Eminent British Statesmen, The Cabinet
    Cyclopedia*, ed. Dionysious Lardner (London: Longman, Rees *et al.*, 1838)
    I: 10. All further references are to this edition.

21. Thomas Carlyle, *Sartor Resartus, Centenary Edition, The Works of Thomas Carlyle*,
    (London: Chapman & Hall, 1897) I: 54. John Forster, 'Life of Arnold',
    Examiner (12 Oct 1844) 644. 'Letters of Thomas Carlyle to John Forster', 18
    November 1847, Forster Collection, Huntington Library, San Marino,
    California.

22. Carlyle to Forster, 6 March 1865; Dickens to Forster, 13 May 1854,
    Huntington Library.

23. Dickens to Forster, 13 May 1854; Dickens to Forster, 15 May 1854,
    Huntington Library. Whitwell Elwin, 'John Forster', *Forster Collection*,
    p. xvii.

24. Charles Dickens to John Forster, 22 April 1848, *The Letters of Charles Dickens,
    Pilgrim Edition*, ed. Graham Storey and K. J. Fielding (Oxford: Clarendon
    Press, 1981) v: 288. Carlyle to Forster, ?1848, Forster Collection, Hunting-
    ton Library. For a further reference to *Goldsmith* see Mrs Gaskell, *Life of
    Charlotte Brontë*, ch. XXVIII. During the period between Forster's political-
    historical biographies and *Goldsmith* (1836–48), he also published a series of
    biographical essays in the *Edinburgh Review* and *Quarterly Review* on Dryden,

Steele, Defoe and Foote. They were reprinted as *Historical and Biographical Essays* (1858). For a discussion of their features see James A. Davies, 'Striving for Honesty: An Approach to Forster's Life,' *Dickens Studies Annual*, 7 (1970) 34–8.

25. Edward Fitzgerald, *The Letters of Edward Fitzgerald*, ed. Terhune (Princeton University Press, 1980) iii: 123, 173. Samuel R. Gardiner, 'Mr. John Forster', *Academy*, vol. 9 (5 Feb 1876) 122.

26. R. H. Super, 'Preface', *Walter Savage Landor* (New York University Press, 1954) p. vii.

27. Elizabeth Lynn Linton, 'Walter Savage Landor, A Biography', *North British Review*, no. 50, n.s. no. 11 (July 1869) 299, 300. All further references are to this source.

28. John Forster, *Walter Savage Landor, A Biography* (London: Chapman & Hall, 1869) i: 2. The biography was revised in 1876 and published as vol. 1 in *The Works and Life of Walter Savage Landor*.

29. [Charles Dickens], 'Landor's Life', *All the Year Round*, no. 34, n.s. (24 July 1869) 182. All further references are to this source. In his life of Dickens, Forster says this essay was Dickens's 'last paper for his weekly'. *Life of Dickens* (London: J. M. Dent, 1966) ii: 408.

30. Sidney Colvin, *Landor* (New York: Harper and Brothers, 1881) p. v. Malcolm Elwin, *Savage Landor* (NY: Macmillan, 1941) p. xviii; [Dickens], 'Landor's Life', *All the Year Round*, no. 34 (24 July 1869) 185. James A. Davies, 'Striving for Honesty', *Dickens Studies Annual*, 7 (1978) 142–3.

31. Among the most interesting recent assessments are James A. Davies, 'Forster and Dickens: The Making of Podsnap,' *Dickensian*, 70: 374 (Sept 1974) 145–58 [Special Forster issue], and Davies's 'Striving for Honesty', *DSA*, 7 (1978) 34–48. This focuses on the *Life of Dickens* but also stresses Forster's development of biography, although it overemphasizes the 'aggressively polemical and judiciously slanted' nature of Forster's writing (p. 34).

32. Georgina Hogarth to Mrs Fields, 29 January 1872, in 'Preface', *The Letters of Charles Dickens, Pilgrim Edition*, ed. Madeline House and Graham Storey (Oxford: Clarendon, 1965) i: xv. Cf. Dickens to Forster, 8 January 1845 and 22 April 1848. *Letters of Charles Dickens*, ed. House and Storey.

33. 'Life of Dickens', *Saturday Review*, xxxiv (1872) 668; George Eliot, *The George Eliot Letters*, ed. Gordon S. Haight (Yale University Press, 1955) v: 226; Collins in Kenneth Robinson, *Wilkie Collins* (London: Bodley Head, 1951) p. 260. George Gissing, *Charles Dickens, A Critical Study* (1898: London: Blackie and Son, 1929) p. 59. All further references are to this edition. Also see Gissing, *The Private Papers of Henry Ryecroft* (Westminster: Archibald Constable, 1903) pp. 215–16. For Carlyle's response see letter dated 16 February 1874 in *Dickens, The Critical Heritage*, ed. Philip Collins (London: Routledge & Kegan Paul, 1971) pp. 566–7; for Fitzgerald, see *Letters*, ed. Terhune, iii: 387, 403. Georgina Hogarth had a different and more curious reaction to the life. She referred to it as 'exhaustive as a *Biography* – leaving nothing to be said ever more, in my opinion. But, I believe, it was universally felt to be incomplete as a *Portrait* – because the scheme of the Book . . . prevented his making use of any letters – or scarcely any, besides those addressed to himself.' 22 March 1878 to Mrs J. T. Fields in 'Preface', *Letters*

of Dickens, Pilgrim Edition, p. ix. *The Saturday Review* provided a typically critical, arch comment: 'the real man Dickens seems persistently to elude us' xxxiv (1872) 668. A defence of the life is found in Andrew Lang's commentary in the *Academy* for 21 February 1874.

34. R. H. Horne, *Temple Bar*, xlvi (1876) 494.

35. Madeline House and Graham Storey, 'Preface', *Letters of Charles Dickens, Pilgrim Edition*, i: xi. A summary of Forster's alterations is found on pp. xi–xvii. Other nineteenth-century biographers who altered letters include Lockhart, J. W. Cross and, later, Strachey. For a comment on this tradition, and the Romantic theory of biography, see above in the present study, pp. 76–7. See also Alec W. Brice, 'The Compilation of the Critical Commentary in Forster's *Life of Dickens*', *Dickensian*, 70 (1974) 188–9.

36. John Forster, *The Life of Charles Dickens* (1872–4; London: J. M. Dent, new augmented edn, 1966) ii: 316–17. This is the 1876 revised edition published in two, not three volumes. All further references are to this accessible edition indicated by year unless otherwise noted. For a critique of this edition see 'Editing Dickens', *Times Literary Supplement*, no. 3, 397 (6 April 1967) 285.

37. See Sylvère Monod, 'John Forster's Life of Charles Dickens and Literary Criticism', *English Studies Today*, 4th series (Roma, 1966) 366.

38. John B. Castieau, 'Forster's Fictions', *Dickensian*, xii, 10 (Oct 1916) 264; Dickens to Forster, *Letters*, Nonesuch edn (London: 1916) ii: 83.

39. Leslie Stephen, *Swift*, English Men of Letters, ed. John Morley (1882; NY: Harper and Brothers, 1902) pp. vi–vii. Henry Craik, 'Preface to the First Edition', *The Life of Jonathan Swift*, 2nd edn (London: Macmillan, 1894) i: xiv–xv.

40. David Woolley summarizes many of these details in 'Forster's *Swift*', *Dickensian*, 70: 374 (Sept 1974) 191–204.

41. Elwin, letter of 22 February 1876 in Woolley, 'Forster's *Swift*', 198. Ironically, Elwin added in a letter to John Murray at this time that Forster's illness affected his judgement and that with the exception of *Goldsmith* and *Dickens* none of his books returned a profit for his publishers. The issue between Elwin and Murray was whether or not to continue *Swift*.

42. Woolley, ibid., p. 198. John Forster, *The Life of Jonathan Swift, Vol. 1, 1667–1711* (London: John Murray, 1875) p. 100. All further references are to this edition.

43. Hesketh Pearson, *Hesketh Pearson By Himself* (New York: Harper & Row, 1965) pp. 324, 240, 263.

44. Harold Nicolson, *The Development of English Biography*, p. 135.

CHAPTER 3: VERSIONS OF THE LIFE: GEORGE ELIOT AND HER BIOGRAPHERS

1. Hayden White argues that 'every set of events can be emplotted in any number of ways without doing violence to their "factuality"', in 'The Problem of Style in Realistic Representation: Marx and Flaubert', *The Concept of Style*, ed. Berel Lang (University of Pennsylvania Press, 1979) p. 228. Modernism, White explains in the same essay, is the capacity of

language to 'intrude itself into discourse as a content alongside of whatever referent may be signalled on the surface of the text' (p. 229). This idea has important consequences for the way we read biography as I show in a discussion of figurative language and narrative in Chapter 5. Katherine Frank advances a different explanation for multiple lives in her essay 'Writing Lives: Theory and Practice in Literary Biography', *Genre*, 13:4 (Winter 1980) 499–516. She believes they appear because of the chasm between narrative (popular) lives and analytical (scholarly) lives. The former tells a story, the latter interprets a life and we need both (pp. 506–8). William McKinley Runyan provides a defence of multiple lives via 'perspectivism' in his article, 'Alternate Accounts of Lives: An Argument for Epistemological Relativism', *biography*, 3:3 (Summer 1980) 209–24.

2. Francis Bacon, *Novum Organum* (London: William Pickering, 1844) p. 170. Thomas S.Kuhn, *The Structure of Scientific Revolutions* (1962; University of Chicago Press, 1970) p. 7.

3. Leon Edel, 'Biography and the Science of Man', *New Directions in Biography*, ed. Anthony M. Friedson (Honolulu: University of Hawaii Press, 1981) p. 10. An example of Proust's importance can be found in the discourse on aesthetics found in *Time Regained* of *Remembrance of Things Past*, pp. 917–52. The role of biographer is identical to that of the artist who must go behind the individual's 'vanity . . . passions . . . spirit of imitation' and habits to reach 'the depths where what has really existed lies unknown within us'. Proust, *Time Regained*, tr. Andreas Mayor, *Remembrance of Things Past*, tr. CK. Scott Moncreiff, Terence Kilmartin, Andreas Mayor (New York: Random House, 1981) p. 932. Compare Leon Edel, 'The Figure Under the Carpet', *Telling Lives*, ed. Marc Pachter (Washington: New Republic Books, 1979) pp. 16–34.

4. Charles Olson, *W. H. Auden, The Life of A Poet* (New York: Harcourt Brace Jovanovich, 1979): Humphrey Carpenter, *W. H. Auden: A Biography* (London: George Allen & Unwin, 1981).

5. Meryle Secrest, *Being Bernard Berenson* (New York: Holt, Rinehart & Winston, 1979) pp. 49–53; Ernest Samuels, *Bernard Berenson, The Making of a Connoisseur* (Harvard University Press, 1979) pp. 67–9. On the controversy generated by these two lives see William Mostyn Owen, *Burlington Magazine*, CXXIII: 938 (May 1981) 317–18 and Peter Plagens, 'Biography', *Art in America*, 68 (Oct 1980) 13–15.

6. Lytton Strachey, 'Gibbon', *Portraits in Miniature* (London: Chatto & Windus, 1931) p. 160. Strachey continued to argue that 'facts relating to the past, when they are collected without art, are compilations; and compilations no doubt may be useful; but they are no more History than butter, eggs, salt and herbs are an omelette' (p. 160). Alfred North Whitehead, *Science and The Modern World* (1925; New York: Mentor Books, 1962) p. 70; Richard Ellmann uses the phrase 'character forming' in 'Literary Biography', *Golden Codgers: Biographical Speculations* (New York: Oxford University Press, 1973) p. 5.

7. Mathilde Blind, *George Eliot* (London: W. H. Allen, 1883) endpaper [p. 219]. All further references are to this edition.

8. See for example the account in *Blackwood's* for February 1881.

9. John Walter Cross, *George Eliot's Life as Related in Her Letters and Journals*, New

Edition (Edinburgh: Blackwood, 1885) p. v. All further references are to this edition.

10. Leslie Stephen, 'Biography', *Men, Books, and Mountains, Essays by Leslie Stephen*, intro. S. O. A. Ullmann (London: Hogarth Press, 1956) pp. 132, 140–1. The essay originally appeared in the *National Review*, xxii (1893).

11. Leslie Stephen, *George Eliot* (London: Macmillan, 1902; rpt New York: AMS Press, 1973) p. 36. All further references are to this edition.

12. Jessie Lawrence to Leslie Stephen, 9 Oct. 1902, Macmillan Archives, British Library, London.

13. Robert Gittings, *The Nature of Biography* (Seattle: University of Washington Press, 1978) passim.

14. Anne Fremantle, *George Eliot* (London: Duckworth, 1933) p. 65. All further references are to this edition.

15. These terms appear in Tzvetan Todorov, *The Poetics of Prose*, tr. Richard Howard (1971; Ithaca: Cornell University Press, 1977) p. 135.

16. Gordon S. Haight, *George Eliot, A Biography* (Oxford: Clarendon Press, 1968) p. 22. All further references are to this edition.

17. Gordon S. Haight, *George Eliot and John Chapman*, 2nd edn (1940; New Haven: Archon Books, 1969) p. vii.

18. Jerrold Seigel, *Marx's Fate, The Shape of A Life* (Princeton University Press, 1978) p. 4.

19. Ruby V. Redinger, *George Eliot: The Emergent Self* (New York: Alfred A. Knopf, 1975) p. 126. All further references are to this edition.

20. Leon Edel, 'The Poetics of Biography', *Contemporary Approaches to English Studies*, ed. Hilda Schiff (London: Heinemann, 1977) p. 42.

CHAPTER 4: WRITERS AS BIOGRAPHERS

1. Sigmund Freud, *Leonardo Da Vinci*, tr. A. A. Brill (New York: Random House, 1947) p. 109. Cf. Harold Bloom on poets: 'to live, the poet must *misinterpret* the father, by the crucial act of misprision, which is the re-writing of the father'. *A Map of Misreading* (New York: Oxford University Press, 1975) p. 19.

2. Katherine Frank suggests that the preponderance of 'narrative biographies', those that concentrate on telling rather than interpreting a life, is the result of their being written by novelists. She cites John Wain, Angus Wilson and Margaret Drabble. While I disagree with her broad categories – narrative v. analytic biographies – and her simplistic generalizations ('nearly all analytic writers are literary critics and scholars') – Frank's reference to the 'fictional dimension' of scene, climax reversal, setting and character in biographies by novelists is useful. However, I believe there is a stronger, psychological cause for the singular nature of such biographies which are simultaneously interpretative and creative. See Katherine Frank, 'Writing Lives: Theory and Practice of Literary Biography', *Genre*, 13: 4 (1980) 513.

3. Virginia Woolf, 'The New Biography', *Collected Essays* (London: Hogarth Press, 1967) iv: 234; Elizabeth Gaskell to George Smith, 31 May 1855, *The Letters of Mrs. Gaskell*, ed. J. A. V. Chapple and Arthur Pollard (Manchester University Press, 1966) p. 345. Hereafter identified as *Letters* in the text. In a

letter dated 5 June 1855 Gaskell explained to Smith that 'I determined that in our country-leisure this summer, I could put down everything I remembered about this dear friend and noble woman, before its vividness had faded from my mind' (*Letters*, p. 347). Gaskell was, however, actually afraid of making such an account public.

4. Patrick Brontë in *Letters*, ed. Chapple and Pollard, p. 361.
5. 'Our Weekly Gossip', *Athenaeum*, 1545 (6 June 1857) p. 727; see p. 726 for the letter of apology and retraction. For an account of the various editions of *The Life of Charlotte Brontë*, see L. R. Chambers, 'The Bibliography of Mrs. Gaskell's Life of Charlotte Brontë', *Brontë Society Transactions*, 17: 3 (1978) 217–21. Briefly, the first edition appeared on 25 March 1857 but objections and writs for libel halted sales of a second edition which was published 9 May 1857. On 30 May 1857 a letter of apology appeared in the press and by 22 August 1857 a corrected third edition was available which, by August 1858, went into a fourth edition published in one volume. For a general account of the context of the biography see Angus Easson, *Elizabeth Gaskell* (London: Routledge & Kegan Paul, 1979) ch. 5.
6. Elizabeth Barrett Browning, 'Aurora Leigh,' title page, Gaskell, *The Life of Charlotte Brontë*, ed. Alan Shelston (Harmondsworth: Penguin Books, 1975) p. 43; Southey, ibid., p. 173. All further references are to this edition which reprints the first edition plus the various revisions that appeared in the third edition.
7. Mrs Gaskell to John Greenwood, 12 April 1855, *Letters*, ed. Chapple and Pollard, p. 337. To George Smith on 4 June 1855 she expressed the same concern: 'she would have disliked my doing so [visiting her while ill] . . . but I think I could have overcome that, and perhaps saved her life' (*Letters*, p. 346). For a parallel reading of the biography see Elizabeth Hardwick, 'The Brontës', *Seduction and Betrayal*, *Women in Literature* (New York: Random House, 1974) pp. 3–29.
8. Virginia Woolf, *The Letters of Virginia Woolf*, VI: 1936–1941, ed. Nigel Nicolson (London: Hogarth Press, 1980) p. 259. Elizabeth Gaskell to Tottie Fox, [27] August 1850, *Letters*, ed. Chapple and Pollard, p. 130.
9. Gaskell, *Life of Charlotte Brontë*, ed. Shelston, p. 281. Rewritten, the passage reads 'Whatever may have been the nature and depth of Branwell's sins, – whatever may have been his temptation, whatever his guilt – there is no doubt of the suffering which his conduct entailed upon his poor father and his innocent sisters. The hopes and plans they had cherished long . . . were cruelly frustrated' (p. 554).
10. *Letters*, pp. 432, 454. For an account of these alterations, see Alan Shelston, 'Introduction', Gaskell, *Life of Charlotte Brontë*, ed. Shelston, pp. 9–37, 527–8.
11. Elizabeth Gaskell, *Mary Barton*, ed. Stephen Gill (Harmondsworth: Penguin Books, 1970) p. 457; Coral Lansbury, *Elizabeth Gaskell: The Novel of Social Crisis* (New York: Barnes & Noble, 1975) p. 129.
12. Angus Easson, 'Two Suppressed Opinions in Mrs. Gaskell's Life of Charlotte Brontë', *Brontë Society Transactions*, 16: 4 (1974) 281–3.
13. George Henry Lewes, 15 April 1857 in *The George Eliot Letters*, ed. Gordon S. Haight (Yale University Press, 1954) II: 315. Lewes records that Eliot read the biography out loud between 9–15 April 1857.

14. [George Eliot], 'Life of Sterling', *Westminster Review*, 57, n.s. vol. 1 (Jan–April 1852) 250, 247.
15. Michael Sadleir summarized the situation in the following manner: Thackeray's death gave Trollope 'the opportunity of "rounding off" at once his personality and his literary position. While Thackeray lived, [Trollope] . . . would have always have been . . . only a disciple to a man he venerated.' *Trollope, A Commentary* (New York: Farrar, Straus, 1947) p. 255.
16. William James noted the Hawthorne parallel. See William Veeder, *Henry James – The Lesson of the Master* (University of Chicago Press, 1975) p. 248. On this subject also see Thaddeo K. Bibiiha, *The James–Hawthorne Relations, Bibliographical Essays* (Boston: G. K. Hall, 1980). On the preference of James for Turgenev see Peter Buitenhuis, *The Grasping Imagination, The American Writings of Henry James* (University of Toronto Press, 1970) p. 106.
17. Morley to Trollope in *Letters of Anthony Trollope*, ed. Bradford Booth (London: Oxford University Press, 1951) pp. 410–11. Morley to James in Peter Buitenhuis, *The Grasping Imagination*, p. 105.
18. Anthony Trollope, *Thackeray* (1879: New York: Harper & Brothers, n.d.) p. 3. For details and background information see Robert A. Colby, 'Trollope as Thackerayan', forthcoming, *Dickens Studies Annual*.
19. Anthony Trollope, *An Autobiography*, ed. Michael Sadleir and Frederick Page (1883; Oxford University Press, 1980) p. 185; see also pp. 243–5 and 249–50 for additional comments on Thackeray.
20. Henry James, *Hawthorne* (1879; London: Macmillan, 1967) p. 22.
21. Trollope, *Thackeray*, p. 31; James, *Hawthorne*, p. 45.
22. Trollope, *Thackeray*, pp. 65, 204, 114, 118; James, *Hawthorne*, pp. 35, 117.
23. Trollope, *Thackeray*, pp. 120, 19.
24. 'He who knew Thackeray will have a vacancy in his heart's inmost casket, which must remain vacant till he dies. One loved him almost as one loves a woman, tenderly and with thoughtfulness. One loved him thus because his heart was tender, as is the heart of a woman.' Trollope, 'W. M. Thackeray', *Cornhill Magazine* (Feb 1864), in Michael Sadleir, *Trollope, A Commentary* (1927; London: Oxford University Press, 1961) p. 253.
25. James, *Hawthorne*, pp. 72, 126.
26. See Henry James, *Henry James Letters*, ed. Leon Edel, vol. II (Harvard University Press, 1975) pp. 240, 266–8. See also his letter to Thomas Sargent Perry, ibid., pp. 274–5. The section listing the failures of American culture in *Hawthorne* echoes the Preface to *The Marble Faun*.
27. Trollope, *Letters*, p. 412.
28. James Thomson in David Skilton, *Anthony Trollope and His Contemporaries* (London: Longman, 1972) p. 34. See also 'Mr. Trollope on Thackeray', *Pall Mall Gazette*, 18 (Oct 1879) 12, and other criticism cited in Robert Colby's forthcoming article.
29. Similar to the function of *Hawthorne* for James is Van Wyck Brooks's biography, *The Pilgrimage of Henry James* (1925) which rehearses – through his interpretation of James's expatriate life – Brooks's own anxieties and failings.
30. In his biography of James, Leon Edel states that James disliked Story and wrote the biography out of financial need and in response to pressure from Story's children. Leon Edel, *Henry James, The Master* (Philadelphia: J. B. Lippincott, 1972) p. 157. For Edel's full discussion of the biography, see

228228 *Notes and References*

pp. 157–162. James, *Letters of Henry James*, ed. Percy Lubbock (New York: Charles Scribner's Sons, 1920) I: 431–2. On the autobiographical dimension of Trollope's biographies see my essay 'Trollope as Biographer', *Prose Studies*, 5:3 (Dec 1982) 318–25.

31. Despite the subtitle of *Orlando, A Biography*, Leon Edel is alone in seriously analysing the work in terms of history of the form. He refers to it as 'a fable for biographers' in *Literary Biography* (1957; New York: Doubleday, 1959) p. 139. See also James Naremore, 'Orlando and the "New Biography" ', *The World Without A Self, Virginia Woolf and the Novel* (Yale University Press, 1973) pp. 190–218. On history and *Orlando* see Howard Harper, *Between Language and Silence, The Novels of Virginia Woolf* (Baton Rouge: Louisiana State University Press, 1982) pp. 163–203.

32. Thomas S. Kuhn, *The Structure of Scientific Revolutions* (1962; University of Chicago Press, 1970) p. 7; Virginia Woolf, to Vita Sackville-West, 9 October 1927, *Letters of Virginia Woolf*, ed. Nigel Nicolson (London: Hogarth Press, 1977) III: 429.

33. Woolf to Sackville-West, 3 May 1938, *Letters*, ed. Nicolson (London: Hogarth Press, 1980) VI: 226; Woolf, *Letters*, III: 429, 430. For a summary of the Woolf–Sackville-West relationship see Jean O. Love, 'Orlando and Its Genesis: Venturing and Experimenting in Art, Love and Sex', *Virginia Woolf, Revolution and Continuity*, ed. Ralph Freedman (University of California Press, 1980) pp. 189–218.

34. Virginia Woolf, *Orlando, A Biography* (London: Hogarth Press, 1928) p. 62. All further references are to this edition.

35. Virginia Woolf, 'The New Biography', *Collected Essays* (London: Hogarth Press, 1967) IV: 231.

36. On revisions of time and fact in *Orlando* see Charles G. Hoffmann, 'Fact and Fantasy in *Orlando*', *Texas Studies in Language and Literature*, 10 (Fall 1968) 435–44.

37. Woolf, 'The New Biography', *Collected Essays*, IV: 230; Woolf in Hoffman, 'Fact and Fantasy', p. 442; Woolf, 'The New Biography', *Collected Essays*, IV: 229.

38. Virginia Woolf, 'The New Biography', *Collected Essays* (London: Hogarth Press, 1967) IV: 233–4; Harold Nicolson, *Some People* (1927; New York: Vintage Books, 1957) p. 39; Woolf, 'The New Biography', *Collected Essays*, IV: 232, 233.

39. Lytton Strachey in Virginia Woolf, *The Diary of Virginia Woolf*, ed. Anne Olivier Bell and Andrew McNeillie (London: Hogarth Press, 1980) III: 32, 156–7. 'I often glide into intimacy with Lytton about books', she wrote in her *Diary* (III: 138). On Woolf and Strachey discussing matters biographical see *Letters*, III: 242 where she explicitly refers to *Elizabeth and Essex*.

40. A. J. A. Symons, 'Tradition and Biography', *Essays and Biographies*. ed. Julian Symons (London: Cassell, 1969) pp. 6–7; Geoffrey Scott, *Portrait of Zélide* (1925; New York: Charles Scribner's Sons, 1926) p. 216.

41. Evelyn Waugh, 'Preface to American Edition' (1946) *Edmund Campion* (1935; Garden City, New York: Image/Doubleday, 1956) pp. 7–8. The biography won the Hawthornden Prize, won by Vita Sackville-West for *The Land* in 1927.

42. George Gissing to Clara Collett, November 1895 in Gillian Tindall, *The Born Exile: George Gissing* (London: Temple-Smith, 1974) [p. 7].

CHAPTER 5: BIOGRAPHY AND THEORY: STEPS TOWARDS A POETIC

1. Frank Brady, 'The Strategies of Biography and Some 18th Century Examples', *Literary Theory and Structure*, ed. Frank Brady *et al.* (Yale University Press, 1973) pp. 245, 247. James L. Clifford, *From Puzzles to Portraits, Problems of a Literary Biographer* (University of North Carolina Press, 1970) pp. 99–112; Michael Holroyd in Dennis W. Petrie, *Ultimately Fiction, Design in Modern American Literary Biography* (Purdue University Press, 1981) p. 81.
2. Rene Wellek and Austin Warren, 'Literature and Biography', *Theory of Literature* (1948; new rev. edn, New York: Harcourt Brace and World, 1956) pp. 75–80; Boris Tomasevskij, 'Literature and Biography', tr. Herbert Eagle, *Readings in Russian Poetics*, ed. Ladislav Mateja and Krystyna Pomorska (Ann Arbor: Michigan Slavic Publications, 1978) pp. 47–55. Tomasevskij admits one use for biography, however, when he writes 'what the literary historian really needs is the biographical legend created by the author himself. Only such a legend is a *literary fact*' (p. 55).
3. See for example Harold Nicolson, *The Development of English Biography* (1927), Edgar Johnson, *One Mighty Torrent, The Drama of Biography* (1937), Richard Altick, *Lives and Letters* (1965) and A. O. J. Cockshut, *Truth to Life, The Art of Biography in the Nineteenth Century* (1974). An early exception was James Field Stanfield's, *An Essay on the Study and Composition of Biography* (Sunderland, 1813).
4. Leon Edel, 'The Poetics of Biography', *Contemporary Approaches to English Studies*, ed. Hilda Schiff (London: Heinemann, 1977) pp. 53, 56, 42, 55.
5. Ralph Rader, 'Literary Form in Factual Narrative: The Example of Boswell's *Johnson*', *Essays in Eighteenth Century Biography*, ed. Philip B. Daghlian (Indiana University Press, 1968) p. 38. In spite of his many useful and valuable comments on the literariness of biography and factual narrative, Rader stops short of citing the power of metaphor, preferring the more indefinite term, 'image'. However, he accurately perceives the function of figurative language in reading biography when he states that 'the image constructs the facts, and the facts in turn construct the image' (p. 17). This reciprocity will be explored in my section on metaphor and metonymy. Edmund Wilson, *Letters on Literature and Politics, 1912–1972*, ed. Elena Wilson (New York: Farrar, Straus & Giroux, 1977) p. 479.
6. Leon Edel, 'A Manifesto', *biography*, I (Winter 1978) 2.
7. Stephen Spender, *World Within World* (New York: Harcourt Brace, 1951) p. 285. Hayden White, 'The Fictions of Factual Representation', *Tropics of Discourse, Essays in Cultural Criticism* (Baltimore: Johns Hopkins Press, 1978) p. 125. My argument here opposes Dennis W. Petrie's claim that 'biographers seem to fear "consciously rhetorical prose" as much as modern fiction writers seem to revel in it'. *Ultimately Fiction*, pp. 120–1. Barbara Herrnstein Smith in her work *On the Margins of Discourses, The Relation of Literature to Language* (University of Chicago Press, 1978) is closer to my approach which understands biography as a prose art creating authorized fictions through the act of discourse. Also see Edward W. Said, *Beginnings, Intention and Method* (New York: Basic Books, 1975) pp. 156–63.

8. Virginia Woolf, 'De Quincey's Autobiography', *Collected Essays* (London: Hogarth Press, 1967) IV: 6.
9. Hayden White, 'The Fictions of Factual Representation', *Tropics of Discourse*, pp. 125, 134, 127. For a similar view of language see Tzvetan Todorov, *The Poetics of Prose*, tr. Richard Howard (1971; Cornell University Press, 1977) pp. 80–9.
10. Virginia Woolf, *Orlando* (London: Hogarth Press, 1928) p. 110; Thomas Carlyle, 'Richter', *Edinburgh Review*, XLVI (1827) 177.
11. Park Honan, 'The Theory of Biography', *Novel*, 13: 1 (Fall 1979) 109–20. All further references are to this version of the essay.
12. Paul Ricoeur, *The Rule of Metaphor*, tr. Robert Czerny (1975; University of Toronto Press, 1977) p. 7. All further references are to this edition. On the power of metaphor see Ricoeur's useful essay, 'Metaphor and The Main Problem of Hermeneutics', *New Literary History*, 6 (1974/75) 95–110.
13. Lytton Strachey, 'John Aubrey', *Portraits in Miniature* (New York: Harcourt Brace, 1931) p. 29.
14. Lytton Strachey, *Eminent Victorians* (1918: New York: Capricorn Books, 1963) p. v. All further references are to this edition; Michael Timko, 'The Victorianism of Victorian Literature', *New Literary History*, 6 (1974/75) 609. All further references are to this version of the essay.
15. Holroyd, *Lytton Strachey* (London: Heinemann, 1967) I: 349, 391–4.
16. Lytton Strachey to Clive Bell in Holroyd, *Lytton Strachey*, II: 11. The contradictions of the self appear as a major theme in the two-volume life of Strachey by Holroyd. See I: 11–12, 44–5, 169–70, 269–70, 361–2; II: 17, 102–3, 126–7, 334.
17. Lytton Strachey, 'Traps and Peace Traps', in Charles Sanders, *Lytton Strachey, His Mind and Art* (Yale University Press, 1957) pp. 290–1.
18. George Eliot, *Middlemarch*, ed. Gordon S. Haight (Boston: Houghton Mifflin, 1956) ch. 10, p. 63.
19. James Boswell, *Life of Johnson*, ed. G. B. Hill, rev. L. P. Powell (Oxford: Clarendon Press, 1934) I: 30, 486; III: 191.
20. James Boswell, *The Correspondence and Other Papers of James Boswell Relating to the Making of the Life of Johnson*, ed. Marshall Waingrow (New York: McGraw-Hill, 1969) p. 96. Hereafter identified as *Corresp.* Boswell, *Life of Johnson*, ed. Hill, I: 5; II: 40; Waingrow, 'Introduction', *Corresp.*, pp. xlvi–xlvii.
21. *Corresp.*, pp. 111–12; Boswell, *Life of Johnson, i*: 30; *Corresp.*, p. 146. David L. Passler argues for yet another dominant metaphor, the sinuous curve, in *Time, Form and Style in Boswell's Life of Johnson* (Yale University Press, 1971) pp. 55–8.
22. Aristotle, 'Poetics', *The Basic Writings of Aristotle*, tr. and ed. Richard McKeon (New York: Random House, 1941) p. 1479, 11.5–8. Aristotle adds that 'a good metaphor implies an intuitive perception of similarity in dissimilars' (ibid.) Ricoeur, *The Rule of Metaphor*, pp. 33, 237.
23. Virginia Woolf, *The Waves* (1923; New York: Harcourt Brace and World, 1959) p. 259. Cf. Michael Holroyd's recent comment: 'the aim of most biographies these days is to explore the connection they make with their subject, and give it a literary pattern, a shape'. 'History and Biography', *Salmagundi*, 46 (Fall 1979) 25.

24. Jacques Lacan, 'The Insistence of the Letter in the Unconscious', *Structuralism*, ed. Jacques Ehrmann (Garden City, New York: Doubleday, 1970) p. 119. Roman Jakobson, 'The Metaphoric and Metonymic Poles', *Critical Theory Since Plato*, ed. Hazard Adams (New York: Harcourt Brace Jovanovich, 1971) p. 1114.

25. James Boswell, *Boswell's London Journal, 1762–63*, ed. Frederick A. Pottle (New York: McGraw-Hill, 1950) p. 260. James Boswell, *Life of Johnson*, ed. G. B. Hill, rev. L. F. Powell, I: 392, 38. All further references are to this edition.

26. See William C. Dowling, *Language and Logos in Boswell's Life of Johnson* (Princeton University Press, 1981) especially ch. III, 'Structure and Absence'.

27. P. N. Furbank, *E. M. Forster, A Life* (New York: Harcourt Brace Jovanovich, 1978) I:104. All further references are to this edition.

28. George Lakoff and Mark Johnson, 'Metonymy', *Metaphors We Live By* (University of Chicago Press, 1980) p. 39.

29. Robert Bisset, *Life of Edmund Burke* (London: George Cawthorn, 1798) p. 3.

30. Tzvetan Todorov, *The Poetics of Prose*, tr. Howard, pp. 135–6. Cf. Susan Sontag's statement: 'The knowledge we gain through art is an experience of the form or style of knowing something, rather than a knowledge of some thing (like a fact or a moral judgment) in itself.' *Against Interpretation* (New York: Dell, 1969) p. 30. William C. Dowling expresses a similar view of biography and form in this passage on the fictionality of Boswell's *Johnson*. Discomfort with the *Life* disappears, he writes, 'only when we see that the true subject of the *Life*, as of all biographies, is the impossibility of the biographical enterprise, not presence but the illusion of presence ultimately revealed as an illusion, the dilemma of narrative trying and failing to reach through to a world beyond itself. To say that the *Life* is the greatest of biographies is to say that it confronts this dilemma more directly . . . than any other.' *Language and Logos in Boswell's Life of Johnson*, p. 97.

31. Leon Edel, 'Biography and the Narrator', *The New Republic*, 152 (6 March 1965) 26.

32. William C. Dowling, 'Boswell and the Problem of Biography', *Studies in Biography*, ed. Daniel Aaron (Harvard University Press, 1978) p. 87. Dowling in this essay and in his two books on Boswell is one of the few critics to analyse the problem of biographical narration in detail. See especially, pp. 80–7, ibid.

33. For a discussion of the problem of objectivity and interpretation see Dowling, *Language and Logos in Boswell's Life of Johnson* (Princeton University Press, 1981) pp. 12–22 and passim. On narrative contracts see Jonathan Culler, *Structuralist Poetics* (1975; London: Routledge & Kegan Paul, 1977) pp. 192–202.

34. Robert Martin Adams called *Joyce* 'the best literary biography of our time'; Dwight Macdonald expressed the hope that it 'will become a model for future scholarly biographies'; Frank Kermode praised it as 'superlatively good'. All quoted on jacket cover, Richard Ellmann, *James Joyce* (1959; New York: Oxford Univeristy Press, 1965). All further references to this edition. More recently, Edward Mendelson has complained that it is a life described through literary criticism and written as though it were a psychological

novel. See Mendelson, 'Authorized Biography and Its Discontents', *Studies in Biography*, ed. Aaron, pp. 21–2.

35. Sybille Bedford, *Aldous Huxley, A Biography* (London: Chatto & Windus, 1973) I: xi, xv. All further references are to this edition.

36. For examples of the confusion in the text see I: 232–4, 255–6, 277–84; II: 11–12, 169–75, 250–1. Additional comments on the narration can be found in James Olney, 'Most Extraordinary: Sybille Bedford and Aldous Huxley', *South Atlantic Quarterly*, 74 (Summer 1975) 376–86 and in George Steiner, 'The Last Victorian', *The New Yorker*, 17 February 1975, pp. 103–6.

37. Bernard Crick, 'Introduction', *George Orwell. A Life* (London: Secker & Warburg, 1980) p. xxiv.

38. Leon Edel, 'The Figure Under the Carpet', *Telling Lives. The Biographer's Art*, ed. Marc Pachter (Washington: New Republic Books, 1979) pp. 24–34; Phyllis Rose, *Woman of Letters, Virginia Woolf* (New York: Oxford University Press, 1978) pp. viii–ix. Arthur Penrhyn Stanley, 'Preface', *Life and Correspondence of Thomas Arnold, D.D.*, 12th edn (London: John Murray, 1881) I: vii. The biography originally appeared in 1844. Yeats in Justin Kaplan, 'The Naked Self and Other Problems', *Telling Lives*, p. 46.

39. Izaak Walton, 'Life of Hooker' in Donald Stauffer, *English Biography Before 1700* (1930; New York: Russell and Russell, 1964) p. 95.

40. Freud to Arnold Zweig, 31 May 1936, *The Letters of Sigmund Freud to Arnold Zweig*, ed. Ernest L. Freud, tr. Elaine and William Robson-Scott (New York: Harcourt Brace World, 1970) p. 127.

41. Northrop Frye, *The Great Code, The Bible and Literature* (Toronto: Academic Press, 1982) p. 43. On the individual becoming the universal, see pp. 46–7, 220.

42. Justin Kaplan, 'The "Real Life" ', *Studies in Biography*, ed. Aaron, p. 7. A. O. J. Cockshut in a parallel statement declared 'it is always useful, before considering in detail what a man really was, to consider his myth', *Truth to Life*, p. 87.

43. Brigid Brophy, *Prancing Novelist, A Defence of Fiction in the Form of a Critical Biography in Praise of Ronald Firbank* (London: Macmillan, 1973) p. 106. All further references to this edition. For a summary of her relentless corrections to earlier biographies, see p. 115.

44. Kaplan, 'The "Real Life" ', *Studies in Biography*, ed. Aaron, p. 2.

45. James Clifford, ' "Hanging Up Looking Glasses at Odd Corners": Ethno-biographical Prospects', *Studies in Biography*, ed. Aaron, p. 45. All further references are to this version of the essay.

46. Robert Scholes, *Structuralism in Literature, An Introduction* (1974: Yale University Press, 1976) p. 197. On this topic also see Culler, *Structuralist Poetics*, p. 263. In ch. 1 of *Orlando* the narrator writes '(. . . that was the way his mind worked now, in violent see-saws from life to death, stopping at nothing in between, so that the biographer must not stop either, but must fly as fast as he can and so keep pace with the unthinking passionate foolish actions and sudden extravagant words in which, it is impossible to deny, Orlando at this time of his life indulged.)' (p. 44). An example of a biography following a rhythmic structure is Karl Miller's *Cockburn's Millennium* (London: Duckworth, 1975).

47. Otto Rank, 'The Artist's Fight with Art', *The Myth of the Birth of the Hero and*

Other Writings, ed. Philip Freund (New York: Vintage Books, 1964) p. 201. James Atlas, biographer of Delmore Schwartz, once quipped 'reading biographies is like meeting famous people; it puts a familiar image in jeopardy', *New York Times Book Review*, 14 December 1980, p. 1.

48. On language and myth see Ernst Cassirer, *Language and Myth*, tr. Susanne K. Langer (1946; New York: Dover Publications, 1953) and Albert Cook, *Myth and Language* (Indiana University Press, 1981) p. 266. Thomas Mann, 'Freud and the Future', *Myth and Mythmaking*, ed. Henry A. Murray (New York: George Braziller, 1960) p. 373.

CHAPTER 6: EXPERIMENT IN BIOGRAPHY

1. Harold Nicolson, *The Development of English Biography* (London: Hogarth Press, 1927) pp. 154–8; Leon Edel, 'Biography and The Science of Man', *New Directions in Biography*, ed. Anthony M. Friedson (Honolulu: University of Hawaii Press, 1981) pp. 6–7. Edel enunciates four useful principles for the writing of biography on pp. 8–10. For a counter view, strongly opposed to the influence of psychology on biography, see Edward Mendelson, 'Authorized Biography and its Discontents', *Studies in Biography*, ed. Aaron, pp. 9–26. On biography and anthropology see *The Biographical Process*, ed. Frank E. Reynolds and Donald Capps (The Hague: Mouton, 1976) passim.
2. William Bingley, *Animal Biography* in Donald A. Stauffer, *The Art of Biography in 18th Century England, Bibliographical Supplement* (Princeton University Press, 1941) p. 19. 'To the female reader', Bingley added, 'I must remark, that every indelicate subject is scrupulously excluded.'
3. Sir Egerton Brydges, 'Introduction', *Imaginative Biography* (London: Saunders and Otley, 1834) n.p.
4. Frank Kermode, *The Sense of an Ending, Studies in the Theory of Fiction* (New York: Oxford University Press, 1967) p. 64.
5. Erikson outlines his life-cycle in *Childhood and Society*, 2nd edn (New York: W. W. Norton, 1963) pp. 48–108, 247–74. Richard Noland, 'Psycho-history, Theory and Practice', *Massachusetts Review*, 18 (Summer 1977) 307.
6. Edward Mendelson, 'Authorized Biography', *Studies in Biography*, ed. Aaron, pp. 20, 24.
7. Norman Holland, *Poems in Persons, An Introduction to the Psychoanalysis of Literature* (1973; New York: W. W. Norton, 1975) p. 142. For a fuller discussion see Nolan, 'Psycho-history', *Massachusetts Review*, 18 (Summer 1977) 295–322.
8. Jerrold Seigel, *Marx's Fate, The Shape of A Life* (Princeton University Press, 1978) pp. 4, 7, 9, 8. See Robert Gittings, *The Nature of Biography* (Seattle: University of Washington Press, 1978) pp. 42–3. On the importance of economic and social factors see pp. 54–5.
9. For recent discussions see James William Anderson, 'The Methodology of Psychological Biography', *Journal of Interdisciplinary History*, XI: 3 (Winter 1981) 455–75; Donna Arzt, 'Psychohistory and Its Discontents', *biography*, 1:3 (1978) 1–36; Jacques Barzun, *Clio and the Doctors* (University of Chicago Press, 1974); Gertrude Himmelfarb, 'The New History', *Commentary*, 59 (Jan 1975) 72–8; Thomas Flanagan, 'Problems of Psychobiography', *Queen's*

Quarterly, 89:3 (Autumn 1982) 576–610; David Stannard, *Shrinking History, On Freud and the Failure of Psychohistory* (New York: Oxford University Press, 1980). For a defence of psychohistory see Cushing Strout, 'Ego Psychology and the Historians', *The Veracious Imagination* (Middletown, Conn.: Wesleyan University Press, 1981) pp. 223–44. For an explanation of psychohistory see Bruce Mazlish, 'What is Psychohistory?', *Varieties of Psychohistory*, ed. George M. Kren and Leon H. Rappoport (New York: Springer, 1976) pp. 17–37.

10. Bruce Mazlish, *James and John Stuart Mill, Father and Son in the 19th Century* (New York: Basic Books, 1975) p. 434. All further references are to this edition. For an elaboration of the father–son theme in late nineteenth and early twentieth-century literature see my essay, 'From Fathers and Sons to Sons and Lovers', *Dalhousie Review*, 59:2 (Summer 1979) 221–38.

11. Richard Sennett, *The Fall of Public Man* (1976; New York: Vintage Books, 1978) pp. 219–24.

12. Margot Peters, 'Group Biography', *New Directions in Biography*, ed. Anthony M. Friedson, p. 44. On page 46 Peters notes the shift in social sciences to group rather than individual therapy, away from the couch to the community. The idea of family appears to dominate group biographies which have also been labelled 'prosopography'. See Lawrence Stone, 'Prosopography', *Daedalus* (Winter 1971) 46–9.

13. James R. Mellow, *Charmed Circle, Gertrude Stein and Company* (New York: Praeger, 1974) p. 7. All further references are to this edition.

14. Norman and Jeanne MacKenzie, *The Fabians* (New York: Simon & Schuster, 1977) p. 411.

15. Karl Miller, 'Eminent Romantics', *New York Review of Books*, 36:13 (16 Aug 1979) 31; Leon Edel, *Bloomsbury, A House of Lions* (Philadelphia: J. B. Lippincott, 1979) p. 271. All further references are to this edition.

16. Peter Stansky and William Abrahams, 'Foreword', *The Unknown Orwell* (London: Constable, 1972) pp. ix, x. All further references are to this edition.

17. Stansky and Abrahams do not cover the years 1937 to 1950 but remain faithful to their original conception of tracing Orwell's life only up to *Homage to Catalonia*. Bernard Crick's *George Orwell, A Life* (London: Secker & Warburg, 1980), covers the entire life.

18. Mendelson, 'Authorized Biography', *Studies in Biography*, p. 20.

19. Of the title Field writes 'it is an admission and declaration of inconclusive evidence, of freedom from the fat of irrelevant fact, and that in itself could be disturbing to a subject such as mine, who has been known to praise biographies only for their documentation'. 'Any given truth', Field later remarks, 'may stand very well by itself but be substantively modified upon being placed in proximity to another given truth, and even a statement which is patently false may more often than not involve capillary truths and histories which are interesting in their own right.' These admissions reveal the dawning awareness by biographers of the limitations and possibilities of their art. Andrew Field, *Nabokov: His Life in Part* (1977; Harmondsworth: Penguin Books, 1978) pp. 5–6, 33. An earlier example of this method of the subject participating in the account, although not actually integrated into the text, is Robert Graves and Liddell Hart, *T. E. Lawrence to his Biographers*

(London: Cassell, 1938). The volume consists of commentary by Lawrence to the authors of his two authorized biographies in response to queries and manuscript drafts. Graves, for example, sent Lawrence the first eleven chapters of *Lawrence and the Arabs* and received copious annotations and comments.

20. George D. Painter, *Marcel Proust, A Biography* (1959; London: Chatto & Windus, 1966) I: xiii.

21. Ford Madox Ford, *Joseph Conrad: A Personal Remembrance* (London: Duckworth, 1924) p. 180.

22. See for example, pp. 107–8, 247. This well-paced biography condenses the narrative to analyse the writing in a confident, interpretative voice. The biography incorporates many of the ideas I have stressed, from biography as a corrective genre to the use of central images and emplotment, here the story of the discovery of a vocation by Gibbon and his preparation for the labour of a life. Patricia B. Craddock, *Young Edward Gibbon, Gentleman of Letters* (Baltimore: Johns Hopkins Press, 1982).

23. Jean Gattégno, *Lewis Carroll, Fragments of a Looking-Glass*, tr. Rosemary Sheed (1974; New York: Thomas Crowell, 1976) p. 5.

24. Sartre in Douglas Collins, *Sartre as Biographer* (Harvard University Press, 1980) p. 177. Also see ch. 1, especially pp. 21–3. Analogous to Sartre's technique is the method of Thomas Mann's artist-biographer in *Doctor Faustus*. Sartre, 'Sur L'Idiot de la famille', *Situations*, II (Paris: Gallimard, 1976) p. 94.

25. Steven Millhauser, *Edwin Mullhouse: The Life and Death of an American Writer, 1943–1954* by Jeffrey Cartwright (New York: Alfred A. Knopf, 1972) pp. 41, 79. Earlier ventures in this form include Dimitri Mercjkowski's *The Romance of Leonardo Da Vinci* (1902), Carl Van Vechten's *Peter Whiffle* (1922) and John P. Marquand's *The Late George Apley* (1937).

26. David Fischer, *Historians' Fallacies, Towards A Logic of Historical Thought* (New York: Harper & Row, 1970) p. 311.

CHAPTER 7: CONCLUSION

1. Marcel Proust, *Time Regained*, tr. Andreas Mayor, *Remembrance of Things Past*, tr. C. K. Scott Moncreiff, Terence Kilmartin, Andreas Mayor (New York: Random House, 1981) III: 924–5; Hegel, *Reason in History: A General Introduction to the Philosophy of History*, tr. Robert S. Hartman (Indianapolis: Bobbs-Merrill, 1953) p. 75.

2. James Olney, 'Autobiography and the Cultural Moment', *Autobiography, Essays Theoretical and Critical*, ed. James Olney (Princeton University Press, 1980) p. 20.

3. Ernest Kris, *Psychoanalytic Explorations in Art* (1952; New York: Schocken Books, 1971) p. 83. See also ch. 2. Kris's idea restates the moral dimension of biography first established by Plutarch, restated in the Introduction to *The British Plutarch* (1776): 'By having before our eyes the *principles* of men of honour and probity enforced by *example*, we shall be animated to fix upon some great model to be the rule of our conduct' (p. vii).

4. Laurence Sterne, *Tristram Shandy*, ed. James Work (1760–7; New York: Odyssey Press, 1940) p. 109. Virginia Woolf in Charles G. Hoffmann, 'Fact and Fantasy in *Orlando*', *Texas Studies in Language and Literature*, 10 (Fall 1968) 442. Leon Edel, 'The Poetics of Biography', *Contemporary Approaches to English Studies*, ed. Hilda Schiff (London: Heinemann, 1977) p. 42.

5. Roger North, *Lives of . . . Francis, Dudley and John North* (London: H. Colburn, 1826) i: xiv.

6. Frank Kermode, *The Genesis of Secrecy, On the Interpretation of Narrative* (Harvard University Press, 1979) p. 114. Cushing Strout, 'Letter', *New York Review of Books*, 16 December 1982, p. 59. On the current debate among historians see Gordon S. Wood, 'Star Spangled History', *New York Review of Books*, 12 August 1982, pp. 4–9 and the letters in response, 'Writing History', *New York Review of Books*, 16 December 1982, pp. 58–9. Also of interest are Donald P. Spence, *Narrative Truth and Historical Truth* (New York: W. W. Norton, 1982) and William R. Siebenschuh, *Fictional Techniques and Factual Works* (Athens, Georgia: University of Georgia Press, 1983). Both of these studies focus on style and its impact on fact.

7. Samuel Johnson (21 August 1733), 'The Journal of A Tour to the Hebrides', in Boswell, *Life of Johnson*, 2nd edn, ed. G. B. Hill and L. F. Powell (Oxford: Clarendon Press, 1964) v: 79. Lytton Strachey, 'Macaulay', *Portraits in Miniature* (London: Chatto & Windus, 1931) pp. 169–70. For a comment on the value of biography synthesizing culture and history by showing how 'cultural tensions and contradictions may be internalized, struggled with and resolved' see David Brian Davis, 'Some Recent Directions in American Cultural History', *American Historical Review*, 73 (Feb 1968) 705.

Index